HORACE MANN

ON THE CRISIS IN EDUCATION

Horace Mann

HORACE MANN
on the Crisis in Education

Edited, with an Introduction by
LOUIS FILLER

EVIL AND INTELLIGENCE

*"The more I see of our present civilization, and of the
only remedies for its evils, the more I dread intellectual eminence, when separated from virtue. We are in a sick world, for
whose maladies the knowledge of truth, and obedience to it, are
the only healing."*

THE ANTIOCH PRESS · 1965

TABLE OF CONTENTS

A QUESTION OF OBSOLESCENCE:
HORACE MANN AND OURSELVES

1. *Writings and Influence*

There are certain matters of moment to us which seem intangible, but which are not intangible at all. There are ways to measure their status, their content, their influence, or any other factors which may be important to us. Such is the question of Horace Mann's actual status, his actual content, his actual influence. I am well aware that no respectable encyclopedia would omit his name or fail to comment on his achievements. But there is a difference between comment and influence. Of course, anybody can deny anything, and often get away with it. I recall a young faculty wife at one institution I visited who contemplated joining us in a seminar on social problems. She seemed upset by some of the preliminary discussion which suggested that there *were* social problems. Juvenile delinquency? Housing? Race problems? Poverty? Education? There had always been dissatisfied people and people who needed help, she said. What wanted emphasis was our high standard of living, the patent progress which characterized American life. "By and large," affairs had never gone better with us as a nation. The young woman did not abide with us a sufficient while to help us determine whether her generalizations stood up under analysis. Whether subsequent events in her life sustained her in her views, I will never know.

Nevertheless, I assert that Horace Mann's influence on American life and education is close to nil, and that we are all the worse for it. I solicit evidence that either assertion is false, and will be pleased to learn that this is the case. I have offered these contentions in various places, and, in connection with the first part of my claim, have received not denials but explanations. My wide, if random, sample tells me that Mann is held to have too well attained his aims. He wanted universal education, and he won it. He believed in teacher training, and he won that, too. Encyclopedias quite properly record these facts. What more can anyone do for Mann today?

Seen from this point of view, nothing, I am sure. We have numerous apostles of more and bigger schools. One dean, quoting some dean's publication, perhaps, asked me where we were going to get the money to build all the dormitories his university needed. My question, whether we possibly ought to be considering how to *curb* student populations in the interest of student quality, left him blank. There do not seem to be funds on the market for such a purpose. Yet I believe this question brings me nearer Horace Mann's purposes than the question of more dormitories ever will.

Horace Mann wrote prolifically on educational subjects* and in his own time was considered a living classic of exposition. It was only in our own twentieth century that he was flatly superseded by other educational theorists and practitioners, and became a name instead of a man. Education became a mighty establishment in the land: the nation's number one business, as some educators like to remind us, employing more people than any other business and involving formidable numbers of "plants." Education proliferated graduate schools, presses, publications. Yet the present volume is the first substantial collection of Mann's writings since his widow and son ceased their labors.

Here is my major piece of evidence that Mann's *influence*, at least, is almost, if not entirely, lost. We apparently do not feel a need for his thoughts. We certainly do not need his encouragement to universal education; there are educators enough to agitate us in its behalf. We hardly need his arguments in furtherance of teacher training. The graduate schools of education have schools of experts to deal with every aspect of this matter, and to create new arguments favoring it.

II. *Dewey and Anti-Dewey*

If we had wished to know more about Mann's other ideas on education, we would have found ways of learning what they were. There are profound social currents which determine what we know and do not know. And also what we do not *wish* to know. As a by-product of my work, I have taught over 1500 teachers in one or another

---

* On other subjects, too, notably slavery; and if this present collection should be well received, there might properly be a further selection of Mann's writings covering other aspects of his social thought. As I will indicate, Mann never for a moment imagined that educational thought could be separated from social thinking.

graduate program, from New York to San Francisco. It early dawned upon me that they were incapable of discussing basic problems of education: they could not argue the right and wrong of John Dewey's tenets, or the pros and cons of "progressive education." Unable to spark discussions on such themes, I sought to discover why this was the case. I pointed out that the educational argument had not been conducted on a specialist's level, but pervaded the popular magazines as well, the Sunday supplements, and even the daily press. Many of my students concluded that the subject was too controversial for their regular workday peace of mind. In some cases, they observed that they had *deliberately* avoided contact with it, in order not to confuse their local aims and relationships.

Education is indivisible. You cannot, for example, have a false study of history in the grammar schools and a sound study of history in the graduate schools. Yet, though I believe false principles are presently promulgated at both levels, I believe, also, that there is a general desire for better than we get. I should like to avoid reference to cynics and oafs who infest our educational establishments, as they do all other avenues of life. We have a will to live as well as a will to die, and if we accept essentially evil principles, or, among administrators, some essentially evil principals, it is not because we prefer them but because we do not think we can get any better ones. We make do with what seem to us the best available resources.

III. *Mann and Mortality*

As for Horace Mann, we have assumed that the principles which guided his crusade for education are patently impractical and obsolete.

The essence of Mann's program was moral. He believed—and we might just as well face this fact now as ever—he believed that people had souls, and that these souls could be perverted to produce devils. He believed, not only that education carried moral responsibilities, but that, prosecuted without them, it could only produce more evil than it had inherited: that an educated devil was vastly more formidable and appalling than an uneducated one.

He believed that a democracy required democratic education. A person who could vote and not think was a danger to society. But this fact (he thought) created a stupendous need for educated teachers with a reverence for valid social principles. They must lead children aright and share responsibility with the parents themselves for their upbringing.

Mann's outlook, then, was religious and social, and I hold that their validity today is implicitly in question. This would explain why his works—the works of America's outstanding name in education— have not been available, and why the principles which direct them do not permeate the works of writers who fill the education journals with articles, who win doctorates in education, or who simply enter class-rooms in order to match children and young adults on a curricular basis.

Do you believe that you have a soul, or are you, perhaps like the intelligent, college-bred airline hostess I met, with an M.A. in English and course credit beyond, who lives from trip to trip, with approxi-mately one lover a year, and a program for world travel at practically no expense? When she is too old for hostess work, she will turn to conducting tours. Her one imponderable is that she could go blind and have a problem of adjustment. She thinks she is of a new breed of people, and that there are many people like herself, male and female, and with her general perspectives.

Do you believe that we, as individuals, can influence students to be better human males and females, or that we can hold the social line against those with egotistical and shallow material goals? Do you believe there *are*, truly any goals which are social and universal, and that they are worth fighting for, at the expense of immediate satisfac-tions and status symbols? The two causes which have recently won substantial numbers of followers have been peace and civil rights, and both have their martyrs. But our subject is not martyrdom, it is educa-tion: the principles we live and work under, whatever our hopes and intentions. If you believe that people are expendable and that tradition is a nonsensical waste of our few moments of pleasurable life, you will hardly want to waste them on austere living, tradition-bound life, in-vestment in the future: a future which will be the stamping ground for other bipeds.

Whatever you believe, Horace Mann believed that morality was at the base of a valid education, and that the physical universe was a patent witness to the need for principled living, healthful living, social living. He believed that the human body was an awesome labyrinth of eternal laws, which, transgressed, resulted in social and individual ill. I am sure that all this sounds old-fashioned and commonplace; but it must be spelled out. It raises the question of what may be new-fashioned and more effective.

iv. *Education and Results*

The reader will not go far in this selection of Mann's writings before he discovers that their author was anything but abstract in his argument. Mann observed experience with the hard head of a lawyer and a student of life. He studied cause and effect. Moreover, he had a gift for anecdote and analogy, many of which are likely to grow in the reader's mind and sparkle more intensely on recollection. The reader is likely to notice how modern are many of the situations with which Mann deals. Mann, too, had to cope with careless and indifferent teachers who sheathed themselves behind formal presentations. He, too, remarked cunning and otherwise offensive characteristics in students— characteristics which had somehow to be controlled. Mann had a faith in the intrinsic capacities of children, and he believed that society could produce a competent and dedicated teaching personnel, if it would define sound discipline for the children and suitable emoluments for the instructors. But he believed, too, that neither discipline nor emoluments would by themselves shape adequate educational goals and means for attaining them. Let us assume Mann was wrong in his moralistic strictures. What is *right*? Who are the educators who produce results which his approach does not comprehend?

I recall a young high-school teacher who complained that his students were not interested in his presentations—that they followed his materials docilely, rather than with enthusiasm and cooperative creativity. Yet he himself used prepared materials of a strictly formal variety. Was he himself "interested"?—interested enough, for example, to expand his preparations with live materials out of newspapers and out of his own and his students' experiences? Why should they be "interested," when his own offerings were unprobed, unconnotative, and reflecting the active intelligence of a TV dinner?

Another young teacher, a young woman of bohemian habits and program, complains of her students' limited "participation" in classroom activities, which strike her as "uncreative." I think she misunderstands her students' nature. They pay less attention to her lessons than they do to *her*, and they dream not of becoming like the wooden people of her wooden story: the fake George Washingtons and Abraham Lincolns. They long, rather, for the day when they will have grown up to enjoy her opportunities and programs. Children are keen, for better or worse. They are observant. The young woman is less complex than her charges, and (unfortunately) she is one of their models, one of the aspirations of their nascent manhood and womanhood.

Seen so, the old progressive-education-versus-basics argument dwindles in significance, unless you actually believe that one shibboleth rather than another will produce educational results. A course of study which does not cope with the problem of character—what can we expect of it? Horace Mann, for one, did not avoid its challenge. We may criticize his solutions, but we cannot avoid the defense of our own.

This effort of Mann's, his attempt to define an education for whole living, was, I think his greatest achievement. With or without him, the schools of his generation had to multiply. There were increasing numbers of children who had to be processed, and there was an increasingly urban civilization which required a modernized school system. But many of our educational "developments" have been no more than accommodations to physical growth.* Mere growth is not educational health or achievement, and we forget the common entrepreneurs of education who no more than increase the size of their schools. We have not so much forgotten Horace Mann as we have avoided his vital and uncomfortable educational tenets. Yet our own educational crisis continues, obscured by states-rights and civil rights issues. That crisis will continue so long as those issues are not linked with individual and social goals: with problems of educational achievement, human deportment, and other non-specialist considerations.

v. *Kew Gardens*

Take, for example, the question of gentility, which happens to have literary and cultural aspects, as in the cases of Henry James and Henry Adams and their circles. The idea of being a lady or a gentleman has not been over-popular in our time, but recently it has been taken by students to be positively distasteful and bizarre. Many of them do not even care to be ladies and gentlemen in the "true" sense of the word: the boor with the heart of gold. Horace Mann, on the contrary, thought that manners were what helped to distinguish people from beasts. In this connection, I have come to wonder what duties anyone owed to anybody. For instance, what duties does a man owe to a female who is not a lady? One girl says she sometimes does not want to be treated like a lady in any sense of the word, whatever it means to her. Good enough; but how *does* she want to be treated, by someone who is not

---

* My "Main Currents in Progressivist American Education," *History of Education Journal*, Winter, 1957, pp. 33ff., seeks to distinguish adjustment processes from educational innovations which were intended to affect the quality of instruction.

her lover, who is, in fact, nothing to her at all? Here, it seems to me,
is an excellent justification for someone who wants only to mind his
own business: who neither cares to rape the female nor to be bothered
with her presence. There was a time when a male who was also a man
took, so to speak, all womankind under his protection. He could not
tolerate a world in which women could be degraded and treated as
beasts. But can he "defend" a female who perhaps does not care to be
defended?—who might resent his solicitude, or be suspicious of his
motives, knowing men as she does?

The tenants of Kew Gardens, in Queens, New York, were perhaps
right, after all, to have minded their own business when they observed
a female apparently being murderously assaulted by a male—I say
"apparently," for how could they know what the situation really was?
How could they *know*?*

When social standards erode, even the concerned individual is
made more and more uncertain of his place and responsibilities in
society. He learns caution. And I put it to the reader:

Horace Mann believed that men and women students should be
rigidly restricted in their associations, and he believed that students
should inform on one another and give no countenance to wrong-
doing, as he defined it. I have no doubt that such regulations were
authoritarian then and would be fantastic today. But is their ob-
verse more feasible, especially at the expense of a school campus and
reputation? Ought campus tramps, for example, to be accorded courtesy
and respect, and conniving narcotics experimenters to be given the run
of a tax-free institution? One big-city gadfly of reputation and opportunity and advancing age thinks he has the right to homosexual
privileges with young people, so long as he does not "exploit" or "hurt"
the objects of his fugitive affections. Do you "structure" an examination
of his individual experiences, or do you keep your nose out of his private
affairs, as you did at Kew Gardens?

Whatever else we say of Horace Mann, he faced issues and he took
stands. I do not say we can follow him in all his thinking and practices.
I suspect we must deviate from quite a few of them. Mann believed in
phrenology. His sense of realism did not permit him to credit the

---

* One housewife, "knowingly if quite casually," said she thought it was a lovers
quarrel. Lovers quarrels can, after all, be occasionally quite hectic. Incidentally,
the reporter who broke the story confessed that his first reaction to it was "one
of professional satisfaction"; see A. M. Rosenthal, *Thirty-Eight Witnesses* (New
York, 1964), pp. 44, 47.

products of fancy; he thought fiction and poetry inferior to scientific works. He had other debatable or obsolete views. But any objective considerations must remind us that not a little of our own thinking is destined for obsolescence. It is not for our up-to-dateness that we warrant respect. GNP, role-playing, New Frontier, explication, basics—such slogans and concepts fade into history. It is for our drive toward reality, our sense of principle, our faithfulness to our heritage, our will to valid change that we deserve regard. How much regard we will attract is undetermined, but there is little question about how much regard Horace Mann merits. He is a great window on his own times and its deepest experiences. He was keen, witty, endlessly energetic, and inspiring. One measure of our advance toward the good society will be the degree to which we show capacity to appreciate, as educators and as human beings, how much it was that he left us.

Antioch College, 1965   Louis Filler

NOTE ON THE TEXT

The selections and extracts here included are taken from the five-volume edition of Horace Mann's *Life and Works* (1865-1891), largely prepared and edited by his wife Mary Mann, and later, by her son George C. Mann. Also helpful has been her *Thoughts Selected from the Writings of Horace Mann* (1867). Materials, however, have been freely edited, so that they would present Mann's views and essays with strength and clarity, and with the highest possible relevance to the present time. The astonishing fact, to me, has been to discover how readily Mann's work responded to editing, how little of his work obscured the dynamic quality of his thought, once one penetrated beneath the surface differences in attitudes and goals created by a passing century. Titles and subtitles have been recast, or newly coined, in order to highlight the similiarities between the educational and social problems of Mann's generation and our own. No liberties, of course, have been taken with his own ideas and phrasings. None were needed. Cleansed of by-views and emphases which would perhaps interest a solitary thesis-writer but no one else, they stand forth as challenging experiences and observation, in our time and in his.   L.F.

CHRONOLOGY

1789. School-district system legalized in Massachusetts. Ensuing decentralization hurt public interest and diminished financial support of education.

May 4, 1796. Horace Mann born, in Franklin, Massachusetts.

1816. Mann prepared for college; after six months of study, he entered Brown University as a sophomore.

1819. Mann graduated with honors; studied law briefly; became a tutor in Latin and Greek at Brown.

1821. Studied law at Litchfield, Connecticut; in 1823 was admitted to the bar at Dedham, Massachusetts.

1827. Began service in the House of Representatives of the Massachusetts Legislature. That year, it sanctioned the establishment of high schools, but none was erected at the time.

September 12, 1830. Mann married Charlotte Messer, the daughter of Asa Messer, President of Brown University. She died childless, August 1, 1832. Her death was a blow to Mann which impelled him to reorganize his life and perspectives.

1833. Mann moved his law practice to Boston; was elected to the Massachusetts Senate. He became acquainted with, and developed interests with, such reformers as Dorothea Dix and Charles Sumner.

1835-37. Served as president of the Massachusetts Senate.

April 20, 1837. The Legislature passed an education bill which provided for a state board of education to employ a secretary at an annual salary of $1,000. He was to report annually to the board. Mann gave up law to accept the post.

1837. Issued first of twelve great annual reports (1837-1848), on aspects of his work and program.

1838. Acquired a private gift of $10,000, conditional on the Massachusetts Legislature's matching that sum, for the establishment of state teachers institutions and normal schools. Within two years Massachusetts had established three normal schools, the first of their kind in the United States. Mann also reinvigorated the 1827 law establishing high schools. During his tenure as secretary, fifty high schools were created. He activated another law of 1827 ending sectarian religious education in the public school system, for which he was severely criticized. Established *Common School Journal.*

1839. Persuaded the Massachusetts legislature to establish six-month minimum school year. Established first normal school in the United States, Lexington, Massachusetts.

May 1, 1843. Married Mary Tyler Peabody, one of the famous "Peabody sisters." Journeyed to Europe where he studied European education.

During five-month stay, visited England, Ireland, Scotland, Holland, Belgium, France, Germany, and Switzerland.

1848. Mann resigned position as secretary to the Massachusetts Board of Education, to succeed John Quincy Adams, who had just died, in the House of Representatives in Washington. Mann developed his antislavery convictions and served its partisans in and out of Congress.

September 15, 1852. Mann nominated for Governor of Massachusetts by a Convention of the Free Democracy. On the same day, he was chosen president of Antioch College, and accepted the latter office.

1853. Took up his administrative duties at Yellow Springs, Ohio. Also taught political economy, intellectual philosophy, moral philosophy, and natural theology. In addition, he continued to lecture and write.

August 2, 1859. Horace Mann died in Yellow Springs, Ohio.

Thoughts from Horace Mann

ASSIMILATION

Intelligence, and wisdom, and virtue, cannot be poured out of one mind into another, as water from a vessel. The increment comes by assimilation, not transfusion. Ideas, knowledge, may be brought within reach of the mind, but if they are not digested, and prepared by a process of the spirit itself upon them, they give no more vigor and power to the mind than sacks of grain nourish the jaded beast when they are fastened to his back.

POSSESSING THE STORES OF KNOWLEDGE

As each generation comes into the world devoid of knowledge, its first duty is to obtain possession of the stores already amassed. It must overtake its predecessors before it can pass by them.

IDEAS

When the common stock of knowledge is enlarged, all men are enlarged; because, if gigantic ideas are given even to a pygmy, the pygmy becomes a giant.

ATHEISM AND DUTY

Even on the atheistic hypothesis of no God, it could be shown that Duty is expedient; but on the theistic hypothesis of a God, it can be demonstrated that the knowledge and performance of Duty are the highest moral necessities for every human being.

VISIBLE MECHANISM AND INVISIBLE CHEMISTRY

[W]oe to the people or the man who, through ignorance or through defiance, contends against the visible mechanism or the invisible chemistry of Nature's laws. Whoever will not learn and obey these laws, her lightnings blast, her waters drown, her fires consume, her pestilences extinguish; and she could crush the whole human race beneath her wheels, nor feel shock or vibration from the contact.

WEAK-BODIED SAINTS

No combatants are so unequally matched as when one is shackled with error, while the other rejoices in the self-demonstrability of truth; yet when virtue contends with vice for the extirpation of social abuses, or for the advancement of great reforms, how often do the strong-bodied reprobates vanquish the weak-bodied saints!

JAILS AND SCHOOLS

Jails and state prisons are the complement of schools: so many less as you have the latter, so many more must you have of the former.

APPLICATION OF PRINCIPLES

We want principles, not only developed,—the work of the closet,—but *applied*; which is the work of life. Between the recluse, who never emerges from his study, however well he may reason on human nature, and the active man, who prepares the machinery and puts it in operation, there is the same difference as between one who describes a wolf and one who tames the animal.

BIGOTS

The prayer of Christ was, "Thy kingdom come." The prayer of every bigot is, "*My* kingdom come."

CHANGING MORALITY

Men who take any enlarged view of the course of nations, and the destiny of the human race, see that a new era has opened upon the world. The history of the future is to be widely different from that of the past. The stream of time is changing its direction. It is about to pass through moral regions, such as in its whole previous course, since it broke from the original fountain, it has never traversed before. We must prepare ourselves to move with safety through the new realms we are entering.

VIRTUE A GROWTH

Are not great mistakes committed in the government of children, by acting upon the supposition that they can grow strong in virtuous resolutions *in a single day?* If all our active affections, whether good or bad, are the result of growth, then opportunity must be allowed for the seeds to germinate after they have been sown.

HAVE HEATHENS SOULS?

After the discovery of America, the question was started among the ecclesiastics of Spain, whether the aborigines of North America had souls. It was warmly debated *pro* and *con*, and the arguments were so equally balanced that no decision was had on the question. But it was wisely suggested that perhaps they had souls, and therefore missionaries should be sent to them. This course was adopted. We would recommend a similar decision. If, peradventure, the children have moral and religious natures, they ought to be cultivated.

RIGHTS AND DUTIES

In this country we seem to learn our rights quicker than our duties.

HEALTH AND EDUCATION

Soundness of health is preliminary to the *highest* success in any pursuit. In every industrial avocation it is an indispensable element, and the highest intellectual eminence can never be reached without it. It exerts a powerful influence over feelings, temper, and disposition, and through these upon moral character. Yet, incredible as it may seem, the means of acquiring vigor, endurance, quickness, have been sought for, not by the clergyman, the lawyer, the artist, the cultivator of letters, the mother, but by the wrestler, the buffoon, the runner, the opera-dancer. There are ten professors of pugilism in our community to one of physical education in our seminaries of learning.

POWERS OF THE MIND

It is my design to show that the world has lost even more by not understanding the powers and laws of the mind than was lost by an ignorance of the powers and laws of matter, and that there are obvious and practical uses of the natural powers of the mind which will confer far greater blessedness upon the race than has been conferred by a knowledge of astronomy, navigation, chemistry, and all the radiant circle of the useful sciences.

THE MIRACLE OF CONSCIENCE

A conscientious man, subjected by adverse fortunes to some vehement temptation, which, day after day, seems more and more to bend his affrighted and struggling conscience to its purpose, until with strong and divine resistance he casts off the clinging viper, experiences a change through all his soul, as great in kind, if not in degree, as can ever be felt in passing from one world to another.

CHANCE AND CAUSE

A philosopher uses the word *chance* not to denote an effect without a cause, but to denote an effect of whose cause he is ignorant. Both in the philosophical and material world all is power and motion, and wherever there is power or motion there is law to govern it.

ELOQUENCE

When an audience of a thousand men, of diverse tastes, of hostile creeds, and of conflicting desires, are, as it were, uplifted from the earth by the might and majesty of eloquence. . . it is nothing but the breaking away of each mind, for the time being, from the fastenings of these habitual associations, which at other times bind it to its monotonous, mill-horse circle of thought.

PLEASURES OF KNOWLEDGE

When the Pennsylvania Dutchman said that all he wanted his boys to know was, how to count a hundred dollars and to row a boat to New Orleans, he did not think that if others had not known vastly more than this, there would have been no dollars to count, nor New Orleans to go to.

LANGUAGE, LOVELY AND UNLOVELY

Some languages are musical in themselves, so that it is pleasant to hear any one read or converse in them, even though we do not understand a word that we hear. Such is the Italian. Others are full of growling, snarling, hissing sounds, as though wild beasts and serpents had first taught the people to speak. Such, to a painful extent, are those of the Saxon stock, from which the greater part of our own is derived. A few poets, however, by their wonderful powers of culling and collocating, have been able to tune the jaggy hoarseness of the English throat, horrid with croak and gutteralness, into the sweet utterance of many a page of gently-flowing verse, musical with swell and cadence of melodious sounds. When the language is unmusical, the only remaining beauty with which we can invest it is that of a distinct articulation. Nothing is more painful to a cultivated and delicate ear, than the jargon which has the harshness of the adult's voice, with the articulateness of the infant's.

SCHOOL-HOUSES

We can now call to mind several cases which we have witnessed in travelling over the state, where barns, piggeries, and other outbuildings have been erected according to the most approved style of Gothic architecture, and the abode of brute animals decorated with the profusion of ornament which belongs to that finical order. But the models of the old school-houses did not come from the classic land of the East; their origin was aboriginal,—not copied from Greece or Rome, but rather from the Pequots and Narragansetts. Not only would many of our school-houses furnish an illustration in geography, because five steps would carry the pupil through the five zones, but astronomy also could be studied in them to advantage, for through the rents in the roof the stars might all be seen as they came to the zenith.

GOOD BEHAVIOR

Manners easily and rapidly mature into morals.

TO BOYS

Do not trouble the birds. Let them sing and fly without fear from you. Do not kill them, do not catch and imprison them. Let them go abroad in all the joyousness of their brief summer's life. If you wish for something to do in the spring days, dig a hole in some suitable place by the road-side, three or four feet across and a foot and a half deep; throw back part of the earth; then go into the fields or woods, catch a wild tree, the prettiest you can find, and fasten its roots carefully in the cage that you have made for them, and your children's children, or the poor wayfaring man, a century hence, may thank you for the shade which you have provided. Is not this better than catching birds?

READ ALWAYS

Resolve to edge in a little reading every day, if it is but a single sentence. If you gain fifteen minutes a day, it will make itself felt at the end of the year.

DUTY A HAPPINESS

In vain do they talk of happiness who never subdued an impulse in obedience to a principle. He who never sacrificed a present to a future good, or a personal to a general one, can speak of happiness only as the blind do of colors.

BIRD LEARNING

In learning to read, we might derive a lesson from the mocking-birds.

If, in learning to sing the songs of other birds, they fall into a mistake, in a moment the gush of sound is checked, and they go back, again and again if necessary, until they catch and can repeat—and *verbatim et literatim*—the notes they aspire to imitate. They also practice long and faithfully, and they have wisdom enough to do this when they are young. Speaking of the ferruginous mocking-bird, Audubon says, "It sings well. The young begin their musical studies in autumn, repeating passages with as much zeal as ever did Paganini. It scarcely possesses the faculty of imitation, but is a *steady performer*." These birds begin their studies young, in the autumn of the year in which they are hatched, and before the silken and flexible fibres of their throats toughen into whale-bone. They repeat, innumerable times, what they hear, and the development of their "Full powers of song" is not reached until after long application.

NATURAL LANGUAGE

Whether a man has one temperament or another, is described all over him,—in his hair, in his eyes, in his complexion, in the style of his features, and in the firmness or sponginess of his flesh. I say, therefore, the proofs of a man's temperament are written all over him. He cannot help himself, any more than a horse can help showing how old he is by his teeth, or an ox by his horns, or a rattlesnake by his rattles. We know, too, that there is such a thing as a natural language, which is more truthful and unambiguous than the English language, or any other that was ever invented. This natural language consists in the peculiar tones of the voice, in the expression of the countenance, and in the gestures, the air and carriage, of a man,— all betokening the spirit within. These outward signs declare what thoughts and emotions have made up the inward history of our lives; they declare what thoughts and emotions we are now indulging, and what, probably, we shall continue to indulge.

SCIENCE AND RELIGION

In every instance where science has revealed a new truth which conflicted, not with the Bible, but with the current interpretations of the Bible,—instead of inquiring whether the alleged discoveries were or were not true, many clergymen have denounced it, and poured vengeance upon its supporters. Hence a disastrous alienation has ensued between science and religion; or rather, between the disciples of science and the ministers of religion; for between true science and true religion there can never be any conflict. As all truth is from God, it necessarily follows that true science and true religion can never be at variance. The works of God, and the providence of God, can never conflict with any revelation from God.

SPIRITUAL WRECKS

There are no wrecks of things so precious as those which lie at the bottom of the spiritual ocean. The serfs of Europe, the vassals and Pariahs of Oriental despotism, the barbarians of Africa, have lived and died, scarcely leaving any more trace behind them than their contemporary swarms of insects in the marshes of the Nile or the Ganges.

RIPENESS OF MEN

As an apple is not in any proper sense an apple until it is ripe, so a human being is not in any proper sense a human being until he is educated.

CAUSALITY

Causality is the mightiest intellectual power bestowed on man. No such intellectual difference exists between men, as between the man who has it and the man who has it not. The extremes of its presence or its absence mark the extremes of greatness and of imbecility. Idiots have but a germ or minimum of it, and hence they are idiots.

FANATICISM AND REFORM

Resistance to improvement contradicts the noblest instincts of the race. It begets its opposite. The fanaticism of reform is only the raging of the accumulated waters caused by the obstructions which an ultra conservatism has thrown across the stream of progress; and revolution itself is but the sudden overwhelming and sweeping away of impediments that should have been seasonably removed. The French Revolution was a frightful spectacle of a too rapid effort at reform. The present condition of England and Ireland is a spectacle still more frightful of an almost inflexible conservatism.

UNQUALIFIED IGNORANCE

An ignorant man is always able to say yes or no immediately to any proposition. To a wise man, comparatively few things can be propounded which do not require a response with qualifications, with discrimination, with proportion.

IGNORANCE UNLEASHED

Ignorance has been well represented under the similitude of a dungeon, where, though it is full of life, yet darkness and silence reign. But in society the bars and locks have been broken; the dungeon itself is demolished; the prisoners are out; they are in the midst of us. We have no security but to teach and renovate them.

AGITATORS

Agitation is a part of the sublime order of nature. In thunder, it shakes the stagnant air, which would otherwise breed pestilence. In tempests, it purifies the deep, which would otherwise exhale miasma and death. And in the immortal thoughts of duty, of humanity, and of liberty, it so rouses the hearts of men that they think themselves inspired by God; and not the mercenary clamor of the market-place, nor the outcries of politicians, clutching at the prizes of ambition, can suppress the utterances that true men believe themselves heaven-committed to declare.

CASTE

The law of caste includes within itself every form of iniquity, because it lives by the practical denial of human brotherhood.

NATIVE LOVE OF LIBERTY

All the noblest instincts of human nature rebel against slavery. Whenever we applaud the great champions of liberty, who, by the sacrifice of life in the cause of freedom, have won the homage of the world, and an immortality of fame, we record the testimony of our hearts against it. Wherever patriotism and philanthropy have glowed brightest, wherever piety and a devout religious sentiment have burned most fervently, there has been the most decided recognition of the universal rights of man.

NO EDUCATION FOR THE SLAVE

Of all the remorseless and wanton cruelties ever committed in this world of wickedness and woe, I hold that to be the most remorseless and wanton which shuts out from all the means of instruction a being whom God has endued with the capacities of knowledge, and inspired with the divine desire to *know*. Strike blossom and beauty from the vernal season of the year, and leave it sombre and cheerless; annihilate the harmonies with which the birds of spring make vocal the field and the forest, and let exulting Nature become silent and desolate;—do all this, if you will, but withhold your profane hand from those creative sources of knowledge which shall give ever-renewing and ever-increasing delight through all the cycles of immortality, and which have the power to assimilate the finite creature more and more nearly to the infinite Creator.

IGNORANCE BREEDS ERROR

He who shuts out truth, by the same act opens the door to all the error that supplies its place. Ignorance breeds monsters to fill up all the vacancies of the soul that are unoccupied by the verities of knowledge. He who dethrones the idea of law, bids chaos welcome in its stead. Superstition is the mathematical complement of religious truth, and just so much less as the life of a human being is reclaimed to good, just so much more it is delivered over to evil. The man or the institution, therefore, that withholds knowledge from a child or from a race of children, exercises the awful power of changing the world in which they live just as much as if he should annihilate all that is most lovely and good in this planet of ours, or transport the victim of his cruelty to some dark and frigid zone of the universe, where the sweets of knowledge are unknown, and the terrors of ignorance hold their undisputed and remorseless reign.

ABOLITIONISTS OF WHAT?

Before we can decide upon the honor or the infamy of the term "Abolitionist," we must know what things they are which he proposes to abolish. We of the North, you say, are abolitionists; but abolitionists of what? Are we abolitionists of the inalienable, indefeasible, indestructible rights of man? Are we abolitionists of knowledge, abolitionists of virtue, of education, and of human culture? Do we seek to abolish the glorious moral and intellectual attributes which God has given to his children, and thus, as far as it lies in our power, make the facts of slavery conform to the law of slavery, by obliterating the distinction between a man and a beast? Do our laws and our institutions seek to blot out and abolish the image of God in the human soul? Do we abolish the marriage covenant? Do we ruthlessly tear asunder the sacred ties of affection by which God has bound the parent to the child and the child to the parent? Do we seek to abolish all those noble instincts of the human soul, by which it yearns for improvement and progress? and do we quench its sublimest aspirations after knowledge and virtue? A stranger would suppose, from hearing the epithets of contumely that are heaped upon us, that we were abolitionists of all truth, purity, knowledge, improvement, civilization, happiness, and holiness. On this subject, perversion of language and of idea has been reduced to a system, and the falsehoods of our calumniators exclude truth with the exactness of a science. If we are abolitionists, we are abolitionists of human bondage; while those who oppose us are abolitionists of human liberty.

BOOK OF LIFE OR OF DEATH?

Priests appealed to the Bible, in Galileo's time, to refute the truths of astronomy. For more than two hundred years the same class of men appealed to the same authority to disprove the science of geology. And now this authority is cited, not to disprove the law of physical nature merely, but to deny a great law of the human soul,—a law of human consciousness,—a law of God written upon the tablet of every man's heart, authenticating and attesting his title to freedom. Let those who reverence the Bible beware how they suborn it to commit this treason and perjury against the sacred rights of man and the holy law of God. Whatever they gain for the support of their doctrine, will be so much subtracted from the authority of the Scriptures. If the Bible has crossed the Atlantic to spread slavery over a continent where it was not known before, then the Bible is a book of death, and not a book of life.

SPIRIT OF THE AGE

There is one hazard which the South invokes and defies, which to her high-minded and honor-loving sons, should be more formidable than all the rest. She is defying the spirit of the age. She is not only defying the judgment of contemporaries, but invoking upon herself the execrations of posterity.

LIVING WITH EARTHQUAKES

There is a spot near the Mississippi River famous for the frequency of its earthquakes. A gentleman who visited there some years ago, told me that soon after entering a hotel, at a place called New Madrid, his attention was suddenly arrested by the rattling of the crockery, the jarring of the household furniture, and the shaking of the chair in which he sat. Starting up in trepidation, he sprang for the door. "O,"

said his landlord, "don't be alarmed. *It is nothing but an earthquake.*"
These phenomena, it seems, had become so common as to have lost
their power of exciting alarm. So, I fear, it is in regard to the late
commotions in Europe, and especially in regard to some of the marvellous doings of Congress in our own country. From their astounding
character, and their rapid succession, I fear we are becoming insensible
to their importance, like the inhabitants who dwell at the base of
Mount Aetna, whom neither the rumbling of the mountain, nor the
lava rivers which pour down its side, can awake from their stupor,
until, like Pompeii or Herculaneum, they are buried in the ruins.

PARTY DICTATION

Perhaps I do not know what I was made for; but one thing I certainly never was made for, and that is, to put principles on and off,
at the dictation of a party, as a lackey changes his livery at his master's
command.

ERRORS OF EDUCATION

The unpardonable error of education has been, that it has not begun
with simple truths, with elementary ideas, and risen by gradations
to combined results. It has begun with teaching systems, rules, schemes,
complex doctrines, which years of analysis would scarcely serve to
unfold. All is administered in a mass. The learner, not being able to
comprehend, has endeavored to remember, and thus has been put
off with a fact, in lieu of a principle explanatory of an entire class
of facts. In this way we pass our errors and our truths over to our
successors done up in the same bundle, they to others, and so onward.
to be perpetual sources of error, alienation, and discord.

TEACHERS

Every teacher ought to know vastly more than he is required to teach,
so that he may be furnished, on every subject, with copious illustration and instructive anecdote; and so that the pupils may be disabused
of the notion that they are so apt to acquire, that they carry all
knowledge in their satchels. Every teacher should be possessed of
a facility at explanation. . . . In Dr. Johnson's Dictionary, the word
"Network" is defined to be "any thing reticulated or decussated, with
interstices between the intersections." Now who, ignorant of the word
"network" before, would understand it any better by being told that
it is " any thing reticulated or decussated, with interstices between

the intersections?" . . . If this is not, as Milton says, "dark with excess of bright," it is, at least, "darkness visible." A few years since, a geography was published in this State—the preface of which boasted of its adaptation to the capacities of children;—and, on the second page, there was this definition of the words "zenith and nadir:" "zenith and nadir, two Arabic words *importing their own signification.*" A few years since, an English traveller and bookmaker, who called himself Thomas Ashe, Esq., visited the Big Bone Licks, in Kentucky, where he found the remains of the mammoth, in great abundance, and whence he carried away several wagon-loads of bones. In describing the size of one of the shoulder-blades of that animal, he says, it "was *about as large as a breakfast table!*" A child's mind may be dark and ignorant before, but, under such explanations as these, darkness will coagulate, and ignorance be sealed in hermetically.

DIFFICULTIES OF AN EDUCATOR

Sometimes I cannot repress laughter at the ridiculousness of my own position. When I devote not a little time to preparation, and then visit a place and strive to expound the great subject of education, and labor, and preach, and exhort, and implore, I seem to myself as if I were standing, on some wintry day, with the storm beating upon me, ringing the door bell of a house that no one lives in, or perhaps where the dwellers are all sound asleep, or too much absorbed in their own minds to hear the summons of one who comes to tell them that a torrent from the mountains is rushing down upon them.

FACETS

Man is improvable. Some people think he is only a machine, and that the only difference between a man and a mill is, that one is carried by blood and the other by water.

Insult not another for his want of the talent you possess; he may have talents which you want.

Reproof is a medicine, like mercury or opium; if it be improperly administered, it will do harm instead of good.

Do not think of knocking out another person's brains because he differs in opinion from you. It would be as rational to knock yourself on the head because you differ from yourself ten years ago.

There is hardly any bodily blemish which a winning behavior will not conceal, or make tolerable; and there is no external grace which ill nature or affectation will not deform.

All mental growth is organization, not accretion; it comes from within outwards, and does not consist in enlargement by external application—aggregation.

Lost, yesterday, somewhere between sunrise and sunset, two golden hours, each set with sixty diamond minutes. No reward is offered, for they are gone forever!

Attention—*ad-tendo*, a bending or stretching towards any object of interest. It marks the degrees of intensity with which we devote our minds to any subject or thing.

I think I restrict myself within bounds in saying, that so far as I have observed in this life, ten men have failed from defect in morals where one has failed from defect in intellect.

The "lower orders" are those who do nothing for the good of mankind.

1.

Horizons

EDUCATION

If ever there was a cause, if ever there can be a cause, worthy to be upheld by all of toil or sacrifice that the human heart can endure, it is the cause of Education. It has intrinsic and indestructible merits. It holds the welfare of mankind in its embrace, as the protecting arms of a mother hold her infant to her bosom. The very ignorance and selfishness which obstruct its path are the strongest arguments for its promotion, for it furnishes the only adequate means for their removal.

MOTIVES

In the education of children, *motives are everything,* MOTIVES ARE EVERY-THING. . . . Let us take a child who has only a moderate love of learning, but an inordinate passion for praise and place; and we therefore allure him to study by the enticements of precedence and applause. . . . If he ever had any compassionate misgivings in regard to the effect which his own promotion may have upon his less brilliant, though not less meritorious fellow-pupils, then we seek to withdraw his thoughts from his virtuous channel, and to turn them to the selfish contemplation of his own brilliant fortunes in future years; if waking conscience ever whispers in his ear, that that pleasure is dishonorable which gives pain to the innocent; then we dazzle him with the gorgeous vision of triumphal honors and applaud-ing multitudes;—and when, in after-life, this victim of false influences deserts a righteous cause because it is declining, and joins an unrighteous one because it is prospering, . . . then we pour out lamentations, in prose and verse, over the moral suicide!

DANGERS AND NECESSITY OF DEMOCRACY

I rejoice that power has passed irrevocably into the hands of the people, although I know it has brought imminent peril upon all public and private interests, and placed what is common and what is sacred alike in jeopardy. The wealthy, the high-born, the privileged, had had it in their power to bless the people; but they had cursed them. Now, they and all their fortunes are in the hands of the people. The poverty which they have entailed is to com-mand their opulence. The ignorance they have suffered to abound, is to adjudicate upon their rights. The appetites they have neglected, or which they have stimulated for their own indulgence, are to invade the sanctuary of their homes. In fine, that interest and concern for the welfare of inferiors, which should have sprung from motives of philanthropy, must now be extorted from motives of self-preservation. As a famine teaches mankind to be industrious and provident, so do these great developments teach the more favored classes of society that they never can be safe while they neglect the welfare of any portion of their social inferiors.

OUR EDUCATION: ITS DIGNITY
AND ITS DEGRADATION

From *Lectures on Education*

"The meed of praise has been very liberally and justly awarded to Washington Irving for his valuable contributions to our scanty stock of polite literature; yet it may well be questioned, whether the injury done to the cause of common education in the character of Ichabod Crane has not more than cancelled the whole debt." R. B. Hubbard, Principal, Worcester, Mass., High School (1843).

The Act of April 20, 1837 which created the Massachusetts Board of Education was a major milestone in American education. It brought Horace Mann actively into the field as the Board's secretary. The next year, the State Legislature provided that a Common-School convention should be held annually, in each county, and that the secretary should attend every one. Mann conscientiously made a circuit of these meetings, delivering a new lecture on subjects he thought meriting priority. The following is drawn from his lecture of 1840. He drew a dreary picture of the history of education, and probably a biased one. He saw education through the eyes of a republican, to whom all limitations upon universal instruction were intolerable. Thus, American ideals and perspectives in the field crowned its past and future. But they would not mature themselves; they would be a product of courageous effort, wakeful vigilance.

In treating any important and comprehensive subject, it will inevitably happen that some portions of it will be found less interesting than others;—inferior in beauty, dignity, elevation. In every book we read, some chapters will be less animating and instructive than the rest; in every landscape we survey, some features less impressive and grand; in every journey we take, some stages more dreary and laborious. Yet we must accept them together, as a whole,—the poor with the good. This is my apology for presenting to you, at the present time, a class of views, which,—whether they excite more or less interest,—will derive none of it from flattering our self-complacency.

In this stage of the inquiry, it seems proper to consider in what relative esteem or disesteem the subject of education has heretofore been held, and is now held, in the regards of men. Let us seek an answer to such questions as these:—Have men assigned to the cause of education a high or a low position? What things have they placed above it; and what things, (if any,) have they placed below it? How have its followers been honored or rewarded? What means, instrumentalities, accommodations, have been provided for carrying on the work? In fine, when its interests have come in competition with other interests, which have been made to yield? It is related of a certain king, that, when embarked on a voyage, attended by some of his courtiers, and carrying with him some of his treasures, a storm arose, which made it necessary to lighten the ship;—whereupon, he commanded his courtiers to be thrown overboard, but saved his money. How is it with parents, who are embarked with fortune and family on this voyage of life;—when they need a better schoolhouse to save their children from ill health, or a better teacher to rescue them from immorality and ignorance; or even a slate or a shilling's worth of paper to save them from idleness;—have we any parents amongst us, or have we not, who, under such circumstances, will fling the child overboard, and save the shilling?

A ten-pound weight will not more certainly weigh down a five-pound weight, than a man will act in obedience to that which, on the whole, is his strongest motive. When, therefore, we would ascertain the rank which education actually holds in the regards of any community, we must not merely listen to what that community says; we must see what it does. This is especially true, in our country, where this cause has so many flatterers, but so few friends. Not by their *words*, but by their *works*, shall ye know them, is a test of universal application. Nor must we stop with inspecting the form of the system which may have been anywhere established; we must see whether it be a live system, or an automaton.

A practical unbelief as to the power of education,—the power of physical, intellectual and moral training,—exists amongst us. As a people, we do not believe that these fleshly tabernacles,—which we call tabernacles of clay,—may, by a proper course of training, become as it were tabernacles of iron; or, by an improper course of training, may become tabernacles of glass. We do not believe, that if we would understand and obey the Physical Laws of our nature, our bodies might be so compacted and toughened; that they would outlast ten cast-iron bodies; or, on the other hand, that by ignorant and vicious management, they may become so sleazy and puny, that a body of glass, made by a glass-blower, would outlast ten of them. We have no practical belief that the human intellect, under a course of judicious culture, can be made to grow brighter and brighter, like the rising sun, until it shall shed its light over the dark problems of humanity, and put ignorance and superstition to flight;—we do not believe this, as we believe that corn will grow, or that a stone will fall; and yet the latter facts are no more in accordance with the benign laws of nature than the former. We manifest no living, impulsive faith in the scriptural declaration, "Train up a child in the way he should go, and when he is old he *will not* depart from it." The Scripture does not say that he *probably* will not depart from it; or that in nine cases out of ten he will not depart from it; but it asserts, positively and uncon-ditionally, that he WILL NOT depart from it;—the declaration being philosophically founded upon the fact, that God has made provision for the moral welfare of all his creatures, and that, when we do not attain to it, the failure is caused by our own ignorance or neglect. It is not more true that a well-built ship will float in sea-water instead of diving to the bottom, then it is that spiritually-cultivated affections will buoy up their possessor above the low indulgences of sensuality, and avarice, and profaneness, and intemperance, and irreverence to-wards things sacred.

We also appeal to the history of the past, and aver that among the most enlightened nations of the earth, education has done little or nothing towards producing a state of individual and social well-being, at once universal and permanent;—and now, in this infancy of the world, we rashly prescribe limits to what may be done, from what has been done,—which is about as wise as it would be to say of an infant, that because it never has walked or talked, it never will walk or talk.

My purpose and hope, on the present occasion, are, to vindicate the cause of education from this charge of imbecility; and to show that it has prospered less than other causes have prospered, for the sole and simple, but sufficient reason, that it has been cherished less than other causes have been cherished,—not only in former times and in other countries, but in our own time and country, that is, *always and everywhere.*

I affirm generally, that, up to the present age and hour, the main current of social desires and energies,—the literature, the laws, the wealth, the talent, the character-forming institutions of the world,—have flowed in other channels, and left this one void of fertilizing power. Philosophers, moralists, sages, who have illumined the world with the splendor of their genius on other subjects, have rarely shed the feeblest beam of light upon this. Of all the literature of the ancients which has come down to us, only a most meagre and inconsiderable part has any reference to education. Examine Homer and Virgil, among the poets; Herodotus, Josephus or Livy, among the historians; or Plutarch among the biographers; and you would never infer that, according to their philosophy, the common mass of children did not grow up noble or hateful by a force of their own, like a cedar of Lebanon, or a wild thorn-tree.

The most important and most general fact which meets us, on approaching the subject, is, that, until within less than two centuries of the present time, no system of *free* schools for a whole people was maintained anywhere upon earth; and then, only in one of the colonies of this country,—that colony being the feeble and inconsiderable one of Massachusetts, containing at that time only a few thousand inhabitants.

Among several of the most powerful nations of antiquity, where laws on the subject of education existed, there were no *Public* Schools. Rome, which so long swayed the destinies of the world, and at last sunk to so ignominious a close, had no *Public* Schools. Its schools were what we call *Private*,—undertaken on speculation, and by any person, however unsuitable or irresponsible.

Among the Jews, there seems to be no evidence that there were schools even for boys. It is supposed that even arithmetic was not taught to them, and so universally was the education of females neglected, that even the daughters of the priests could not read and write. Girls, however, were instructed in music and dancing.

The part of education most attended to by all the ancient nations, was that which tended to strengthen and harden the body. Even this, however, was hardly worthy of being called *physical* education, because it was conducted without any competent notions of anatomy or physiology. As war was the grand object which nations proposed to themselves, the education of male children was conducted in reference to their becoming soldiers. In modern times we have gone to the other extreme,—educating the mind, or rather parts of the mind, to the almost total neglect of the body. A striking illustration of these facts is, that the places appropriated to bodily exercises among the Greeks, were called *Gymnasia*; while the Germans, who excel in the cultivation of classical literature, call those schools where mind is cultivated, to the almost entire neglect of the body, by the same name. There can be no true education without the union of both.

The *subject-matter* of education, was, of course, very limited amongst all ancient nations. Their encyclopædia of knowledge would have been but a *primer*, in size, compared with ours. The *seven* liberal arts taught in the celebrated schools of Alexandria, in the time of our Saviour, were grammar, rhetoric, dialectics, arithmetic, geometry, astronomy, and music; and these constituted the complete circle of liberal knowledge. As eloquence conferred a celebrity inferior only to success in arms, it was more assiduously cultivated than any of the other studies. But rhetoric gives only a power over men, while natural philosophy gives a power over nature. In no one respect is the contrast or disparity between ancient and modern times more remarkable than in their ignorance of, and our acquaintance with the natural sciences.

It would be unjust to pass unnoticed a few illustrious educators among the ancients, who existed, not in accordance with, but in defiance of the spirit of the age in which they lived. One of the earliest, and probably the most remarkable of these, was Pythagoras, a Greek, born between five and six hundred years before Christ. He opened a school in the southern part of Italy, and proved the power of education by the results of his labors. Under his instructions, his pupils became men of the most exemplary and noble character; and going out from his school into the different cities of Magna Græcia, they effected the most beneficent revolutions in the social relations of life, and the public institutions of society. Music with him was a prominent means of culture. Each day began and ended with songs, accompanied by the lyre or some other instrument. Particular songs, with corresponding metres and tunes, lively or plaintive, religious or mirthful, were prepared, as excitants or antidotes for particular passions or emotions.

Following Pythagoras, were Socrates, Plato and Aristotle among the Greeks, and Quintilian among the Romans,—great men, indeed, but with not enough of great men around them to correct their errors; and hence it may be questioned whether the authority of their names has not propagated, through succeeding times, more of error than of truth. This is doubtless true of Aristotle, if not of some of the rest.

Little was done by any of the ancient nations for the honor or emolument even of the best of teachers. We know that Socrates was put to death for his excellences; and, according to some accounts, Pythagoras fell in a public commotion which had been raised by a factious hostility to his teachings. Julius Cæsar was the first who procured for Grecian scholars an honorable reception at Rome, by conferring the right of citizenship upon them.* Augustus encouraged men of learning by honorable distinctions and rewards, and exempted teachers from holding certain public offices; but, at one time, a hundred and seventy years before Christ, Grecian philosophers and rhetoricans were expelled from Rome by a decree of the censors.

Quintilian, one of the most eminent and successful of teachers, is supposed to have been the first, and perhaps the only one, among the ancients, who disused and condemned whipping in school; but his power seems, for many centuries, to have been among the lost arts. He taught in the last half of the first century of the Christian era.

Scattered up and down,—but with vast intervals,— among Grecian and Roman writings, we now and then catch a glimpse of this multiform subject;—as when Polybius speaks of the influence of music in refining the character of the Arcadians; or when Horace says that the cultivation of the Fine Arts prevents men from degenerating into brutes;—but considering the vast expanse,—ages of time and millions of minds,—over which these few beams of light were thrown, what right have we to say, that the power and beneficence of education had any opportunity to make known their transforming and redeeming prerogatives, in ancient times?

It occurs to me here to make a single remark in reference to the limited number of those who enjoyed the advantages of education among the ancients. I have elsewhere expounded that beautiful law, in the Divine economy, by which the improvement of the society around us is made indispensable to our own security,—because no man, living in the midst of a vicious community, can be sure that all the virtuous influences which he imparts to his own children will not be neutralized and lost, by the counter influences exerted upon them by others. The sons of Themistocles, Aristides, Pericles, Thucydides, and even of Socrates himself, were contaminated by the corruptions of the times, and thus defeated their paternal hopes. The parent who wishes to bring up his own children well, but refuses to do all in his power to perfect the common, educational institutions around him, should go with his family into voluntary exile,—he should fly to some Juan Fernandez, where no contagion of others' vices can invade his solitude and defeat his care.

---

* Perhaps it is not generally known that Julius Cæsar wrote a Latin Grammar.

Shortly after the commencement of the Christian era, all idea of general popular education, and almost all correct notions concerning education itself, died out of the minds of men. A gloomy and terrible period succeeded, which lasted a thousand years,—a sixth part of the past duration of the race of man! Approaching this period from the side of antiquity, or going back to view it from our own age, we come, as it were, to the borders of a great Gulf of Despair. Gazing down from the brink of this remorseless abyss, we behold a spectacle resembling rather the maddest orgies of demons, than any deeds of men. Oppression usurped the civil throne. Persecution seized upon the holy altar. Rulers demanded the unconditional submission of body and soul, and sent forth ministers of fire and sword to destroy what they could not enslave. Innocence changed places with guilt, and bore all its penalties. Even remorse seems to have died from out the souls of men. As high as the halls of the regal castle rose into the air, so deep beneath were excavated the dungeons of the victim, into which hope never came. By the side of the magnificent Cathedral was built the Inquisition; and all those who would not enter the former, and bow the soul in homage to men, were doomed by the latter to have the body broken or burned. All that power, wealth, arts, civilization had conferred upon the old world,—even new-born, divine Christianity itself,—were converted into instruments of physical bondage and spiritual degradation. These centuries have been falsely called the Dark Ages; they were not *dark*; they glare out more conspicuously than any other ages of the world; but, alas! they glare with infernal fires.

What could education do in such an age? Nothing! nothing! Its voice was hushed; its animation was suspended. It must await the revival of letters, the art of printing, and other great revolutions in the affairs of the world, before it could hope to obtain audience among men.

In the Augustan age of English literature,—in the days of Johnson, Goldsmith, Swift, Pope, Addison,—in all the beautiful writings of these great men, almost nothing is said on the subject of education. Not anywhere is there a single expression showing that they, or either of them, had any just conception of its different departments, and of the various and distinct processes by which the work of each is to be carried on. Dr. Johnson has a few paragraphs scattered up and down over his voluminous writings; but by far the most labored passage he ever prepared on the subject was a forensic argument for Boswell,

defending the brutal infliction of corporal punishment so common
in those days. To show the opinion of this great man respecting the propriety of giving an education to the laboring and poor
classes, let me quote a sentence or two from his "Review of Free
Inquiry."

"I know not whether there are not many states of life, in which
*all knowledge less than the highest wisdom will produce discontent
and danger*. I believe it may be sometimes found that *a little learning
to a poor man is a dangerous thing*."

"Though it should be granted that those who are *born to poverty
and drudgery* should not be *deprived by an improper education of
the opiate of ignorance*, yet," &c.

One of these expressions of Dr. Johnson seems to have been
caught from a celebrated couplet of Pope:

> "A little learning is a dangerous thing,
> *Drink deep or taste not the Pierian spring;*
> There, shallow draughts intoxicate the brain,
> But drinking deeper sobers us again."

One would like to know what extent of acquired knowledge
would constitute *"deep drinking,"* in the sense of this authority; or, in
surveying the vastness of the works of God, whether all that Pope
himself knew, though it were multiplied a hundred-fold, would not
be "a dangerous thing." The doctrine of this passage is as false in
the eye of reason, as the simile is in the creed of a *teetotaler*!

Pope has another oft-quoted passage, in the last line of which,
namely,—

> "Just as the twig is bent, the tree's inclined,"—

he uses the word "twig" in a false sense, as it properly means the
end of a limb, and not the stem or shoot which expands into a tree.
In this he was probably misled by the strength of his associations,
because the twigs, or ends of limbs, performed so important a part
in the work of education in his day, that they had become to him
the type and symbol of the whole process. At the most, Pope merely
symbolizes the general truth; he nowhere proposes to tell us what
modes or processes of cultivation will stimulate its aspiring tendencies,
or bow it downward to the earth;—he never pretends to instruct us
how the tiny germs just breaking from the shell, or the tender shoot
just peering from the earth, may be reared into the lofty tree, bearing
a forest-like crown of branches upon its top, and having limbs and

trunk of such massiveness and cohesive strength, that they will toss off the storm and survive the thunderbolt.

Consider, too, my friends, another general but decisive fact, showing in what subordinate estimation this paramount subject has been held. The human mind is so constituted that it cannot embrace any great idea, but, forthwith, all the faculties strive to aggrandize and adorn and dignify it. Let any principle or sentiment be elevated by the public voice,—whether rightfully or wrongfully,—to a station of pre-eminence or grandeur, in the eyes of men, and it is at once personified, and, as it were, consecrated. The arts go, as on a pilgrimage, to do it reverence. Music celebrates it in national songs. Sculpture embodies it in enduring substance, and clothes it in impressive forms. Painting catches each flashing beam of inspiration from its look, transfers it to her canvas, and holds it fast for centuries, in her magic coloring. Architecture rears temples for its residence and shrines for its worship. Religion sanctifies it. In fine, whatever is accounted high or holy in any age, all the sentiments of taste, beauty, imagination, reverence, belonging to that age, enoble it with a priesthood, deify its founders or law-givers while living, and grant them apotheosis and homage when dead. Such proofs of veneration and love signalized the worship of the true God among the Jews, and the worship of false gods among pagans. Such devotion was paid to the sentiment of Beauty among the Athenians; to the iron-hearted god of War among the Romans; to Love and knightly bearing in the age of chivalry.

Without one word from the historian, and only by studying a people's relics, and investigating the figurative expressions in their literature and law, one might see reflected, as from a mirror, the moral scale on which they arranged their idea of good and great. Though history should not record a single line in testimony of the fact, yet who, a thousand years hence, could fail to read, in their symbols, in their forms of speech, and in the technical terms of their law, the money-getting, money-worshipping tendencies of all commercial nations, during the last and the present centuries? The word "sovereign," we know, means a potentate invested with lawful dignity and authority; and it implies subjects who are bound to honor and obey. Hence, in Great Britain, a gold coin, worth twenty shillings, is called a *"sovereign;"* and happy is the political sovereign who enjoys such plenitude of power and majesty, and has so many loyal and devoted subjects as this vicegerent of royalty. An ancient English coin was called an *angel.* Its value was only ten shillings, and yet it was named after a messenger from heaven. In the Scriptures, and in political law, a *crown* is the emblem and personification of might and majesty, of glory and blessedness. The synonyme of all these is a piece of silver worth six shillings and seven pence. As the king has his representative in a sovereign, so a duke has his in a ducat,—the inferior value of the latter corresponding with the inferior dignity of its archetype. As Napoleon was considered the mightiest ruler that France ever knew, so, for many years, her highest coin was called a *Napoleon*; though now, in the French mint, they strike double-Napoleons. God grant that the world may never see a double-Napoleon of flesh and blood! Our forefathers subjected themselves to every worldly privation for the sake of liberty,—and when they had heroically endured toil and sacrifice for eight long years,—and at last achieved the blessing of independence,—they showed their veneration for the Genius of Liberty by placing its image and superscription— upon a *cent!*

So, too, in our times, epithets the most distinctively sacred are tainted with cupidity. Mammon is not satisfied with the heart-worship of his devotees; he has stolen the very language of the Bible and the Liturgy; and the cardinal words of the sanctuary have become the business phraseology of bankers, exchange-brokers, and lawyers. The word "good," as applied to character, originally meant benevolent, virtuous, devout, pious;—now, in the universal dialect of traffic and credit, a man is technically called *good* who pays his notes at maturity; and thus, this almost divine epithet is transferred from those who laid up their treasures in heaven, to such as lay up their treasures on earth. The three-days' respite which the law allows for the payment of a promissory note or bill of exchange, after the stipulated period has expired, is called *"grace,"* in irreverent imitation of the sinner's chance for pardon. On the performance of a broken covenant, by which a mortgaged estate is saved from forfeiture, it is said, in the technical language of the law, to be saved by *"redemption."* The document by which a deceased man's estate is bequeathed to his survivors, is called a *testament*; and were the glad tidings of the New Testament looked for as anxiously as are the contents of a rich man's last will and testament, there would be no further occasion for the Bible Societies. Indeed, on opening some of our law-books, and casting the eye along the running titles at the top of the pages, or on the marginal notes, and observing the frequent recurrence of such words as "covenant-broken," "grace," "redemption," "testament," and so forth, one might

very naturally fall into the mistake of supposing the book to be a work
on theology, instead of the law of real estate or bank stock.

I group together a few of these extraordinary facts, my friends,
to illustrate the irresistible tendency of the human mind to dignify,
honor, elevate, aggrandize, and even sanctify, whatever it truly respects and values. But education,—that synonyme of mortal misery
and happiness; that abbreviation for earth and heaven and hell,—
where are the conscious or unconscious testimonials to its worth?
What honorable, laudatory epithets, what titles of enconium or of
dignity, have been bestowed upon its professors? What, save such titles
as pedagogue, (which, among the Romans, from whom we derived
it, meant a slave,) and pedant, and knight of the birch and ferrule?
What sincere or single offering has it received from the hand or voice
of genius? Traverse the long galleries of art, and you will discover no
tribute to its worth. Listen to all the great masters of music, and you
will hear no swelling notes or chorus in its praise. Search all the
volumes of all the poets, and you will rarely find a respectful mention
of its claims, or even a recognition of its existence. In sacred and
devotional poetry, with which all its higher attributes so intimately
blend and harmonize, it has found no place. As proof of this extraordinary fact, let me say that, within the last five years, I have been
invited to lecture on the subject of education, in churches of all the
leading religious denominations of New England; and perhaps in the
majority of instances the lecture has been preceded or followed by the
devotional exercises of prayer and singing. On these occasions, probably every church hymn-book belonging to every religious sect amongst
us has been searched, in order to find fitting and appropriate words
wherein to utter fitting and appropriate thoughts on this sacred theme.
But, in all cases, the search has been made in vain. I think I hazard
nothing in saying that there is not a single psalm or hymn, in any
devotional book of psalms and hymns, to be found in our churches,
which presents the faintest outline of this great subject, in its social,
moral and religious departments, or in its bearing upon the future
happiness of its objects. On these occasions, the officiating clergyman
has looked through book and index, again and again, to make a
suitable selection; he has then handed the book to me, and I have done
the same,—the audience all the while waiting, and wondering at the
delay,—and at last, as our only resource, we have been obliged to
select some piece that had the word "child" or the word "young" in it,
and make it do.

In contrast with this fact, think of the size of a complete collection of Bacchanal songs, or of martial music;—these would make libraries; but the Muse of education is yet to be born.

In regard to all other subjects, histories have been written. The facts pertaining to their origin and progress have been collected; their principles elucidated; their modes and processes detailed. As early as the time of Cato, there was the history of agriculture. In modern times we have the history of the silk-worm, the history of cotton, the history of rice and of tobacco, and the history of the mechanic arts; but, in the English language, we have no history of education. Indeed, even now, we can scarcely be said to have any treatise, showing at what favoring hours the sentiments of virtue should be instilled into young hearts; or by what processes of care and nurture, or by what neglect, the chrysales of human spirits are evolved into angels or demons.

Both in Europe and in this country, scientific institutions have been founded, and illustrious men, during successive ages, poured the collected light of their effulgent minds upon other departments of science and of art,—upon language, astronomy, light, heat, electricity, tides, meteors, and so forth, and so forth. Such were the Royal Academy of Sciences, in Paris, founded in 1660; the Royal Society of England, founded in 1663; and the American Academy of Arts and Sciences, founded in 1780;—and what pondorous volumes of reports, essays, and transactions, they have published! But when or where have a nation's sages met in council to investigate the principles and to discuss the modes by which that most difficult and delicate work upon earth,—the education of a human soul,—should be conducted? Yet what is there in philology, or the principles of universal grammar; what is there in the ebb and flow of tides, in the shooting of meteors, or in the motions of the planetary bodies;—what is there, in fine, in the corporeal and insensate elements of the earth beneath, or of the firmament above, at all comparable in importance to those laws of growth and that course of training, by which the destiny of mortal and immortal spirits is at least foretokened, if not foredoomed?

So. too, in regard to those ancient and renowned literary institutions, which have been established and upheld by the foremost nations of Christendom,—the Sorbonne in France; the universities of Oxford and Cambridge and Edinburgh, in Great Britain; and the universities and colleges of this country,—the grand object of all these institutions has been, not to educate the general, the common mass of mind, but to

rear up men for the three learned professions (as they are called),
Physics, Law, and Divinity. For this comparatively narrow and special
purpose, vast legislative endowments and munificent private donations
have been made, and the highest talents have been called from the community, for presidentships and professorships.

The three learned professions, it is true, represent the three great
departments of human interests,—the Medical representing the body, or
corporeal part, through whose instrumentality alone can the spirit
make itself manifest; the Legal profession being designed to establish
social rights, and to redress social wrongs, in regard to property, person,
and character; and the Theological to guide and counsel us in regard
to our moral and religious concernments both for time and for
eternity. But all the learning of all the professions can never be an
adequate substitute for common knowledge, or remedy for common
ignorance. These professions are necessary for our general enlightenment, for guidance in difficult cases, and for counsel at all times; but
they never should aim to supersede, they never can supersede, our
own individual care, forethought, judgment, responsibility. Yet how
little is this truth regarded! How imperfectly do we live up to its
requirements! In respect to the medical profession, we are this year,
this day, and every day, sending young men to college, and from
college to the medical school, that they may acquire some knowledge
of human diseases and their remedies; but, at the same time, we are
neglecting to educate and train our children in accordance with the
few and simple laws upon which wealth depends, and which every
child might be easily led to know and to observe;—and the consequence is, that we are this year, this day, and every day, sowing, in
the constitutions of our children, the seeds of innumerable diseases;
so that the diseases will be ready for the doctors quite as soon as the
doctors are ready for the diseases. Indeed, before the doctor confronts
the disease, or while he is pondering over it, how often does death step
in and snatch the victim away!

At what vast expense, both of time and money, is the legal profession trained, and the judicial tribunals of the land supported! Two
or three, or half a dozen years, spent in preparing for college, four
years at college, and two or three years at a law school, or elsewhere, as
a qualification to practise in the courts; then, the maintenance of the
courts themselves; the salaries of judges, and of prosecuting officers;
the expense of jurors, grand-jurors, and witnesses; the amount of
costs and counsel fees; the vast outlay for prisons, jails, and houses of

correction;— and all this enormous expenditure, in order to adjust disputes, rectify mistakes, and punish offences, nine-tenths of which would have been prevented by a degree of common knowledge easily taught, and of common honesty, to which all children, with scarcely an exception, might be trained.

When the law of hereditary distempers shall be as profoundly investigated as the law which regulates the hereditary transmission of property, then may we expect some improvement in the health and robustness and beauty of the race. Compare all the books written on the transmission from parents to children of physical or moral qualities with the law-books and treatises on the descent of estates. When will the current of public opinion, or the stimulus of professional emolument, create a desire to understand the irreversible ordinances and statutes of Nature, on this class of subjects, as strong as that which now carries a student at law through Fearne on Contingent Remainders?—a book which requires the same faculty for divining ideas, that Champollion had for deciphering Egyptian Hieroglyphics.

And how is it with the clerical profession? They enter upon the work of reforming the human character,—not at the earlier stages of its development,—but when it has arrived at, or is approaching to, its maturity;—a period, when, by universal consent, it has become almost unchangeable by secondary causes. They are reformers, I admit, but in regard to any thing that *grows*, one right *former* will accomplish more than a thousand *re*-formers. It is their sacred mission to prepare a vineyard for the Lord, to dress it, and make it fruitful; but I think no one will say that an army of laborers, sent into a vineyard at midsummer, when brambles and thorns have already choked the vines, and the hedges have been broken down, and the unclean beasts of the forest have made their lair therein;—I think no one will say that an army of laborers, entering the vineyard at such a time, will be able to make it yield so abundant a harvest as one faithful, skilful servant would do, who should commence his labors in the spring-time of the year.

The Constitution of the United States makes no provision for the education of the people; and in the Convention that framed it, I believe the subject was not even mentioned. A motion to insert a clause providing for the establishment of a national university was voted down. I believe it is also the fact, that the Constitutions of only *three* of the thirteen original States made the obligation to maintain a system of Free Schools a part of their fundamental law.

On what grounds of reason or of hope, it may well be asked,

did the framers of our National and State Constitutions expect that the future citizens of this Republic would be able to sustain the institutions, or to enjoy the blessings, provided for them? And has not all our subsequent history shown the calamitous consequences of their failing to make provision for the educational wants of the nation? Suppose it had been provided, that no person should be a voter who could not read or write, and also that no State should be admitted into the Union which had not established a system of Free Schools for all its people; would not our National history and legislation, our State administrations and policy, have felt the change through all their annals? Great and good men though they were, yet this truth, now so plain and conspicuous, eluded their sagacity. They did not reflect that, in the common course of nature, all the learned and the wise and the virtuous are swept from the stage of action almost as soon as they become learned and wise and virtuous; and that they are succeeded by a generation who come into the world wholly devoid of learning and wisdom and virtue. The parents may have sought out the sublimest truths, but these truths are nothing to the children, until their minds also shall have been raised to the power of grasping and of understanding them. The truths, indeed, are immortal, but the beings who may embrace them are mortal, and pass away, to be followed by new minds, ignorant, weak, erring, tossed hither and thither on the waves of passion. Hence, each new generation must learn all truth anew, and for itself. Each generation must be able to comprehend the principles, and must rise to the practice of the virtues, requisite to sustain the position of their ancestors; and the first generation which fails to do this, loses all, and comes to ruin not only for itself but for its successors.

At what time, then, by virtue of what means, is the new generation to become competent to take upon itself the duties of the old and retiring one? At which of Shakespeare's "Seven Ages" is the new generation expected to possess the ability to stand in the places of the departed? Allow that the vast concerns of our society must be submitted to a democracy,—still, shall they be submitted to the democracy of babyhood,—to those whose country, as yet, is the cradle, and whose universe the nursery? Can you call in children from trundling hoops and catching butterflies, organize them into "Young Men's Conventions," and propound for their decision the great questions of judicature and legislation, of civil, domestic, and foreign policy? Or will you take the youth of the land, from sixteen to twenty-one years of age, in the heyday of their blood, with passions unappeasable in their cry for indulgence, and unquenchable by it; without experience, without sobriety of judgment; whose only notions of the complex structure of our government and of its various and delicate relations have been derived from hearing a Fourth-of-July Oration; with no knowledge of this multiform world into which they have been brought, or of their dangers, duties and destiny, as men,—in one word, with no education,—and is it to such as these that the vast concernments of a nation's well-being can be safely intrusted? Safer, far safer, would it be to decide the great problems of legislation and jurisprudence by a throw of dice; or, like the old Roman soothsayers, by the flight of birds. And even after one has passed the age of twenty-one, how is he any better fitted than before to perform the duties of a citizen, if no addition has been made to his knowledge, and if his passions have not been subjected to the control of reason and duty?

I adduce these extraordinary facts, in relation to the founders of our Republic, not in any spirit of disparagement or reprehension, but only as another proof in the chain of demonstration, to show in what relative esteem, how low down the social scale, this highest of all earthly subjects has been held,—and held in a Republic too, where we talk so much about foundations of knowledge and virtue.

And what was the first school established by Congress, after the formation of the general government? It was the Military Academy at West Point. This school is sustained at an annual expense of more than a hundred thousand dollars. It is the Normal School of war. As the object of the common Normal School is to teach teachers how to teach; so the object of this Academy is to teach killers how to kill. At this school, those delightful sciences are pursued which direct at what precise angle a cannon or a mortar shall be elevated, and what quantity and quality of gunpowder shall be used, in order to throw red-hot balls or bomb-shells a given distance, so as, by the one, to set a city on fire, and, by the other, to tear in pieces a platoon of men,—husbands, brothers, fathers. And while it is thought of sufficient importance to nominate the most learned men in the whole land, and to assemble them from the remotest quarters of the Union, to make an annual visit to this School of War, and to spend days and days in the minutest, severest examination of the pupils, to see if they have fully mastered their death-dealing sciences; it is not uncommon to meet with the opinion that our Common Schools need no committees and no examination.

Great efforts have been made in Congress to establish a Naval

School, having in view the same benign and philanthropic purposes, for the ocean, which the Military School has for the land.

At Old Point Comfort, in Virginia, there now is, and for a long time has been, under the direction of the general government, what is called a "School for Practice," where daily experiments are tried to test the strength of ordnance, the explosive force of gunpowder, and the distance at which a Christian may fire at his brother Christian and be sure to kill him, and not waste his ammunition!

At selected points, throughout our whole country, the thousand wheels of mechanism are now playing; chemistry is at work in all her laboratories; the smelter, the forger, the founder in brass and iron, the prover of arms,—all are plying their daily tasks to prepare implements for the conflagration of cities and the destruction of human life. Occasionally, indeed, a Peace Society is organized; a few benevolent men assemble together to hear a discourse on the universal brotherhood of the race, the horrors of war and the blessings of peace; but their accents are lost in an hour, amid the never-ceasing din and roar of this martial enginery. And so the order and course of things will persist to be,—the ministers of the Gospel of Peace may continue to preach peace for eighteen centuries more, and still find themselves in the midst of war, or of all those passions by which war is engendered, unless the rising generation shall be educated to that strength and sobriety of intellect which shall dispel the insane illusions of martial glory; and unless they shall be trained to the habitual exercise of those sentiments of universal brotherhood for the race, which shall change the common heroism of battle into a horror and an abomination.

A deputation of some of the most talented and learned men in this country has lately been sent to Europe, by the order and at the expense of the general government, to visit and examine personally all the founderies, armories and noted fortifications, from Gibraltar to the Baltic;—to collect all knowledge about the forging of iron cannon and brass cannon, the tempering of swords, the management of steam-batteries, and so forth, and so forth—to bring this knowledge home, that our government may be instructed and enlightened in the art—*to kill*. I have not heard that Congress proposes to establish any Normal School, the immediate or the remote object of which shall be to teach "peace on earth and good will to men." "Go ye out into every nation and preach the gospel to every creature," has hitherto been practically translated, "Go ye out into every nation and kill or rob every creature."

We are told that a celestial choir once winged its way from heaven to earth on an errand of mercy and love; but for the communication of that message which burned in their hearts and melted from their tongues, they sought out no lengthened epic or long-resounding pæan; —they chanted only that brief and simple strain, "Peace on earth and good will to men," as if to assure us that these were the selectest words in the dialect of heaven, and the choicest beat in all its music. But long since have these notes died away. Oh! when shall that song be renewed, and every tongue and nation upon earth unite their voices with those of angels in uplifting the heavenly strain?

Again I say, my friends, that the arrangement and denunciation of men is no part of my present purpose. I advert to these world-known facts, for the sole and simple object of showing how the subject of education stands, and has stood, in prosaic and poetic literature, in the refining arts, in history, and in the laws, institutions and opinions of men. I wish hereby to show its relative degradation, the inferiority of the rank assigned to it, as compared with all other interests, or with any other interest; and thus to exhibit the true reasons why, as yet, it has done so little for the renovation of the world. I have spoken only of the general current of events, of opinions and of practices common to mankind. In our own times, in such low estimation is this highest of all causes held, that in these days of conventions for all other objects of public interest,—when men go hundreds of miles to attend railroad conventions, and cotton conventions, and tobacco conventions; and when the delegates of political conventions* are sometimes counted, as Xerxes counted his army, by acres and square miles,—yet such has often been the dispersive effect upon the public of announcing a Common-school Convention, and a Lecture on Education, that I have queried in my own mind whether, in regard to two or three counties, at least, in our own State, it would not be advisable to alter the law for quelling riots and mobs; and, instead of summoning sheriffs and armed magistrates and the *posse comitatus* for their dispersion, to put them to flight by making proclamation of a Discourse on Common Schools.

When we reflect upon all this, what surprises and grieves us most is, that so few men are surprised or grieved.

I think, for instance, that it would be impossible for our people to imitate the example of our neighbors, the inhabitants of Maine,—so

---

* It was said that at the Young Men's Whig Convention, held at Baltimore, in May, 1844, there were *forty thousand* delegates in attendance.

long and so lately a part of ourselves,—where, in the year 1839, there was a general uprising of the whole population, and an appropriation, by an almost unanimous vote of the Legislature, of the sum of *eight hundred thousand dollars*, for the forcible rescue of certain outlands, or outwastes, claimed by Great Britain; while, for three successive sessions, some of the wisest and best men in that State have been striving, in vain, to obtain from that same Legislature the passage of a law authorizing school districts to purchase a school library, by levying a tax upon themselves for the purpose. In the memoirs of the Pickwick Club, it is related that they passed a unanimous vote, that any member of said club should be allowed to travel in any part of England, Scotland or Wales, and also to send whatever packages he might please, *always provided that said member should pay his own expenses.* But the Legislature of Maine would not allow their school districts to buy libraries, *even at their own cost!* What latent capacities for enjoyment and for usefulness, which will now lie dormant forever, might not that sum of *eight hundred thousand dollars* have opened for the people of that State, for their children and their children's children, had it been devoted by enlightened minds to worthy objects!

So, too, to give one more example, you will all recollect that outbreak of South Carolina against the general government, in 1832, when a few of the demi-gods of that State stamped upon the earth, and instantly it was covered with armed men; a State convention was held, laws were enacted, extending the jurisdiction of the courts and investing the Executive almost with a Dictator's power,—all under the pretext of defending State rights,—while, for the last thirty years, her whole appropriation for public schools has been less than *forty thousand dollars per annum*; and out of a white population, *of all ages*, of less than 270,000, there are more than 20,000, above the age of twenty years, who cannot read and write;—as though it could long be possible, without more efficient means for the general diffusion of intelligence and virtue, to have any State rights worth defending.

Compare the salaries given to engineers, to superintendents of railroads, to agents and overseers of manufacturing establishments, to cashiers of banks, and so forth, with the customary rates of remuneration given to teachers. Yet, does it deserve a more liberal requital, does it require greater natural talents, or greater attainments, to run cotton or woollen machinery, or to keep a locomotive from running off the track, than it does to preserve this wonderfully-constructed and complicated machine of the human body in health and vigor; or to prevent the spiritual nature,—that vehicle which carries all our hopes, —from whirling deviously to its ruin, or from dashing madly forward to some fatal collision? Custom-house collectors and postmasters sometimes realize four, five or six thousand dollars a year from their offices, while as many hundreds are grudgingly paid to a school teacher.

The compensation which we give with the hand is a true representation of the value which we affix in the mind; and how much more liberally and cordially do we requite those who prepare outward and perishable garments for the persons of our children, than those whose office it is to endue their spirits with the immortal vestments of virtue? Universally, the price-current of accomplishments ranges far above that of solid and enduring attainments. Is not the dancing-master, who teaches our children to take steps, better requited than he who teaches their feet not to go down to the chambers of death? Were the music-master as wretchedly rewarded and as severely criticised as the schoolmaster, would not his strains involuntarily run into the doleful and lugubrious? Strolling minstrels, catching the eye with grotesque dresses, and chanting unintelligible words, are feasted, *fêted* and garlanded; and when a European dancer, nurtured at the foul breast of theatrical corruption, visits our land, the days of idolatry seem to have returned;—wealth flows, the incense of praise rises, enthusiasm rages like the mad Bacchantes. It is said that Celeste received *fifty thousand dollars*, in this country, in one year, for the combined exhibition of skill and person; and that devotee to Venus, Fanny Ellsler, was paid the enormous sum of *sixty thousand dollars*, in three months, for the same meritorious consideration, or *value received*. In both these cases, a fair proportion was contributed in the metropolis of our own State. At the rate of compensation at which a majority of the female teachers in Massachusetts have been rewarded for their exhausting toils, it would require more than twenty years' continued labor to equal the receipts of Fanny Ellsler for a single night!

One word more, and I will forbear any further to depict these painful contrasts;—I will forbear, not from lack of materials, but from faintness of spirit. Almost from year to year, through the whole period of our history, wealthy and benevolent individuals have risen up amongst us, who have made noble gifts for literary, charitable and religious purposes,—for public libraries, for founding professorships in colleges, for establishing scientific and theological institutions, for sending abroad missionaries to convert the heathen,—some to one form of faith, some to another. For most of these objects, the State has co-operated with individuals; often, it has given on its own account. It has bestowed immense sums upon the University at Cambridge, and Williams College, especially the former. It gave thirty thousand dollars to the Massachusetts General Hospital. It put ten thousand dollars into the Bunker-hill Monument, there to stand forever in mindless, insentient, inanimate granite. But while, with such a bounteous heart and open hand, the State has bestowed its treasures for special, or local objects,—for objects circumscribed to a party or a class,—it had not, for two hundred years, in its parental and sovereign capacity, given any thing for universal education;—it had given nothing, as God gives the rain and the sunshine, to all who enter upon the great theatre of life.

It was under these circumstances, that a private gentleman, to his enduring honor, offered the sum of ten thousand dollars, on condition that the State would add an equal amount, to aid Teachers of our Common Schools in obtaining those qualifications which would enable them the more successfully to cultivate the divinely wrought and infinitely valuable capacities of the human soul. The hope and expectation were, that these teachers would go abroad over the State, and, by the improved *modes* and *motives* which they would introduce into the schools, would be the means of conferring new, manifold and unspeakable blessings upon the rising generation, without any distinction of party or of denomination, of mental, or of physical complexion. This hope and expectation were founded upon the reasonableness of the thing, upon the universal experience of mankind in regard to all other subjects, and upon the well-attested experience of several nations in regard to this particular measure. The proposition was acceded to. This sum of twenty thousand dollars was placed at the disposal of the Board of Education, to carry the purposes of the donor and of the Legislature into effect. Institutions called Normal Schools were established. That their influence might be wholly concentrated upon the preparation of teachers for our Common Schools, the almost doubtful provision, that the learned languages should not be included in the list of studies taught therein, was inserted in the regulations for their government;—not because there was any hostility or indifference towards those languages, but because it was desirable to prepare teachers for our Common Schools, rather than to furnish facilities for those who are striving to become teachers of Select Schools, High Schools, and Academies.

The call was responded to by the very class of persons to whom it was addressed. Not the children of the rich, not the idle and luxurious, not those in pursuit of gaudy accomplishments, came; but the children of the poor,—the daughter of the lone widow whose straitened circumstances forbade sending her to costly and renowned seminaries,—the young man came from his obscure cottage-home, where for years his soul had been on fire with the love of knowledge and the suppressed hope of usefulness;—some accounted the common necessaries of life as superfluities, and sold them, that they might participate in these means of instruction;—some borrowed money and subsidized futurity for the same purpose, while others submitted to the lot, still harder to a noble soul, of accepting charity from a stranger's hand. They came, they entered upon their work with fervid zeal, with glowing delight, with that buoyancy and inspiration of hope which none but the young and the poor can ever feel.

But alas! while this noble enterprise was still in its bud and blossom, and before it was possible that any fruits should be matured from it, it was assailed. In the Legislature of the Commonwealth of Massachusetts, an attempt was made to abolish the Normal Schools, to disperse the young aspirants who had resorted to them for instruction, and crush their hopes; and to throw back into the hands of the donor the money which he had given, and which the State had pledged its faith to appropriate,—the first and only gift which had ever been made for elevating and extending the education of all the children in the Commonwealth.

In the document which purports to set forth the reasons for this measure, the doctrine, that "the art of teaching is a peculiar art," is gainsaid. It is boldly maintained "that every person who has himself undergone a process of instruction, must acquire by that very process the art of instructing others." And in this country, where, without a higher standard of qualification for teachers, without more universal and more efficient means of education than have ever elsewhere existed, all our laws and constitutions are weaker barriers against the assaults of human passion than is a bulrush against the ocean's tide;—in this country, that document affirmed that "perhaps it is not desirable that the business of keeping these schools, [the Common Schools,] should become a distinct and separate profession."

Conceding to the originators and advocates of this scheme for abolishing the Normal Schools, that they were sincerely friendly to the cause of Common Schools, how strikingly does it exhibit the low state of public sentiment in regard to these schools! Those claiming to be their friends,—men, too, who had been honored by their fellow-citizens with a seat in the Legislature,—thought it unnecessary, even in this country, to elevate the teacher's office into a profession!

I will never cease to protest that I am not bringing forward these facts for the purpose of criminating the motives, or of invoking retribution upon the conduct of any one. My sole and exclusive object is to show to what menial rank the majesty of this cause has been degraded; —to show that the affections of this community are not clustered around it; that it is not the treasure which their hearts love and their hands guard;—in fine, that the sublime idea of a generous and universal education, as the appointed means, in the hands of Providence, for restoring mankind to a greater similitude to their Divine Original, is but dawning upon the public mind.

In the first place, the education of the whole people, in a republican government, can never be attained without the consent of the whole people. Compulsion, even though it were a desirable, is not an available instrument. Enlightenment, not coercion, is our resource. The nature of education must be explained. The whole mass of mind must be instructed in regard to its comprehensive and enduring interests. We cannot drive our people up a dark avenue, even though it be the right one; but we must hang the starry lights of knowledge about it, and show them not only the directness of its course to the goal of prosperity and honor, but the beauty of the way that leads to it. In some districts, there will be but a single man or woman, in some towns scarcely half a dozen men or women, who have espoused this noble enterprise. But whether there be half a dozen or but one, they must be like the little leaven which a woman took and hid in three measures of meal. Let the intelligent visit the ignorant, day after day, as the oculist visits the blind man, and detaches the scales from his eyes, until the living sense leaps to the living light. Let the zealous seek contact and communion with those who are frozen up in indifference, and thaw off the icebergs wherein they lie embedded. Let the love of beautiful childhood, the love of country, the dictates of reason, the admonitions of conscience, the sense of religious responsibility, be plied, in mingled tenderness and earnestness, until the obdurate and dark mass of avarice and ignorance and prejudice shall be dissipated by their blended light and heat.

But a duty more noble, as well as more difficult and delicate than that of restoring the suspended animation of society, will devolve upon the physician and friend of this cause. In its largest sense, no subject is so comprehensive as that of education. Its circumference reaches around the outside of, and therefore embraces all other interests, human and divine. Hence, there is danger that whenever anything practical,—any real change,—is proposed, all classes of men will start up and inquire, how the proposed change will affect some private interest, or some idolized theory or opinion of theirs. Suppose a short-sighted, selfish man to be interested as manufacturer, author, compiler, copyright owner, vender, peddler, or puffer, of any of the hundreds of school-books,—from the reading-book that costs a dollar, to the primer that costs four-pence,—whose number and inconsistencies infest our schools, and whose expense burdens our community,— then he will inquire which one of all these books will be likely to meet with countenance or disfavor, in an adjudication upon their merits; and he will strive to turn the scales which confessedly hold the great interests of humanity, one way or the other, as their inclination will promote or oppose the success of his reading-book or his primer. So one, who has entered the political arena, not as a patriot, but as a partisan, will decide upon any new measure by its supposed bearing upon the success of his faction or cabal, and not by its tendency to advance the welfare of the body politic. In relation, too, to a more solemn subject,—how many individuals there are belonging to the hundred conflicting forms of religious faith, which now stain and mottle the holy whiteness of Christianity, who will array themselves against all plans for the reform or renovation of society, unless its agents and instruments are of their selection! And so of all the varied interests in the community,—industrial, literary, political, spiritual. Whatever class this great cause may touch, or be supposed likely to touch, there will come forth from that class, active opponents; or, what may not be less disastrous, selfish and indiscreet friends. I have known the carpenter and the mason belonging to the same school district, change sides and votes on the expediency of erecting a new schoolhouse, after it had been determined, contrary to expectation, to construct it of brick instead of wood. I have known a bookmaker seek anxiously to learn the opinions of the Board of Education respecting his book, in order to qualify himself to decide upon the expediency of its having been established.

How, then, I ask, is this interest to sustain itself, amid these disturbing forces of party and sect and faction and clan? how is it to navigate with whirlwinds above and whirlpools below, and rocks on every side?

In the first place, in regard to mere secular and business interests, we are to do no man wrong; we are to show by our deeds, rather than by our words, that we are seeking no private, personal aims, but public ends by equitable means. We are to show that our object is to diffuse light and knowledge, and to leave those who can best bear these tests to profit most by their diffusion. Let us here teach the lessons of justice and impartiality on what, in schools, is called the *exhibitory* method; that is, by an actual exhibition of the principle we would inculcate; and as, for the untaught schoolboy, we bring out specimens, and models and objects, and give practical illustrations by apparatus and diagram to make him acquainted with the various branches of study; so, in the great school of the world, let us illustrate the virtues of generosity, magnanimity, equity and self-sacrifice, by the shining example of our acts and lives.

But sterner trials than any I have yet mentioned await the disciples of this sacred apostleship. The strong abuses that have invaded us will not be complimented into retirement; they will not be *bowed out* of society; but as soon as they are touched, they will bristle all over with armor, and assail us with implacable hostility. While doing good, therefore, we must consent to suffer wrong. Such is human nature, that the introduction of every good cause adds another chapter to the Book of Martyrs. Though wise as serpents, yet there are adders who will not hear us; and though harmless as doves, yet for that very harmlessness will the vultures more readily swoop upon us. We shall not, indeed, be literally carried to the stake, or burned with material fires; but pangs keener than these, and more enduring, will be made to pierce our breasts. Our motives will be maligned, our words belied, our actions falsified. A reputation, for whose spotlessness and purity we may, through life, have resisted every temptation and made every sacrifice, will be blackened; and a character,—perhaps our only precious possession wherewith to requite the love of family and friends,— will be traduced, calumniated, vilified, and, if deemed sufficiently conspicuous to attract public attention, held up, in the public press, perhaps in legislative halls, to common scorn and derision. What then? Shall we desert this glorious cause? Shall we ignobly sacrifice immortal good to mortal ease? No; never! But let us meet opposition in the spirit of him who prophetically said, "If they have persecuted me, they will also persecute you." For those who oppose and malign us, our revenge shall be, to make their children wiser, better, and happier than themselves. If we ever feel the earthly motives contending with the heavenly in our bosoms,—selfishness against duty, sloth against enduring and ennobling toil, a vicious contentment against aspiring after higher and attainable good,—let us not suffer earth-born to vanquish the immortal. What though it cannot be said,

"A cloud of witnesses around
Hold us in full survey,"

yet the voiceless approval of conscience outweighs the applauses of the world, and will outlast the very air and light through which the eulogiums of mankind, or the memorials of their homage, can be manifested to us.

BOOKS AND LIBRARIES

From Third Annual Report (1829)

"Let good books be read, and the taste for reading bad ones will slough off from the minds of the young, like gangrened flesh from a healing wound."

Mann's views on the proper contents of libraries are controversial, but challenge us in that they embody a *plan*, which can be properly compared with any one which we might wish to offer our own times, Mann derogated the imaginative facilities, but mainly because he was so intensely concerned for the establishment of standards of truth and reverence for humanity. It should be noted that if he inadequately appreciated the writings of Herman Melville, Edgar Allen Poe, and his own brother-in-law, Nathaniel Hawthorne, so did his novel-reading contemporaries. Indeed, a hundred years after, individuals who have been exposed to our education can still set down Poe as a "detective-story writer," and persons have in print referred to "Moby-Dick *and* the Whale." Mann did cope with the popularity of nineteenth century equivalents of comic books and unprincipled writings, as well as fads which gave Ernest Hemingway, Jack Kerouac, and Henry Miller priority over all other imaginative writers. Our much higher percentage of publications per population no more than emphasizes our modern need to weigh their positive services to our civilization.

AFTER the rising generation have acquired habits of intelligent reading in our schools, *what shall they read?* for, with no books to read, the power of reading will be useless; and, with bad books to read, the consequences will be as much worse than ignorance as wisdom is better. What books, then, are there accessible to the great mass of the children in the State, adapted to their moral and intellectual wants, and fitted to nourish their minds with the elements of uprightness and wisdom?

Let any person go into one of our country towns or districts of average size, consisting, as most of them do, of an agricultural population, interspersed with mechanics, and here and there a few manufacturers, and inquire from house to house what books are possessed, and he will probably find the Scriptures and a few school-books in almost every family. These are protected by law, even in the hands of an insolvent; so that the poor are as secure in their possession as the rich. In the houses of professional men,—the minister, the lawyer, the physician,—he would find small professional libraries, intermixed with some miscellaneous works not of a professional character; in the houses of religious persons, a few religious books of this or that class, according to the faith of the owner; in the houses of the more wealthy, where wealth is fortunately combined with intelligence and good taste, some really useful and instructive books; but where the wealth is unfortunately united with a love of display, or with feeble powers of thought, he would find a few elegantly-bound annuals, and novels of recent emission. What he would find in other houses— and these the majority—would be a few, and of a most miscellaneous character; books which had found their way thither rather by chance than by design, and ranging in their character between very good and very bad. Rarely, in such a town as I have supposed, will a book be found which treats of the nature, object, and abuses of different kinds of governments, and of the basis and constitution and fabric of our own; or one on economical or statistical science; or a treatise on general ethics and the philosophy of the human mind; or popular or intelligible explanations of the applications of science to agriculture and the useful arts, of the processes by which the latter are made so eminently serviceable to man. Rarely will any book be found partaking of the character of an encyclopædia, by a reference to which, thousands of interesting questions, as they daily arise, might be solved, and great accessions to the stock of valuable knowledge be imperceptibly made; quite as rarely will any books containing the lives of eminent British or American statesmen be found, or books treating of our ante-Revolutionary history; and, most rarely of all, will any book be found on education,—education at home, physical, intellectual, and those rudiments of a moral and religious education in which all agree,—the most important subject that can possibly be named to parent, patriot, philanthropist, or Christian. And in the almost total absence of books adapted to instruct parents how to educate their children, so there are quite as few which are adapted to the capacities of the children themselves, and might serve, in some secondary degree, to supply the place of the former. Some exceptions would, of course, be expected where so many particulars are grouped under so few heads; but from all I have been able to learn, after improving every opportunity for inquiry and correspondence, I am led to believe, that, as it regards the *private* ownership of books, the above may be taken as a fair medium for the State. In small towns, almost wholly rural in their occupation, the books, though fewer, may generally be better; while in cities and large towns, though more numerous, yet a larger proportion of them is worse. Whatever means exist, then, either for inspiring or for gratifying a love for reading in the great mass of the rising generation, are mainly to be found, if found at all, in public libraries.

As the tastes and habits of the future men and women, in regard to reading, will be only an enlargement and expansion of the tastes and habits of the present children, it seemed to me one of the most desirable of facts, to learn, as far as practicable, under what general influences those tastes and habits are now daily forming. For who can think, without emotion, and who can remain inactive under the conviction, that every day which now passes is, by the immutable law of cause and effect, predestinating the condition of the community twenty, thirty, or forty years hence; that the web of their character and fortunes is now going through the loom, to come out of it, at that time, of worthy or of worthless quality, beautified with colors and shapes of excellence, or deformed by hideousness, just according to the kind of the woof which we are daily weaving into its texture? Every book which a child reads with intelligence is like a cast of the weaver's shuttle, adding another thread to the indestructible web of existence.

In the general want of private libraries, therefore, I have endeavored to learn what number of public libraries exist; how many volumes they contain, and what are their general character, scope, and tendency; how many persons have access to them, or, which is the most material point, how many persons do *not* have access to them; and, finally, how many of the books are adapted to prepare children to be free citizens and men, fathers and mothers, even in the most limited signification of those vastly comprehensive words. It seemed to me, therefore, that nothing could have greater interest or significance than an inventory of the means of knowledge, and the encouragements of self-education, possessed by the present and the rising generation.

Simultaneously with this inquiry I have pursued a collateral one, not so closely, although closely, connected with the main object. A class of institutions has lately sprung up in this State, universally known by the name of Lyceums, or Mechanics' Institutes, before some of which courses of Popular Lectures, on literary or scientific subjects, are annually delivered, while others possess libraries and reading-rooms, and in a very few cases both these objects are combined. These institutions have the same general purpose in view as public libraries, viz. that of diffusing instructive and entertaining knowledge, and of exciting a curiosity to acquire it; though they are greatly inferior to libraries in point of efficiency. As the proportion of young persons who attend these lectures and frequent these reading-rooms, compared with the whole number of attendants, is much greater than the proportion they bear to the whole people, the institutions may justly be regarded as one of the means now in operation for enlightning the youth of the State. At any rate, an inventory of the means of general intelligence which did not include these institutions would justly be regarded as incomplete.

For the purpose of obtaining authentic information on the abovementioned subjects, I addressed to school committees and other intelligent men residing, respectively, in every town in the Commonwealth, a few inquiries, by which I ascertained that, omitting the ten Circulating Libraries, containing about twenty-eight thousand volumes, it appears that the aggregate of volumes in the public libraries of all kinds in the State is about three hundred thousand. This is also exclusive of the Sabbath-school Libraries, which will be adverted to hereafter. To these three hundred thousand volumes but little more than one hundred thousand persons, or one-seventh part of the population of the State, have any right of access, while more than six hundred thousand have no right therein.

Of the towns heard from, there are one hundred (almost one third of the whole number in the State) which have neither a town, social, nor district school library therein. What strikes us with amazement, in looking at these facts, is the inequality with which the means of knowledge are spread over the surface of the State; a few deep, capacious reservoirs, surrounded by broad wastes. It has long been a common remark that many persons read too much; but here we have proof how many thousands read too little. For the poor man and the laboring man the art of printing seems hardly yet to have been discovered.

The next question respects the character of the books composing the libraries, and their adaptation to the capacities and mental condition of children and youth. In regard to this point there is, as might be expected, but little diversity of statement. Almost all the answers concur in the opinion that the contents of the libraries are not adapted to the intellectual and moral wants of the young; an opinion which a reference to the titles in the catalogues will fully sustain. With very few exceptions the books were written for adults, for persons of some maturity of mind, and possessed already of a considerable fund of information; and, therefore, they could not be adapted to children, except through mistake. Of course, in the whole collectively considered there is every kind of books; but probably no other kind, which can be deemed of a useful character, occupies so much space upon the shelves of the libraries as the historical class. Some of the various histories of Greece and Rome; the History of Modern Europe, by Russell; of England, by Hume and his successors; Robertson's Charles V.; Mavor's Universal History; the numerous histories of Napoleon, and similar works, constitute the staple of many libraries. And how little do these books contain which is suitable for children! How little do they record but the destruction of human life, and the activity of those misguided energies of men which have hitherto almost baffled the beneficent intentions of Nature for human happiness! Descriptions of battles, sackings of cities, and the captivity of nations, follow each other with the quickest movement, and in an endless succession. Almost the only glimpses which we catch of the education of youth present them as engaged in martial sports, and in mimic feats of arms, preparatory to the grand tragedies of battle; exercises and exhibitions, which, both in the performer and the spectator, cultivate all the dissocial emotions, and turn the whole current of mental forces into the channel of destructiveness. The reader sees inventive genius, not employed in perfecting the useful arts, but exhausting itself in the manufacture of implements of war; he sees rulers and legislators, not engaged in devising comprehensive plans for universal welfare, but in levying and equipping armies and navies, and extorting taxes to maintain them; thus dividing the whole mass of the people into the two classes of slaves and soldiers, enforcing the degradation and servility of tame animals upon the former, and cultivating the ferocity and bloodthirstiness of wild animals in the latter. The highest honors are conferred upon men in whose rolls of slaughter the most thousands of victims are numbered; and seldom does woman emerge from her obscurity, indeed, hardly should we know that she existed, but for her appearance to grace the triumphs of the conqueror. What a series of facts would be indicated by an examination of all the treaties of peace which history records! they would appear like a grand index to universal plunder. The inference which children would legitimately draw from reading like this would be, that the tribes and nations of men had been created only for mutual slaughter, and that they deserved the homage of posterity for the terrible fidelity with which their mission had been fulfilled. Rarely do these records administer any antidote against the inhumanity of the spirit they instil. In the immature minds of children, unaccustomed to consider events under the relation of cause and effect, they excite the conception of magnificent palaces or temples for bloody conquerors to dwell in, or in which to offer profane worship for inhuman triumphs, without a suggestion of the bondage and debasement of the myriads of slaves, who, through lives of privation and torture, were compelled to erect them; they present an exciting picture of long trains of plundered wealth, going to enrich some city or hero, without an intimation, that, by industry and the arts of peace, the same wealth could have been earned more cheaply than it was robbed; they exhibit the triumphal return of warriors, to be crowned with honors worthy of a god, while they take the mind wholly away from the carnage of the battlefield, from desolated provinces and a mourning people. In all this, it is true, there are many examples of the partial and limited virtue of patriotism, but few only of the complete virtue of philanthropy. The courage held up for admiration is generally of that animal nature which rushes into danger to inflict injury upon another; but not of that divine quality which braves peril for the sake of bestowing good,—attributes, than which there are scarcely any two in the souls of men more different, though the baseness of the former is so often mistaken for the nobleness of the latter. Indeed, if the past history of our race is to be much read by children, it should be rewritten; and while it records those events which have contravened all the principles of social policy, and violated all the laws of morality and religion, there should, at least, be some recognition of the great truth, that among nations, as among individuals, the highest welfare of all can only be effected by securing the individual welfare of each: there should be some parallel drawn between the *historical* and the *natural* relations of the race; so that the tender and immature mind of the youthful reader may have some opportunity of comparing the right with the wrong, and some option of admiring and emulating the former instead of the latter. As much of history now stands, the examples of right and wrong, whose nativity and residence are on opposite sides of the moral universe, are not merely brought and shuffled together, so as to make it difficult to distinguish between them, but the latter are made to occupy almost the whole field of vision; while the existence of the former is scarcely noticed. It is as though children should be taken to behold, from afar, the light of a city on fire, and directed to admire the splendor of the conflagration, without a thought of the tumult and terror and death reigning beneath it.

Another very considerable portion of these libraries, especially where they have been recently formed or replenished, consists of novels, and all that class of books which is comprehended under the familiar designations of "fictions," "light reading," "trashy works," "ephemeral," or "bubble literature," &c. This kind of books has increased immeasurably within the last twenty years. It has insinuated itself into public libraries, and found the readiest welcome with people who are not dependent upon libraries for the books they peruse. Aside from newspapers, I am satisfied that the major part of the *unprofessional* reading of the community is of the class of books designated. Amusement is the object,—mere *amusement*, as contradistinguished from instruction in the practical concerns of life; as contradistinguished from those intellectual and moral impulses, which turn the mind, both while reading and after the book is closed, to observation and comparison and reflection upon the great realities of existence.

What gives additional importance to this subject is the fact, that by far the most extensive portion of this reading for amusement consists of the perusal of fictitious works. The number of books and articles, which, under the names of romances, novels, tales in verse or prose,—from the elaborate work of three volumes to the hasty production of three chapters or three pages,—is so wide-spread and ever-renewing, that any computation of them transcends the power of the human faculties. They gush from the printing-press. Their authors are a nation. When speaking of the reading public, we must be understood with reference to the subject-matter of the reading. In regard to scientific works on government, political economy, morals, philosophy, the reading public is very small. Hardly one in fifty, amongst adults, belongs to it. For works of biography, travels, history, it is considerably larger. But in reference to fictitious works, it is large and astonishingly active. It requires so little acquaintance with our language, and so little knowledge of sublunary things and their relations, to understand them; and the inconvenience of failing to understand the word, a sentence, or page, is so trivial; so exactly do they meet the case of minds that are ignorant, indolent, and a little flighty, that they are welcomed by vast numbers. Other books are read slowly, commenced, laid aside, resumed, and perused in intervals of leisure. These are run through with almost incredible velocity. Take a work on morals, of the same size with a novel; the reading of the former will occupy a month, the latter will be dispatched without intervening sleep. Of works unfolding to us the structure of our own bodies, and the means of preserving health, and of the constitution of our own minds, and the infinite diversity of the spiritual paths, which the mind can traverse, each bringing after it, its own peculiar consequences; of works laying open the complicated relations of society, illustrative of the general duties belonging to all, and of the special duties arising from special positions; of works making us acquainted with the beneficent laws and properties of Nature, and their adaptations to supply our needs and enhance our welfare,—of works of these descriptions, editions of a few hundred copies only are printed, and then the types are distributed, in despair of any further demand; while of fictitious works, thousands of copies are thrown off at first, and they are stereotyped in confidence that the insatiable public will call for new supplies. It was but a few years after the publication of Sir Walter Scott's poems and novels, that fifty thousand copies of many of them had been sold in Great Britain alone. Under the stimulus which he applied to the public imagination, the practice of novel-reading has grown to such an extent, that his imitators and copyists have overspread a still wider field, and covered it to a greater depth. In this country, the reading of novels has been still more epidemic, because, in most parts of it, so great a portion of the people can read, and because, owing to the extensiveness of the demand, they have been afforded so cheaply, that the price of perusal has often been less than the value of the light by which they were read.

To give some idea of the difference in the sales of different kinds of works, it may be stated, that of some of Bulwer's and Marryatt's novels, from ten to fifteen thousand copies have been sold in this country; while of that highly valuable and instructive work, Spark's "American Biography," less than two thousand copies, on an average, have been sold; and of Prescott's "Ferdinand and Isabella," only about thirty-six hundred. The latter is considered a remarkably large sale, and is owing, in no inconsiderable degree, to the superior manner in which that interesting history was written.

So far as it respects fictitious writings, the explanation of their weakening and dispersive influence is palpable to the feeblest comprehension. All men must recognize the wide distinction between *intellect* and *feeling*, between *ideas* and *emotions*. These two classes of mental operations are inherently distinct from each other in their nature; they are called into activity by different classes of objects; they are cultivated by different processes; and as one or the other predominates in the mental constitution, widely different results follow both in conduct and character. All sciences are the offspring of the intellect. On the other hand, there cannot be poetry or eloquence without emotion. From the intellect come order, demonstration, invention, discovery; from the feelings, enthusiasm, pathos, and sublime sentiments in morals and religion. The attainments of the greatest intellect are gathered with comparative slowness, but each addition is a permanent one. The process resembles that by which material structures are reared, which are laboriously built up, brick by brick, or stone by stone, but, when once erected, are steadfast and enduring. But the feelings, on the other hand, are like the unstable elements of the air or ocean, which are suddenly roused from a state of tranquillity into vehement commotion, and as suddenly subside into repose. When rhetoricians endeavor to excite more vivid conceptions of truth by means of sensible images, they liken the productions of the intellect to the solidity and stern repose of time-defying pyramid or temple; but they find symbols for the feelings and passions of men in the atmosphere, which obeys the slightest impulse, and is ready to start into whirlwinds or tempest at once. To add to the stock of practical knowledge, and to increase intellectual ability, requires voluntary and long-sustained effort; but feelings and impulses are often spontaneous, and always susceptible of being roused into action by a mere glance of the eye, or the sound of a voice. To become master of an exact, coherent, full set, or complement of ideas, on any important subject, demands fixed attention, patience, study; but emotions or passions flash up suddenly, and while they blaze they are consumed. In the mechanical and useful arts, for instance, a knowledge of the structure and quality of materials, of the weight and motive power of fluids, of the laws of gravitation, and their action upon bodies in a state of motion or rest, is acquired by the engineer, the artisan, the machinist, —not by sudden intuition, but by months and years of steady application. Arithmetic, or the science of numbers; geometry, or the science of quantities; astronomy, and the uses of astronomical knowledge in navigation, must all have been profoundly studied,—the almost innumerable ideas which form these vast sciences must have been discovered and brought together, one by one,—before any mariner could leave a port on this side of the globe and strike, without failure, the smallest town or river on the opposite side of it. And the same principle is no less true in regard to jurisprudence, to legislation, and to all parts of social economy, so far as they are worthy to be called sciences. But that part of the train of our mental operations which we call the emotions or affections, those powers of our spiritual constitution denominated the propensities and sentiments, which give birth to appetite, hope, fear, grief, love, shame, pride, at the very first, produce a feeling, which is perfect or complete of its kind. An infant cannot reason, but may experience as perfect an emotion of fear as an adult. Mankind, for thousands of years, have been advancing in the attainments of intellect; but the fathers of the race had feelings as electric and impetuous as any of their latest descendants. In every intellectual department, therefore, there must be accurate observation in collecting the elementary ideas,—these ideas must be compared, arranged, methodized, in the mind,—each faculty, which has cognizance of the subject, taking them up individually, and, as it were, handling, assorting, measuring, weighing them, until each one is marked at its true value, and arranged in its right place, so that they may stand ready to be reproduced, and to be embodied in any outward fabric or institution, in any work of legislation or philosophy, which their possessor may afterwards wish to construct. Such intellectual processes must have been performed by every man who has ever acquired eminence in the practical business of life, or who has ever made any great discovery in the arts or sciences, except, perhaps, in a very few cases, where discovery has been the result of happy accident. It is this perseverance in studying into the nature of things, in unfolding their complicated tissues, discerning their minutest relations, penetrating to their centres, that has made such men as Lord Bacon, Sir Isaac Newton, Dr. Franklin, Watt, Fulton, Sir Humphry Davy, and Dr. Bowdich,—men, the light of whose minds is now shed over all parts of the civilized world as diffusively and universally as the light of the sun, and as enduring as that light. And so it is in all the other departments of life, whether higher or humbler; not more in the case of the diplomatist, who is appointed an ambassador to manage a difficult negotiation at a foreign court, than in that of the agent who is chosen by a town, because of his good sense and thorough knowledge of affairs, to conduct a municipal controversy. It is such habits of thought and reflection upon the actual relations of things as they exist, and as

God has constituted them, that we are indebted for the men who know how to perform each day the duties of each day, and, in any station, the duties of that station; men, who, because of their clear-sightedness and wisdom, are nominated as arbitrators or umpires by contending parties, or whose appearance in the jury-box is hailed by the counsellors and suitors of the court; men whose work has not to be done over again, and whose books or reports do not need *errata* as large as themselves. But the feelings or emotions, so far from being dependent on those intellectual habits for their vividness and energy, are even more vivid and energetic when freed from control and direction. The intellect hems in the feelings by boundaries of probability and naturalness. It opposes barriers of actual and scientific truth to their devious wanderings and flights. It shows what things can be, and what things cannot be, and thus arrests the imagination when it would otherwise soar or plunge into the impossible and the preternatural. The savage, with his uncultivated intellect, has fields for the roamings of fancy, which can have no existence to the philosopher; just as an idolater has an immensity for the creations of his superstition, which to the enlightened Christian is a nonenity.

But if it is unfortunate that so many people should addict themselves to the reading of fiction, because their minds are immature and unbalanced, and have no touchstone whereby they can distinguish between what is extravagant, marvellous, and supernatural, and what, from its accordance to the standard of nature, is simple, instructive, and elevating; it is doubly unfortunate that so many excellent young persons should be misled into the same practice, either from a laudable desire to maintain some acquaintance with what is called the literary world, and to furnish themselves with materials for conversation, or from a vague notion that such reading alone will give a polish to the mind, and adorn it with the graces of elegance and refinement. In endeavoring to elucidate the manner in which this indulgence entails weakness upon the understanding, and unfits it for a wise, steady, beneficent course of life, in a world so abounding as this is in solemn realities and obligations, I would most sedulously refrain from uttering a word in disparagement of a proportionate and measured cultivation of what are called polite literature and the polite arts in all their branches. While we have sentiments and affections, as well as thoughts and ideas; while, in the very account of the creation of the world, it is said that some things were made to be *pleasant to the sight,* and others good for sustenance; and while our spiritual natures are endowed with susceptibilities to enjoy the former, as well as with capacities to profit by the latter,—any measures for the elevation of the common mind, which do not recognize the existence and provide for the cultivation of the first class of powers, as well as for the second, would form a community of men, wholly uncouth and rugged in their strength, and almost unamiable, however perfect might be their rectitude. The mind of every man is instinct with capacities above the demands of the workshop or the field,—capacities which are susceptible of pure enjoyments from music and art, and all the embellishments of civilized life, and whose indulgence would lighten the burden of daily toil. All have susceptibilities of feeling too subtle and evanescent to find any medium of utterance, except in the language of poetry and art, and too refined to be called into being, but by the creations of genius. The culture of these sensibilities makes almost as important a distinction between savage and civilized man, as the training of the intellect; and without such cultivation, though the form of humanity may remain, it will be disrobed of many of its choicest beauties. Still, in a world, where, by the ordinances of Providence, utility outranks elegance; where harvests to sustain life must be cultivated before gardens are planted to gratify taste; where all the fascinations of regal courts are no atonement for the neglect of a single duty,—in such a world, no gentility or gracefulness of mind or manners, however exquisite and fascinating, is any substitute for practical wisdom and benevolence. Without copious resources of useful knowledge in our young men and young women; without available, applicable judgment and discretion, adequate to the common occasions and ready for the emergencies of life,—the ability to quote poetic sentiments, and expatiate on passages of fine writing, or a connoisseurship in art, is but mockery. Hence it is to be regretted that so many excellent young persons, emulous of self-improvement, should commit the error of supposing that an acquaintance with the institutions of society, with the real wants and conditions of their fellow-men, and with the means of relieving them, can be profitably exchanged for a knowledge of the entire universe of fiction; or that it is wise, in their hours of study, to neglect the wonderful works of the Creator, in order to become familiar with the fables of men. Intellect must lay a foundation, and rear a superstructure, before taste can adorn it. Without solid knowledge and good sense, there is no substance into which ornament or accomplishment can be inwrought. It is impossible to polish vacuity, or give a lustre to the surface of emptiness.

But far above and beyond all special qualifications for special pursuits is the importance of forming to usefulness and honor the capacities which are common to all mankind. The endowments that belong to all are of far greater consequence than the peculiarities of any. The practical farmer, the ingenious mechanic, the talented artist, the upright legislator or judge, the accomplished teacher, should be only modifications or varieties of the original *man*. The man is the trunk; occupations and professions are only different qualities of the fruit it should yield. There are more of the same things to be taught to all, and learned by all, than there are of different things to be imparted, distributively, to classes consisting of a few. The development of the common nature; the cultivation of the germs of intelligence, uprightness, benevolence, truth, that belong to all,—these are the principal, the aim, the end; while special preparations for the field or the shop, for the forum or the desk, for the land or the sea, are but incidents.

In the first place, it is requisite that every man, considered merely as a man, and without reference to station or occupation, should know something of his own bodily structure and organization, of whose marvellous workmanship it is said, that it is fearfully and wonderfully made,—*wonderfully,* because the infinite wisdom and skill, manifested in the adjustment and expansion of his frame, tend to inspire the mind with devotion and a religious awe; and *fearfully,* because its exquisite mechanism is so constantly exposed to peril and destruction from all the objects and elements around him, that precaution or fear is the hourly condition of his existence.

Did each individual know,—what, with a few suitable books, he might easily learn,—on what observances and conditions the Creator of the body has made its health and strength to depend; did he know that his corporeal frame is a general system, made up by the union of many particular systems,—the nervous, the muscular, the bony, the arterial, the venous, the pulminary, the digestive; that all these bear certain fixed relations to each other, and to the objects and elements of the external world,—it is inconceivable how much of disease and pain and premature death would be averted,— from how much imposition he would be saved, and how much the powers of useful labor, and the common length of life, would be increased. Even from the extension of knowledge on these subjects within the last century, the average length of life has increased one quarter; and yet it now reaches to but little more than half of threescore years and ten. How many persons, annually, are killed by the carbonic gas of burning charcoal, when, did they know of its existence, or how it is formed, they would as soon swallow arsenic as inhale it! How much property is annually destroyed by spontaneous combustion, through an ignorance of the circumstances that cause it! What a population of spectres and ghosts and apparitions has been driven from the abodes of all intelligent men, and might be annihilated with regard to all mankind, by a knowledge of the reflection and refraction of light, and of a few other simple laws of Nature! These terrific races, that once swarmed the earth, have ceased their visits where a few of those principles of science are understood, which every child, if supplied with the means, might easily learn. How pertinaciously have the most diffusive blessings been resisted,—such as the use of lightning conductors, and vaccination, —because devout but ignorant people supposed, that to ward off death, when it came under violent forms, was an impious defiance of the will of Heaven! as though it were not the primary will of Heaven that we should use the means of self-preservation which it has graciously given us. It is not long since, that, in one of our most intelligent cities, a splendid granite church took fire; and when it was found impossible to extinguish the flames in its interior, the chief-engineer forbade the engine-men to play upon the walls, because he knew that water thrown upon heated granite would decompose it, and he wished to save the materials; but hundreds of others, ignorant of this fact, but only knowing that the engineer belonged to a different religious denomination from the worshippers at the church, attributed the prohibition to his spite against an opposing sect of Christians; and, while he took the measure which alone could save the property, they supposed he was maliciously delighting himself with the sight of its destruction. In Scotland, during the last century, the introduction of mills for winnowing grain was violently opposed. The whole argument took a theological cast. It was urged, on one side, that the use of a winnowing mill was a resistance of the Divine Will, because it prevented the wind from "blowing where it listeth." But, on the other side, it was gravely answered, that to prevent the wind from "blowing where it listeth," only contravened the will of the "Prince of the power of the air," and was therefore not only lawful, but laudable. Profit and convenience coming to the support of the latter argument, it prevailed. These are specimens only of the most gross and sottish ignorance. Its less palpable forms are indefinitely more numerous, and their consequences, in the aggregate, indefinitely more disastrous. Let any one read such a work as that of Dick "On the

Diffusion of Useful Knowledge," and he will be able to form some idea how intimately the private, personal happiness of a people is connected with its intelligence.

But these illustrations are endless. The real fact to be pondered is, that, without diffusing information amongst the people, we shall go on in the same way, smiling at the follies of the last generation, and furnishing anecdotes for the next. There are innumerable ways in which a knowledge of the material world would gladden the obscurest dwelling in the land, and disburden the heart of the humblest individual of fears, anxieties, and sorrows. There are innumerable ways in which an instructed and enlightened man turns the course of Nature to his profit and delight and daily comfort, which an ignorant man would no more think of than a savage would think of burning anthracite coal in the winter to warm him, and of preserving ice over summer to cool him.

All children might learn something of Natural History. This department presents an immense variety of objects, calculated to develop their observing and comparing faculties, at a period of life when these faculties are more active than ever afterwards, and to store the mind with an abundance of materials for the judging and reasoning powers to act upon. To portions of this class of objects, divines and moralists are perpetually referring, in order to illustrate the power and wisdom and perfections of God; and yet, how nearly lost are all such illustrations upon minds that know nothing of those laws of vegetable life which clothe "the lilies of the field" in beauty beyond the regal glory of Solomon, nor of that animal mechanism that saves the "sparrow" from falling!

The biography of great and good men is one of the most efficient of all influences in forming the character of children; for, as they are prone to imitate what they admire, it unconsciously directs, while it delights them. Let the mind be supplied with definite, exact ideas on any subject, and we all know by experience, that, when an analogous case arises, the related ideas with which we were familiar before will instantaneously spring up in the mind by the law of association. And when correct ideas present themselves spontaneously in this way, they are, to say the least, far more likely to be embodied in action, than if they had first to be laboriously sought out. Especially is this true in emergencies; and how many of the follies and imprudences of men are first committed on emergencies, so sudden as to exclude reflection! On such occasions, to have prototypes of moral excellence in the mind is something like having precedents or examples in the practical concerns or business of life. Although it is a great truth, that all minds have the capacity of distinguishing between right and wrong, yet life presents innumerable instances where the application of these principles is attended with serious difficulty: in such cases, mere ignorance is always the source of error, and often of ruin. And how many excellent men have lived, how many illustrious examples have been set, of which only a very few of the more favored children of this State have ever heard! all others, therefore, being not so much as invited to follow in the same radiant paths. Why should the examples of benevolence, of probity, of devotion to truth, be lost to so many of our children, whom they might fire with a corresponding love of excellence? Here are real examples of real men, and are, therefore, possible and imitable; and, to the unsophisticated mind of a child, there is as great a difference between real and fictitious personages as there is to a merchant between real and fictitious paper. There never was such an argument in favor of furnishing biographical and scientific truth for children, and against the mass of fictions which are given them for true stories, and not as media or illustrations merely, as the simple question, which ingenuous children so often ask, when reading or hearing a narrative, *Is it true?* It ought to be remembered, that in all the objects and operations of Nature, and in the lives of genuine men, we converse with God and with the course of his providence *at first hand*, and not with mock-shows and counterfeits and hearsays.

There is another kind of reading, which all must admit to be of the very highest importance to our citizens, and of which they are almost universally ignorant; I mean our ante-Revolutionary history. Few, even of our educated men, can claim any familiarity with it; yet there our free institutions germinated. Never, in any other place, nor at any ther time, have the great principles of civil and religious liberty been so ably discussed, or been sustained by such heroic trials and sacrifices, as between the first colonization of this country and the peace of 1783. Our country's independence, the birth of a free people,—one of the greatest epochs in the history of the human race,—was the result. Every boy who is not ruined by a false course of instruction passes through a state of mind, between the ages of sixteen and twenty-one, when a study of the principles and deeds recorded in that history would give him some adequate idea what liberty and law are, what they have cost, and what they are worth.

But when we turn from the outward and material world to the

inward and spiritual life, a wider field for improvement opens before us; for out of the invisible recesses of the mind come all the mighty changes wrought by human power. When an uninstructed person looks upon the outward form of a man, he thinks nothing of the skillfully-adjusted organs, nor of the mysterious functions of vitality, within it. The vibrating nerves, which convey sensation and volition, the contracting muscle, the flowing blood, the health and strength giving processes of nutrition, the dilating lungs, with their adaptations to each other, are all hidden from his untaught gaze. So, when an ignorant man regards the operations of the mind, he discerns only a tumultuary, conflicting tide of wishes and terrors, of pleasures and pains, of doubts and purposes, rising, contending, and subsiding, without order or law. He takes no cognizance of the different powers and faculties with which he has been endowed, of their relative supremacy, of their different spheres of action, nor of their adaptations to his temporal condition; and hence, when he obeys their impulses, it is without the approval of conscience; and when he commands them, it is without the discriminations of reason. Every child, towards the close of his minority, has time and capacity enough, could he be furnished with the means, to acquire much of the knowledge enjoined in that ancient precept, so universally celebrated and sanctioned, "Know thyself."

But, after all, those blessings of knowledge, combined with well-directed feelings, which cannot be enumerated, are infinitely more than any language can express. The greater proportion of the stream of every man's life is hidden in the silent breast, and never emerges into utterance or action. Much as any one may be in the company of the world, he is much more in the company of his own consciousness only. It is the perpetual inflowing of his secret reflections and emotions that mingles sweet or bitter waters in the stream of every man's existence. Whatever reaches the fountains of this stream, is, as far as possible, to be remembered in plans for human amelioration. Few men have battles to fight, or senates to persuade, or kingdoms to rule; but all have a spirit to be controlled, and to be brought into subjection to the social and divine law. The intellect forces the great problems of existence and futurity and destiny upon all; and none will question that much depends upon human means, whether a man shall go through the world and out of it, elated by delusive hopes, or tormented by causeless fears.

Among the agencies that operate to these momentous ends, books, certainly, occupy a conspicuous place. Whoever has read modern biography, with a philosophic eye to the cause of the extraordinary characters it records, must have observed the frequent references that are made to some *book*, as turning the stream of life at some critical point in its course. In one of Dr. Franklin's letters, he says, that, when a boy, he met with a book entitled "Essays to do Good," which led to such a train of thinking, as had an influence on his conduct through life. Sir Walter Scott, in his writings and letters, makes repeated and repeated mention of the fact, that he owed his power of painting past times to the books which he read when young. The notorious Stephen Burroughs, a native of a neighboring State, relates in his autobiography, that he was inflamed with military ardor by the perusal of "Guy, Earl of Warwick;" that he ran away from his father three times,—once before he was fourteen years of age,—and enlisted in a regiment of artillery. Twice he was reclaimed, but, at last, he succeeded in escaping, and in the camp, it has been sometimes said, commenced his life of ignominy. Whoever looks deeper, sees that that ignominious life commenced when he was reading a pernicious book. It would be easy to fill pages with similar facts. "When I see a house," says Dr. Franklin, "well furnished with books and newspapers" (of course he meant instructive, and not mere partisan ones), "there I see intelligent and well-informed children; but, if there are no books nor papers, the children are ignorant, if not profligate." It has been frequently remarked by observing men, that towns in which good libraries have been established show a population of intelligence superior to that of towns where none has existed. In a number of towns, recent attempts to establish libraries for grown people have utterly failed. The men and women, not having acquired a taste for useful reading when children, have lost it for life. Let the same course be followed in regard to the present children, and time is not more certain to bring the day when they shall be men and women, than it is to bring the same feelings of indifference towards mental improvement. On the other hand, I have never heard of a well-selected library for children which has failed from their want of interest in it.

And in what way, except by furnishing good libraries to the people at large, can the reading of frivolous and useless books, of novels of the baser sort, and of that contaminating and pestilential class of works which is now hawked around the country, creating moral diseases, or inflaming and aggravating where it finds them, be prevented? These books no law can destroy or reach. No power of persuasion can ever induce those who have acquired a love of reading them to abandon what gives them pleasure, without some equivalent of pleasure is proffered in its stead. But a supply of good books would confer far more than an equivalent. It would prove a remedy where the disease exists, and an antidote where it threatens. Let good books be read, and the taste for reading bad ones will slough off from the minds of the young, like gangrened flesh from a healing wound. Nor will any severity of legislative enactment, nor any vigilance in the administration of the law, ever succeed in the extirpation of gaming, shows, circuses, theatres, and many low and gross forms of indulgence, without the introduction of some moral and intellectual substitutes.

For the purpose of carrying out a plan of improvement, co-extensive with the wants of the community, and with the limits of the State, no system can be devised at all comparable with the existing arrangement of school districts. Here are corporate bodies, known to the law, already organized and in operation. The schoolhouses are central points of minute subdivisions of territory, which, in the aggregate, embrace every inch of ground in the State. There are but few districts in the State which comprise more than a space of two miles square. On an average, they include less than that extent of territory. Here, then, are central points, at convenient distances, distributed with great uniformity all over the Commonwealth; each one with a little group of children—the hope and treasure of the State—dependent upon it for all the means of public instruction they are ever to enjoy. And these points, though now emitting so dim and feeble a light, may be made luminous and radiant, dispelling the darkness, and filling the land with a glory infinitely above regal splendor. Could the children, who are so widely scattered over the surface of the State, laboring, even in their tender years, upon its hills and by its water-falls,—could they assemble, and present themselves before their rulers, and be, for a moment, endued with a vision of their coming fortunes, and speak of the life of toil to which most of them have been born, of their poverty in the means of self-cultivation, or, what is worse than poverty, of their indifference to it; could they proclaim that every passing day is uttering the irreversable oracles of their fate, who could resist the appeal? And can the thought of such an appeal penetrate the heart with less electric swiftness because they cannot make it?

Again: it is believed that no barbarous nation has ever been known to history,—amongst whom any form of government had been established,—which had not adopted specific measures to educate the heir of sovereignty for the discharge of his regal duties. And can the obligation to prepare for the responsibilities attendant to power be less, where all the citizens, instead of one, are born to the inheritance of sovereignty? By our institutions, the political rights of the father descend to his sons in course of law. But the intellectual and moral qualifications necessary for the discreet use of those rights are intransmissible by virtue of any statute. These are personal, not hereditary; and are, therefore, to be taught anew and learned anew by each successive generation. Hence, as the work of education is never done, the means of education should never be withheld; as the former must be continually renewed, the latter must as continually be supplied.

The instruction and pleasure which the parents themselves would experience from the establishment of a good library in their respective districts are too important to be forgotten, and yet are so obvious as to need only a passing reference.

It seems to be the unanimous opinion of the teachers of all schools, whether public or private, that a School Library would be a most valuable auxiliary in interesting children in their studies. It would inspire the young with the desire to learn, that they might prepare themselves to enjoy what they saw was prized by others. Several of the rudimental studies could be invested, to the eye of the pupil, with new interest and usefulness by its means. If the facts or sentiments contained in the reading-lessons could be illustrated or enlivened by some explanation or anecdote from the library, it would often convert a mechanical routine into a living exercise. If, when the scholars come to the name of Socrates or Luther or Howard, they could turn to a Biographical Dictionary, and find a summary of the lives and deeds of these men, and ascertain their place in chronology and in geography, it would give a sense of reality to the business of the school, while, at the same time, it would acquaint them with important facts. And so of ancient or foreign customs and manners, of memorable events, of remarkable phenomena in Nature, &c. Pupils, who, in their reading, pass by names, references, allusions, without searching, *at the time*, for the facts they imply, not only forego valuable information, which they may never afterwards acquire, but they contract a habit of being contented with ignorance. Under the influence of such a habit, the ardent desire for knowledge, which Nature kindles in the breast of children, will soon be extinguished, and they will come to resemble the irrational creation, which, without thought or emotion, passes by objects of the greatest curiosity and wonder.

Again: access to some library seems indispensable, in all schools where any attention is paid to composition. The ability to express ideas in writing, with vigor and perspicuity, is now deemed so valuable, that, in many places, Composition has been added to the list of Common-school studies. But the earlier exercises of children, in composing (however it may be with the later), can consist of little more than rendering other men's thoughts in their own language. If the most distinguished authors desire to consult books before they attempt the discussion of great subjects, then to require children to write composition, without supplying them with some resources whence to draw their materials, is absurdly to suppose, not only that they are masters of a select and appropriate diction in which to clothe their thoughts and feelings, but also that they possess a degree of originality which even the ablest writers do not claim.

For these and other reasons, some of the most judicious and successful teachers have carried into school any little collection of books belonging to themselves, and have realized great benefit from it. Such collections, however, must generally be scanty, and can rarely, if ever, be the most appropriate and useful; besides, such a practice is, at least, liable to misuse. But a well-selected library,—such as that which is now in a course of preparation under the auspices of the Board,—in which all possible respect is paid to the right of private judgment on questions concerning which an unhappy difference of opinion prevails amongst the best men in the community,—such a library would avoid all danger, and increase every benefit. Every legitimate excitement or encouragement brought to bear upon our children in the schools, not only quickens progress, but diminishes the occasion for discipline.

THE INDISPENSABLE TEACHER

From Fourth Annual Report (1840)

Here Mann's examination of basic school needs rings one of its most modern notes. There is the teacher, there is the child, there is the parent. If they are, individually or collectively, unconcerned, incompetent, or without sound social principles, society itself is in jeopardy. The important fact to be noted is that Mann was not merely earnest and well-wishing, and in no sense the mere moralist. He spoke from a fund of experience which makes his views as formidable today as they were in his own time.

IN regard to management and discipline, a more trying situation, to a person of judgment and good feelings, cannot well be conceived, than that of having the sole charge of a school of sixty, seventy, or eighty scholars, of all ages, where he is equally exposed to censure for the indulgences that endanger good order, and for the discipline that enforces it. One of the inquiries contained in the circular letter to the school committees, in 1838, was respecting the ages of the children attending our public schools. By the answers, it appeared, that, in very many places, the schools were attended by scholars of all ages, between four years and twenty, and, in some places, by those between two years and a half and twenty-five; and thus the general regulations of the school, as to order, stillness, and the observance of a code of fixed laws, were the same for infants but just out of their cradles, and for men who had been enrolled seven years in the militia. Now, nothing can be more obvious than that the kind of government appropriate and even indispensable for one portion of these scholars was flagrantly unsuitable for the other. The larger scholars, with a liberal recess, can keep their seats and apply their minds for three consecutive hours. But to make small children sit both dumb and motionless, for three successive hours, with the exception of a brief recess and two short lessons, is an infraction of every law which the Creator has impressed upon both body and mind. There is but one motive by which this violence to every prompting of nature can be committed, and that is an overwhelming, stupefying sense of fear. If the world were offered to these children as a reward for this prolonged silence and inaction, they would spurn it: the deep instinct of self-preservation alone is sufficient for the purpose. The irreparable injury of making a child sit straight and silent and motionless for three continuous hours, with only two or three brief respites, cannot be conceived. Its effect upon the body is to inflict severe pain, to impair health, to check the free circulations in the system (all which lead to dwarfishness), and to misdirect the action of the vital organs, which leads to deformity. In regard to the intellect, it suppresses the activity of every faculty; and as it is a universal law in regard to them all, that they acquire strength by exercise, and lose tone and vigor by inaction, the inevitable consequence is, both to diminish the number of things they will be competent to do, and to disable them from doing this limited number so well as they otherwise might. In regard to the temper and morals, the results are still more deplorable. To command a child whose mind is furnished with no occupation to sit for a long time silent in regard to speech, and dead in regard to motion, when every limb and organ aches for activity; to set a child down in the midst of others, whose very presence acts upon his social nature as irresistibly as gravitation acts upon his body, and then to prohibit all recognition of or communication with his fellows,—is subjecting him to a temptation to disobedience, which it is alike physically and morally impossible he should wholly resist. What observing person who has ever visited a school where the laws of bodily and mental activity were thus violated has failed to see how keenly the children watch the motions of the teacher; how eagerly, the first moment when his face is turned from them, or any person or object intervenes to screen them from his view, they seize upon the occasion to whisper, laugh, chaffer, make grimaces, or do some other thing against the known laws of school? Every clandestine act of this kind cultivates the spirit of deception, trickery, and fraud; it leads to the formation, not of an open and ingenuous, but of a dissembling, wily, secretive character. The evil is only aggravated when the teacher adopts the practice of looking out under his eyebrows, as it is called, or of glancing at them obliquely, or of wheeling suddenly round, in order to detect offenders in the act of transgression. Such a course is a practical lesson in artifice and strategem, set by the teacher; and the consequence is, that to entrap on the one side and elude on the other soon becomes a matter of rivalry and competition between teacher and pupils. Probably it is within the recollection of most persons, that, after the close of some school-terms, both teacher and pupils have been heard to boast,—the one how many he had insnared, the others how often they had escaped; thus presenting the spectacle of the moral guide to our youth, and the moral subjects of his charge, *boasting* of mutual circumvention and disingenuousness.

Teachers who manage schools with a due observance of those laws with which the Creator has pervaded the human system, are accustomed, when scholars have become restless and uneasy, to send them out to run, or in some way to take exercise, until the accumulation of muscular and nervous energy, which prompted their uneasiness, is expended. They will then return to the schoolroom to sit with composure, or to study with diligence and vigor.

The remedies for these various evils are the establishment of Union Schools, wherever the combined circumstances of territory and population will allow; the consolidation of two or more districts into one, where the union system is impracticable; and, where the population is so sparse as to prevent either of these courses, there to break in upon the routine of the school, either by confining the young children for a less number of hours, or by giving them two recesses each half-day. The health of the body must be preserved, because it is the only medium through which the brightest intellect and the purest morals can bless the world.

If it were possible to measure or gauge the quantity and quality of instruction which the teacher could give under the union system, compared with that which he can give in a school composed of scholars of all ages, and in all stages of advancement, no further proof in favor of a classification of the children into divisions of older and younger would be needed. A teacher well versed in the better modes of instruction, which are beginning to be adopted, will, in most branches, teach each one, of a class of twenty, more in the same time than he could teach any one individual of the same class. What an accession to his usefulness, that is, to the improvement of the children, would thus be gained! And is it not an unpardonable waste of means, where it can possibly be avoided, to employ a man, at $25 or $30 a month, to teach the alphabet, when it can be done much better, at half-price, by a female teacher?

. . . A brief consideration of a few of the qualifications essential to those who undertake the momentous task of training the children of the State will help us to decide the question, whether the complaints of the committees, in regard to the incompetency of teachers, are captious and unfounded; or whether they proceed from enlightened conceptions of the nature of their duties and office, and therefore require measures to supply the deficiency.

1st. One requisite is a knowledge of Common-school studies. Teachers should have a perfect knowledge of the rudimental branches which are required by law to be taught in our schools. They should understand, not only the rules, which have been prepared as guides for the unlearned, but also the principles on which the rules are founded,—those principles which lie beneath the rules, and supersede them in practice, and from which, should the rules be lost, they could be framed anew. Teachers should be able to teach *subjects*, not manuals merely.

This knowledge should not only be thorough and critical, but it should be always ready at command for every exigency,—familiar like the alphabet, so that, as occasion requires, it will rise up in the mind instantaneously, and not need to be studied out with labor and delay. For instance: it is not enough that the teacher be able to solve and elucidate an arithmetical question, by expending half an hour of school-time in trying various ways to bring out the answer; for that half-hour is an important part of the school-session, and the regular exercises of the school must be shortened or slurred over to repair the loss. Again: in no school can a teacher devote his whole and undivided attention to the exercises, as they successively recur. Numerous things will demand simultaneous attention. While a class is spelling or reading, he may have occasion to recall the roving attention of one scholar; to admonish another by word or look; to answer some question put by a third; or to require a fourth to execute some needed service. Now, if he is not so familiar with the true orthography of every word, that his ear will instantaneously detect an error in the spelling, he will, on all such occasions, pass by mistakes without notice, and therefore without correction, and thus interweave wrong instruction with right through all the lessons of the school. If he is not so familiar, too, both with the rules of reading, and with the standard of pronunciation for each word, that a wrong emphasis or cadence, or a mispronounced word, will jar his nerves, and recall even a wandering attention, then innumerable errors will glide by his own ear unnoticed, while they are stamped upon the minds of his pupils. These remarks apply with equal force to recitations in grammar and geography. A critical knowledge respecting all these subjects should be so consciously present with him, that his mind will gratefully respond to every right answer or sign made by the scholar, and shrink from every wrong one, with the quickness and certainty of electrical attraction and repulsion. In regard to the last-named branch, geography, a study which, in its civil or political department, is constantly mutable and progressive, the teacher should understand, and be able to explain, any material changes which may have occurred since the last edition of his text-book; as, for instance, the erection of Iowa into a territorial government by the last Congress; or, during the last year, the restitution of Syria to the Turkish government through the intervention of the Four European Powers. This establishment of a link between past events and present times, this realization of things as lately done or now doing, sheds such a strong light upon a distant scene, as makes it appear to be near us, and thus gives to all the scholars a new and inexpressible interest in their lessons.

However much other knowledge a teacher may possess, it is no equivalent for a mastership in the rudiments. It is not more true in architecture than in education, that the value of the work in every upper layer depends upon the solidity of all beneath it. The leading, prevailing defect in the intellectual department of our schools is a want of thoroughness,—a proneness to be satisfied with a verbal memory of rules, instead of a comprehension of principles, with a knowledge of the names of things, instead of a knowledge of the things themselves; or, if some knowledge of the things is gained, it is too apt to be a knowledge of them as isolated facts, and unaccompanied by a knowledge of the relations which subsist between them, and bind them into a scientific whole. That knowledge is hardly worthy of the name, which stops with things, as individuals, without understanding the relations existing between them. The latter constitutes indefinitely the greater part of all human knowledge. For instance, all the problems of plane geometry, by which heights and distances are measured, and the contents of areas and cubes ascertained, are based upon a few simple definitions which can be committed to memory by any child in half a day. With the exception of the comets, whose number is not known, there are but thirty bodies in the whole solar system. Yet, on the relations which subsist between these thirty bodies is built the stupendous science of astronomy. How worthless is the astronomical knowledge which stops with committing to memory thirty names!

At the Normal School at Barre during the last term the number of pupils was about fifty. This number might have been doubled if the visitors would have consented to carry the applicants forward at once into algebra and chemistry and geometry and astronomy, instead of subjecting them to a thorough review of Common-school studies. One of the most cheering auguries in regard to our schools is the unanimity with which the committees have awarded sentence of condemnation against the practice of introducing into them the studies of the university to the exclusion or neglect of the rudimental branches. By such a practice a pupil foregoes all the stock of real knowledge he might otherwise acquire; and he receives, in its stead, only a show or counterfeit of knowledge, which, with all intelligent persons, only renders his ignorance more conspicuous. A child's limbs are as well fitted in point of strength to play with the planets before he can toss a ball, as his mind is to get any conception of the laws which govern their stupendous motions before he is master of common arithmetic. For these and similar considerations, it seems that the first intellectual qualification of a teacher is a critical thoroughness, both in rules and principles, in regard to all the branches required by law to be taught in the Common Schools; and a power of recalling them in any of their parts with a promptitude and certainty hardly inferior to that with which he could tell his own name.

2nd. The next principal qualification in a teacher is the *art of teaching*. This is happily expressed in the common phrase, *aptness to teach*, which in a few words comprehends many particulars. The ability to acquire, and the ability to impart, are wholly different talents. The former may exist in the most liberal measure without the latter. It was a remark of Lord Bacon, that "the art of well-delivering the knowledge we possess is among the secrets left to be discovered by future generations." Dr. Watts says, "There are some very learned men who know much themselves, but who have not the talent of communicating their knowledge." Indeed, this fact is not now questioned by any intelligent educationist. Hence we account for the frequent complaints of the committees, that those teachers who had sustained an examination in an acceptable manner failed in the schoolroom through a want of facility in communicating what they knew. The ability to acquire is the power of understanding the subject-matter of investigation. Aptness to teach involves the power of perceiving how far a scholar understands the subject-matter to be learned, and what, in the natural order, is the next step he is to take. It involves the power of discovering and of solving at the time the exact difficulty by which the learner is embarrassed. The removal of a slight impediment, the drawing aside of the thinnest veil which happens to divert his steps or obscure his vision, is worth more to him than volumes of lore on collateral subjects. How much does the pupil comprehend of the subject? What should his next step be? Is his mind looking towards a truth or an error? The answer to these questions must be intuitive in the person who is apt to teach. As a dramatic writer throws himself successively into the characters of the drama he is composing, that he may express the ideas and emotions peculiar to each; so the mind of a teacher should migrate, as it were, into those of his pupils, to discover what they know and feel and need; and then, supplying from his own stock what they require, he should reduce it to such form, and bring it within such a distance, that they can reach out and seize and appropriate it. He should never forget that intellectual truths are naturally adapted to give intellectual pleasure; and that, by leading the minds of his pupils onward to such a position in relation to these truths that they themselves can discover them, he secures to them the natural reward of a new pleasure with every new discovery, which is one of the strongest as well as most appropriate incitements to future exertion.

Aptness to teach includes the presentation of the different parts of a subject in a natural order. If a child is told that the globe is about twenty-five thousand miles in circumference, before he has any conception of the length of a mile or of the number of units in a thousand, the statement is not only utterly useless as an act of instruction, but it will probably prevent him ever afterwards from gaining an adequate idea of the subject. The novelty will be gone, and yet the fact unknown. Besides, a systematic acquisition of a subject knits all parts of it together, so that they will be longer retained and more easily recalled. To acquire a few of the facts gives us fragments only; and even to master all the facts, but to obtain them promiscuously, leaves what is acquired so unconnected and loose that any part of it may be jostled out of its place and lost, or remain only to mislead.

Aptness to teach, in fine, embraces a knowledge of methods and processes. These are indefinitely various. Some are adapted to accomplish their object in an easy and natural manner; others in a toilsome and circuitous one; others, again, may accomplish the object at which they aim with certainty and despatch, but secure it by inflicting deep and lasting injuries upon the social and moral sentiments. We are struck with surprise on learning, that, but a few centuries since, the feudal barons of Scotland, in running out the lines around their extensive domains, used to take a party of boys, and whip them at the different posts and landmarks in order to give them a retentive memory as witnesses in case of future litigation or dispute. Though this might give them a vivid recollection of localities, yet it would hardly improve their ideas of justice, or propitiate them to bear true testimony in favor of the chastiser. But do not those who have no aptness to teach sometimes accomplish their objects by a kindred method?

He who is apt to teach is acquainted, not only with common methods for common minds, but with peculiar methods for pupils of peculiar dispositions and temperaments; and he is acquainted with the principles of all methods whereby he can vary his plan according to any difference of circumstances. The statement has been sometimes made, that it is the object of Normal Schools to subject all teachers to one inflexible, immutable course of instruction. Nothing could be more erroneous; for one of the great objects is to give them a knowledge of modes as various as the diversity of cases that may arise, that, like a skilful pilot, they may not only see the haven for which they are to steer, but know every bend in the channel that leads to it. No one is so poor in resources for difficult emergencies as they may arise as he whose knowledge of methods is limited to the one in which he happened to be instructed. It is in this way that rude nations go on for indefinite periods, imitating what they have seen, and teaching only as they were taught.

3rd. Experience has also proved that there is no necessary connection between literary competency, aptness to teach, and the power to manage and govern a school successfully. They are independent qualifications; yet a marked deficiency in any one of the three renders the others nearly valueless. In regard to the ordinary management or administration of the school, how much judgment is demanded in the organization of classes, so that no scholar shall either be clogged and retarded, or hurried forward with injudicious speed, by being matched with an unequal yoke-fellow! Great discretion is necessary in the assignment of lessons, in order to avoid, on the one hand, such shortness in the tasks as allows time to be idle; and, on the other, such over-assignments as render thoroughness and accuracy impracticable, and thereby so habituate the pupil to mistakes and imperfections, that he cares little or nothing about committing them. Lessons, as far as it is possible, should be so adjusted to the capacity of the scholar, that there should be no failure in a recitation not occasioned by culpable neglect. The sense of shame, or of regret for ignorance, can never be made exquisitely keen, if the lessons given are so long, or so difficult, as to make failures frequent. When "bad marks," as they are called, against a scholar, become common, they not only lose their salutary force, but every addition to them debases his character, and carries him through a regular course of training which prepares him to follow in the footsteps of those convicts who are so often condemned, that, at length, they care nothing for the ignominy of the sentence. Yet all this may be the legitimate consequence of being unequally mated or injudiciously tasked. It is a sad sight, in any school, to see a pupil marked for a deficiency, without any blush of shame, or sign of guilt; and it is never done with impunity to his moral character.

The preservation of order, together with the proper despatch of business, requires a mean between the too much and the too little, in all the evolutions of the school, which it is difficult to hit. When classes leave their seats for the recitation-stand, and return to them again, or when the different sexes have a recess, or the hour of inter-mission arrives, if there be not some order and succession of movement, the school will be temporarily converted into a promiscuous rabble, giving both the temptation and the opportunity for committing every species of indecorum and aggression. In order to prevent confusion, on the other hand, the operations of the school may be conducted with such military formality and procrastination,—the second scholar not being allowed to leave his seat until the first has reached the door, or the place of recitation, and each being made to walk on tip-toe to secure silence,—that a substantial part of every school session will be wasted in the wearisome pursuit of an object worth nothing when obtained.

When we reflect how many things are to be done each half-day, and how short a time is allotted for their performance, the necessity of system in regard to all operations of the school will be apparent. System compacts labor; and when the hand is to be turned to an almost endless variety of particulars, if system does not preside over the whole series of movements, the time allotted to each will be spent in getting ready to perform it. With lessons to set; with so many classes to hear; with difficulties to explain; with the studious to be assisted; the idle to be spurred; the transgressors to be admonished or cor-rected; with the goers and comers to observe;—with all these things to be done, no considerable progress can be made, if one part of the wheel is not coming up to the work while another is going down. And if order do not pervade the school as a whole, and in all its parts, all is lost: and this is a very difficult thing; for it seems as though the school were only a point, rescued out of a chaos that still encompasses it, and is ready on the first opportunity to break in and re-occupy its ancient possession. As it is utterly impracticable for any committee to prepare a code of regulations co-extensive with all the details which belong to the management of a school, it must be left with the teacher; and hence the necessity of skill in this item of the long list of his qualifications.

The government and discipline of a school demands qualities still more rare, because the consequences of error in these are still more disastrous. What caution, wisdom, uprightness, and sometimes even intrepidity, are necessary in the administration of punishment! After all other means have been tried, and tried in vain, the chastisement of pupils found to be otherwise incorrigible is still upheld by law and sanctioned by public opinion. But it is the last resort, the ultimate resource, acknowledged on all hands to be a relic of barbarism, and yet authorized because the community, although they feel it to be a great evil, have not yet devised and applied an antidote. Through an ignorance of the laws of health, a parent may so corrupt the constitution of his child as to render poison a necessary medicine; and, through ignorance of the laws of mind, he may do the same thing in regard to punishment. When the arts of health and of education are understood, neither poison nor punishment will need be used, unless in most extraordinary cases. The discipline of former times was inexorably stern and severe; and, even if it were wished, it is impossible now to return to it. The question is, what can be substituted, which, without its severity, shall have its efficiency?

But how important is the relation in which a teacher stands towards a supposed offender! If the grounds of suspicion are presumptive only, how nice the balance of judgment in which they should be weighed, lest, on the one hand, injustice be done by bringing a false accusation against the innocent; or lest, on the other, a real offender should escape through mistaken confidence and charity! If there be sufficient ground to put a pupil upon trial, the teacher in his own person combines the characters of the law-maker, by whom the rule, supposed to be transgressed, was enacted; of the counsel who examines the witnesses; of the jury who decides upon the facts; and of the judge interpreting his own law, and awarding sentence according to his own discretion. And, after all this, he is the executive officer, inflicting the penalty he himself has awarded, unless that penalty is remitted by the pardoning power, which also resides in him. Often, too, this representative or depositary of so many functions is himself the person supposed to be offended; and thus he presents the spectacle of a party in interest trying his own cause, and avenging his own insults against his own dignity. If he suffers the out-door consequences of inflicting punishment to enter his mind, his fears will become his counsellors, and they will be as false as his pride. This specification is not given for the purpose of excepting to that usage which makes the teacher the sovereign of the schoolroom, but only to show what danger of error there must be when teachers are employed who have had neither experience nor instruction, and whose judgment years have not yet begun to ripen. Are there not teachers to whom all the children in the district are intrusted for their education, and for all the momentous and enduring interests connected with that word, to whom scarcely a parent in the district would surrender the care and management of his own children for the same length of time? Yet how much less incapable would the teacher be of governing and controlling a family of five or six children than a school of fifty or sixty! Every child ought to find at school the affection and the wisdom which he has left at home; or, if he has left neither wisdom nor affection at home, there is so much more need that he should find them at school.

A school should be governed with a steady hand, not only during the same season, but from year to year; substantially the same extent of indulgence being allowed, and the same restrictions imposed. It is injurious to the children to alternate between the extremes of an easy and a sharp discipline. It is unjust also for one teacher to profit by letting down the discipline of a school, and thus throw upon his successor the labor of raising it up to its former level.

4th. In two words the statute opens to all teachers an extensive field of duty, by ordaining that all the youth in the schools shall be taught "*good behavior.*" The framers of the law were aware how rapidly good or bad manners mature into good or bad morals; they saw that good manners have not only the negative virtue of restraining from vice, but the positive one of leading, by imperceptible gradations, towards the practice of almost all the social virtues. The effects of civility or discourtesy, of gentlemanly or ungentlemanly deportment, are not periodical or occasional, merely, but of constant recurrence; and all the members of society have a direct interest in the manners of each of its individuals; because each one is a radiating point, the centre of a circle which fills with pleasure or annoyance, not only those who voluntarily enter it, but all those, who, in the promiscuous movements of society, are caught within its circumference. Good behavior includes the elements of that equity, benevolence, conscience, which, in their great combinations, the moralist treats of in his books of ethics, and the legislator enjoins in his codes of law. The school-room and its playground, next to the family table, are the places where the selfish propensities come into most direct collision with social duties. Here, then, a right direction should be given to the growing mind. The surrounding influences which are incorporated into its new thoughts and feelings, and make part of their substance, are too minute and subtile to be received in masses like nourishment; they are rather imbibed into the system unconsciously by every act of respiration, and are constantly insinuating themselves into it through all the avenues of the senses. If, then, the manners of the teacher are to be imitated by his pupils, if he is the glass at which they "do dress themselves," how strong is the necessity that he should understand those nameless and innumerable practices in regard to deportment, dress, conversation, and all personal habits, that constitute the differ-ence between a gentleman and a clown! We can bear some oddity or eccentricity in a friend whom we admire for his talents or revere for his virtues; but it becomes quite a different thing when the oddity or the eccentricity is to be a pattern or model from which fifty or a hundred children are to form their manners. It was well remarked by the ablest British traveller who has ever visited this country, that, amongst us, "every male above twenty-one years of age claims to be a sovereign. He is, therefore, *bound to be a gentleman.*"

5th. On the indispensible, all-controlling requisite of moral char-acter, I have but a single suggestion to make in addition to those admir-able views on this subject which are scattered up and down through the committees' reports. This suggestion relates to the responsibility rest-ing on those individuals who give letters of recommendation or certifi-cates of character to candidates for schools. Probably one-half, perhaps more, of all the teachers in the State are comparatively strangers in the respective place where they are employed. Hence the examining committee, in the absence of personal knowledge, must rely upon testimonials exhibited before them. These consist of credentials brought from abroad, which are sometimes obtained through the partialities of relationship, interest, or sect; or even given lest a refusal should be deemed an unneighbourly act, and the applicant should be offended or alienated by a repulse. But are interests of such vast moment as the moral influence of teachers upon the rising generation to be sacrificed to private considerations of relationship or predilection, or any other selfish or personal motive whatever? It may be very agreeable to a person to receive the salary of a teacher, but this fact has no tendency to prove his fitness for the station: if so, the poorhouse would be the place to inquire for teachers; and what claim to conscience or benevolence can that man have who jeopards the permanent welfare of fifty or a hundred children for the private accommodation of a friend? In regard to pecuniary transactions, it is provided by the laws of the land, that whosoever recommends another as responsible and solvent becomes himself liable for the debts which may be contracted, under a faith in the recommendation, should it prove to have been falsely given. The recommendation is held to be a warranty; and it charges its author with all its losses incurred, within the scope of a fair construction. It is supposed that, without this responsibility, the expanded business of trade and commerce would be restricted to persons possessing a mutual knowledge of each other's trustworthiness or solvency. But why should the precious and enduring interests of morality be accounted of minor importance, and protected by feebler securities than common traffic? Why should the man who has been defrauded by an accredited peddler have his remedy against the guarantor, while he who is instrumental in inflicting upon a district, and upon all the children in a district, the curse of a dissolute, vicious teacher, escapes the condign punishment of general execration? In the contemplation of the law, the school committee are sentinels stationed at the door of every schoolhouse in the State to see that no teacher ever crosses its threshold who is not clothed, from the crown of his head to the sole of his foot, in garments of virtue; and they are the enemies of the human race,—not of contemporaries only, but of posterity,—who, from any private or sinister motive, strive to put these sentinels to sleep in order that one who is profane or intemperate, or addicted to low associations, or branded with the stigma of any vice, may elude the vigilance of the watchmen, and be installed over the pure minds of the young as their guide and exemplar. If none but teachers of pure tastes, of good manners, of exemplary morals, had ever gained admission into our schools, neither the schoolrooms nor their appurtenances would have been polluted as some of them now are with such ribald inscriptions, and with the carvings of such obscene emblems, as would make a heathen blush. Every person, therefore, who indorses another's character, as one befitting a school teacher, stands before the public as his moral bondsman and sponsor, and should be held to a rigid accountability.

Sovereign, reigning over and above all other influences upon the school, is, or rather might be, that of the parents. The father, when presiding at his table, or returning home at evening from the labors of the day; the mother, in that intercourse with her children which begins with the waking hour of the morning and lasts until the hour of sleep,—enjoy a continuing opportunity, by arranging the affairs of the household in such a way as to accommodate the hours of school; by subordinating the little interests or conveniences of the family to the paramount subject of regular and punctual attendance; by manifesting such an interest in the studies of each child, that he will feel a daily responsibility, as well as a daily encouragement in regard to his lessons; by foregoing an hour of useless amusement or a call of ceremony, in order to make a visit to the school; by inviting the teacher to the house, and treating him, not as a hireling, but as a wiser friend; by a conscientious care in regard to their conversation about the school, and their award of praise or blame; in fine, by all those countless modes which parental affection, when guided by reason, will make delightful to themselves, the parents can inspire their offspring with a love of knowledge, a habit of industry, a sense of decorum, a respect for manliness of conduct and dignity of character, prophetic of their future usefulness and happiness and honor.

For one who has not traversed the State, and made himself actually acquainted with the condition of the schools by personal inspection and inquiry, it is impossible fully to conceive the contrasts they now present. I have no hope, therefore, of making myself adequately understood, when I say, that in contiguous towns, and even in contiguous districts, activity and paralysis—it is hardly too much to say life and death—are to be found side by side. Wherever a town or district has been blessed with a few men, or even with a single man, who had intellect to comprehend the bearings of this great subject, and a spirit to labor in the work, there a revolution in public sentiment has been effected, or is now going on. In some districts, last winter, the prosperity of the school became a leading topic of conversation among the neighbors; the presence of visitors, from day to day, cheered the scholars; a public spirit grew up among them, animating to exertion, and demanding courteous, honorable, just behavior; the consequence of which was, that, by a law as certain as that light comes with the rising of the sun, a proficiency surpassing all former example was made; and when the schools drew to a close, a crowd of delighted spectators attended the final examination, which, from the interest and the pleasure of the scene, was prolonged into the night. In some places, the visitors who did not come early to this examination could not obtain admittance on account of the crowded state of the house; and in one, although a cold and driving snow-storm lasted through the day, yet a hundred parents attended, whom the inclemency of the weather could not deter from being present to celebrate this harvest-home of knowledge and virtue; while on the same occasion, in an adjoining town, perhaps in a bordering district, a solitary committee-man dropped grudgingly in to witness a half-hour of mechanical movements, got up as a mock representation of knowledge, and to look at the half-emptied benches of the schoolroom made vacant by deserters. These differences are not imaginary, they are real; and their proximate cause is the interest, or the want of interest, manifested by the parents toward the schools.

It is a celebrated saying of the French philosopher and educationist, Cousin, that "as is the teacher, so is the school." In regard to France and Prussia, where the schools depend so much upon the authority of the government, and so little upon the social influences of the neighborhood where they exist, this brief saying is the embodiment of an important truth; but, with our institutions, there is far less reason for giving it the currency and force of a proverb. Here, every thing emanates from the people: they are the original; all else is copy. If, therefore, the transatlantic maxim, which identifies the character of the school with that of the teacher, be introduced amongst us, it must be with the addition, that "as are the parents, so are both teacher and school."

A visit to the school by the parents produces a salutary effect upon themselves. Although it is feeling which originates and sends forth conduct, yet conduct re-acts powerfully upon feeling; and, therefore, if parents could be induced to commence the performance of this duty, they would soon find it not only delightful in itself, but demanded by the force of habit. Nor is it any excuse for their neglect, that they are incapable, in point of literary attainments, of examining the school, or of deciding upon the accuracy of recitation. If they have no knowledge to bestow in instruction, they all have sympathy to give in encouragement. Indeed, the children must be animated to exertion before they will make any valuable or lasting attainment. This animation the parents can impart, and thus become the means of creating a good they do not themselves possess.

It is surprising that the sagacity of parental love does not discover that a child, whose parents interest the teacher in his welfare, will be treated much better in school than he otherwise would be; and this, too, without the teacher's incurring the guilt of partiality. If the teacher is made acquainted with the peculiarities of the child's disposition, he will be able to manage him more judiciously, and therefore more successfully, than he otherwise could; he will be able to approach the child's mind through existing avenues, instead of roughly forcing a new passage to it; and thus, in many instances, to supersede punishment by mild measures. A wise physician always desires to know the constitution and habit of his patient before he prescribes for his malady; and a parent who should call a medical practitioner to administer to a sick child, but should refuse to give him this information, would be accounted insane. But are the maladies of the mind less latent and subtle and elusive than those of the body? and is a less degree of peril to be apprehended in the former case than in the latter from the prescriptions of ignorance? I have been credibly informed of a case where a child received a severe chastisement in school for not reading distinctly, when the inarticulateness was occasioned by a natural impediment in his organs of speech. The parent sent the child to school without communicating this fact to the teacher; and, under the circumstances of the case, the teacher mistook the involuntary defect for natural obstinacy. This may seem an extreme case, and one not likely to happen; but, doubtless, hundreds of similar though less discoverable ones, in regard to some mental or moral deficiency, are daily occurring. Again: if parents do not visit the school until at or near its close, they may then discover errors or evils whose consequences might have been foreseen on an earlier visit, and thus prevented. It is another fact, eminently worthy of parental consideration, that many young and timid children, unaccustomed to see persons not belonging to the family, are almost paralyzed when first brought into the presence of strangers. An excessive diffidence cripples their limbs, and benumbs all their senses; and it is only by their being gradually familiarized to company, that the fetters of embarrassment can be stripped off, and the shy, downcast countenance be uplifted. After a few years of neglect, that awkwardness and shamefacedness become irremediable: they harden the whole frame, as it were, into a petrification; and their victim always finds himself bereft of his faculties at the very moment when he has most need of freedom and vigor in their exercise. On the other hand, pert, forward, self-esteeming children, who are unaccustomed to the equitable reciprocities of social intercourse, commit the opposite error of becoming rude, aggressive, and disdainful, whenever brought into contact with society. Now, one of the best remedies or preventives which children can enjoy, both for this disabling bashfulness, and for this spirit of effrontery, is the meeting of visitors in school, where a previous knowledge of what the occasion demands helps them to behave in a natural manner, notwithstanding the consciousness that others are present; and where they are relieved from the double embarrassment of thinking both what they are to do, and how it should be done. Especially is it necessary that mothers should accompany sensitive and timid children when they first go to school, to obviate a distrust of the teacher, or a fear of other children, which might otherwise infix in the mind a permanent repugnance to the place. Whatever confers upon the school a single attraction, or removes from it one feature of harshness, clears the avenue for a more ready transmission of knowledge into the pupils' minds.

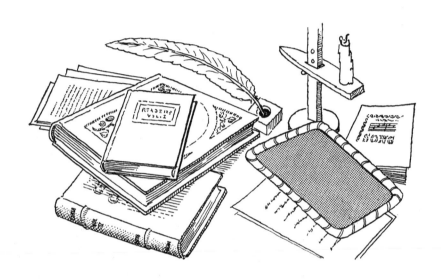

2.

Tools and Problems

THE COST OF EDUCATION

One such man as [Eli] Whitney is worth more than all the common schools of New England ever cost.

A TRADITION OF ILL-HEALTH

So universal and long-continued have been the violations of the physical laws, and so omnipresent is human suffering as the consequence, that the very tradition of a perfect state of health has died out from among men.

REFLECTION-PERCEPTION

As it regards the intellectual man, nothing enlarges or diminishes his power of usefulness more than the predominance of the reflective over the perceptive faculties, or that of the perceptive over the reflective. The reflective man is immeasurably superior to the perceptive one. His analysis is always deeper, so that he not only shows his antagonist to have been wrong, but shallow as well as wrong. I would not say a word against the cultivation of the perceptive powers; but it is most desirable that the reflective ones should maintain the ascendancy. The true office of the former is to supply the materials for the latter to work upon.

CHALLENGES TO A NEW AGE

From Ninth Annual Report (1845)

By 1845, Mann spoke not only with the voice of experience, the voice of urgency; he spoke with the voice of authority. He echoed, too, the sense of triumph, of unconquerableness which could be heard in the sentences of his contemporaries Emerson, Garrison, Wendell Phillips, and Theodore Parker, among others. Democracy could only unfold a wealth of human potential—here one can discern the premises on which a later Reform Era would operate; and, as one would reach its height in a great Civil War, so the other would conclude in World War I. Hidden, then, in Mann's prose is disillusionment. This, however, should not blind us to the fact that the great prophets of reform had earned their optimism honestly: had faced the enigmas of human nature and struggled to repress its less useful aspects, to encourage and sustain those which better profited humanity. Moreover, the prophets of pessimism and despair had not always set examples of dignity and integralness.

T HE extraordinary facts exhibited in my last Report, respecting the manner of apportioning school-money among the districts, have turned public attention to that important subject. Those facts have already induced some towns to make very material modifications in the manner of distributing their money; and they promise to do the same thing in many more. The great doctrine which it is desirable to maintain, and carry out, in reference to this subject, is, *equality of school-privileges for all the children of the town, whether they belong to a poor district or a rich one, a small district or a large one.*

A general interest has been awakened in some towns upon which a deep sleep had fallen before. During no year, since my original appointment, have my advice and assistance been so frequently requested respecting the best methods of arranging and improving our school-system.

Nor is the movement confined to our own Commonwealth. Several States in the south and west seem to be awakening from their lethargy, and inquiring into the detail of means necessary to be adopted for the general education of their people. Within the space of a single month, during the last autumn, I received inquiries from a dozen distinguished men, belonging to a single State, respecting the organic structure of our system, its general administration, and its internal arrangements and management. In the mean time, the great State of New York, by means of her county superintendents, her State Normal School, and otherwise, is carrying forward the work of popular education more rapidly than any other State in the Union, or any country in the world. Within the last year, the State of Rhode Island has entirely renovated her school-system. Under the auspices of that distinguished and able friend of common schools, Henry Barnard, Esq., she is preparing to take her place among the foremost of the States. Within the last few weeks also, the State of Vermont has re-organized her school-system, by passing a law which provides for the appointment of town, *county,* and State superintendents, prescribing the course of duty of each class of officers in regard to the examination of teachers, the visitation of schools, and the general administration of the system.

These indubitable evidences of progress are not only a reward for past exertions, but an incentive to future efforts. But let not complacency in successes already obtained tempt to the relaxation of a single fibre in our endeavors for future advancement. What has been gained must be converted into means for further acquisition. The faithful steward, being intrusted with five talents, therewith gets other five talents.

Our common schools are a system of unsurpassable grandeur and efficiency. Their influences reach, with more or less directness and intensity, all the children belonging to the State,—children who are soon to be the State. They act upon these children at the most impressible period of their existence,—impairing qualities of mind and heart which will be magnified by diffusion, and deepened by time, until they will be evolved into national character,—into weal or woe, into renown or ignominy,—and, at last, will stamp their ineffaceable seal upon our history. The natural philosopher looks at the silky envelopment which an insect has woven for itself; he marks its structure; he recognizes the laws of life which are silently at work within it; and he knows that, in a few days or weeks, that covering will burst, and from it will be evolved a thing of beauty and vivacity, lovely in the eyes of all, or an agent of destruction, fit to be a minister in executing God's vengeance against an offending people. With a profounder insight into the laws of development and growth, and with an eye that embraces an ampler field of time in its vision, the philosopher of humanity looks at the institutions which are moulding the youthful capacities of a nation; he calculates their energy and direction; and he is then able to foresee and to foretell, that, if its course be not changed, the coming generation will be blessed with the rewards of parental forecast, or afflicted with the retributions of parental neglect. Happy are they, who, knowing on what conditions God has made the welfare of nations to depend, observe and perform them with fidelity.

Improvement in schoolhouse architecture—including in the phrase all comfortable and ample accommodations for the schools—is only an improvement in the perishing body in which they dwell. A more perfect organization of the schools themselves, by a wisely-graduated classification of schools and scholars, and by the assignment of such territorial limits as will best combine individual convenience with associated strength, is only an endowment of that perishing body with a superior mechanism of organs and limbs. The more bounteous pecuniary liberality with which our schools, from year to year, are maintained, is only an addition to the nutriment by which the same body is fed, giving enlargement and energy to its capabilities, whether of good or of evil, and empowering it to move onward more swiftly in its course, whether that course is leading to prosperity or to ruin.

The great, the all-important, the only important question still remains: By what spirit are our schools animated? Do they cultivate the higher faculties in the nature of childhood,— its conscience, its benevolence, a reverence for whatever is true and sacred? or are they only developing, upon a grander scale, the lower instincts and selfish tendencies of the race,—the desires which prompt men to seek, and the powers which enable them to secure, sensual ends,—wealth, luxury, preferment,— irrespective of the well-being of others? Knowing, as we do, that the foundations of national greatness can be laid only in the industry, the integrity, and the spiritual elevation of the people, are we equally sure that our schools are forming the character of the rising generation upon the everlasting principles of duty and humanity? or, on the other hand, are they only stimulating the powers which lead to a base pride of intellect, which prompt to the ostentation instead of the reality of virtue, and which give augury that life is to be spent only in selfish competitions between those who should be brethren? Above all others, must the children of a republic be fitted for society as well as for themselves. As each citizen is to participate in the power of governing others, it is an essential preliminary that he should be imbued with a feeling for the wants, and a sense of the rights, of those whom he is to govern; because the power of governing others, if guided by no higher motive than our own gratification, is the distinctive attribute of oppression; an attribute whose nature and whose wickedness are the same, whether exercised by one who calls himself a republican, or by one born an irresponsible despot. In a government like ours, each individual must think of the welfare of the State, as well as of the welfare of his own family, and, therefore, of the children of others as well as his own. It becomes, then, a momentous question, whether the children in our schools are educated in reference to themselves and their private interests only, or with a regard to the great social duties and prerogatives that await them in after-life. Are they so educated, that, when they grow up, they will make better philanthropists and Christians, or only grander savages? For, however loftily the intellect of man may have been gifted, however skillfully it may have been trained, if it be not guided by a sense of justice, a love of mankind, and a devotion to duty, its possessor is only a more splendid, as he is a more dangerous barbarian.

We have had admirable essays and lectures on the subject of morality in our schools. In perusing the reports of school-committees from year to year, nothing has given me so much pleasure as the prominence which they have assigned to the subject of moral education, and the sincerity, the earnestness, and the persistence with which they have vindicated its claims to be regarded as an indispensable part of all common-school instruction. Considered as general speculation, nothing could be better; and yet no one will deny that the want of a corresponding action on this subject still beclouds the prospects of the schools, and ofttimes causes us to tremble for the fate of those who are passing through them. Practically, the duty of cultivating the moral nature of childhood has been neglected, and is still neglected. Profound ethical treatises are written for the guidance of men, after the habits and passions of ninety-nine in every hundred of those men have become too deep-rooted and inveterate to be removed by secondary causes. Volumes are published on the nicest questions of casuistry,—questions which probably will never arise in the experience of more than one in a thousand of the community,—while specific directions and practical aids in regard to the training of children in those every-day domestic and social duties on which their own welfare and the happiness of society depend are comparatively unknown. How shall this great disideratum be supplied? How shall the rising generation be brought under purer moral influences, by way of guaranty and suretyship, that, when they become men, they will surpass their predecessors, both in the soundness of their speculations and in the rectitude of their practice? Were children born with perfect natures, we might expect that they would gradually purify themselves from the vices and corruptions which are now almost enforced upon them by the examples of the world. But the same nature by which the parents sunk into error and sin pre-adapts the children to follow in the course of ancestral degeneracy. Still, are there not moral means for the renovation of mankind which have never yet been applied? Are there not resources whose vastness and richness have not yet been explored? Of all neglected and forgotten duties, in all ages of the world, the spiritual culture of children has been most neglected and forgotten. In all things else, art and science have triumphed. In all things else, principles have been investigated, and instruments devised and constructed, to apply those principles in practice. The tree has been taken in the germ, and its growth fashioned to the wants or the tastes of man. By the skill of the cultivator, the wild grain and the wild fruit have been taken in their seed, and have had their dwarfish-ness expanded into luxuriance, and their bitter and sometimes poison-ous qualities ameliorated into richness of flavor and nutrition. The wild animal, and even the beast of prey, if domestcated when young, and from the lair, have been tamed and trained to the service of man,— the wild horse and the buffalo changed into the most valuable of domestic animals, and the prowling wolf into the faithful dog. But man has not yet applied his highest wisdom and care to the young of his own species. They have been comparatively neglected until their passions had taken deep root, and their ductile feelings had hardened into the iron inflexibility of habit; and then how often have the mightiest agencies of human power and terror been expanded upon them in vain! Governments do not see the future criminal or pauper in the neglected child, and therefore they sit calmly by, until roused from their stupor by the cry of hunger or the spectacle of crime. Then they erect the almshouse, the prison, and the gibbet, to arrest or miti-gate the evils which timely caution might have prevented. The courts and the ministers of justice sit by until the petty delinquencies of youth glare out in the enormities of adult crime; and then they doom to prison or the gallows those enemies to society, who, under wise and well-applied influences, might have been supports and ornaments of the social fabric. For sixteen centuries, the anointed ministers of the gospel of Christ were generally regardless of the condition of youth. And the same remark holds true in regard to the last two centuries, with the exception of three or four only of all the Christian nations; and by far the greater part, even of these, must be excepted from the exception. The messengers of Him who took little children in his arms and blessed them have suffered juvenile waywardness or perversity to mature into adult incorrigibleness and impenitency; and then they have invoked the aid of Heaven to subdue that ferociousness of the passions which even a worldly foresight would have checked. How often has Heaven turned a deaf ear to their prayers, as if to rebuke the neglect and the blindness which had given occasion for them! Who will deny, that, if one tithe of the talent and culture which have been expended in legislative halls, in defining offences, and in devising and denouncing punishments for them; or of the study and knowledge which have been spent in judicial courts, in trying and in sentencing criminals; or of the eloquence and the piety which have preached repentance and remission of sins to adult men and women,—had been consecrated to the instruction and training of the young, the civilization of mankind would have been adorned by virtues and charities and Christian graces to which it is now a stranger?

What an appalling fact it is to every contemplative mind, that even wars and famines and pestilences—terrible calamities as they are acknowledged to be—have been welcomed as blessings and mercies, because they swept away, by thousands and tens of thousands, the pests which ignorance and guilt had accumulated! But the efficiency or sufficiency of these comprehensive remedies is daily diminishing. A large class of men seem to have lost that moral sense by which the liberty and life of innocent men are regarded as of more value than the liberty and life of criminals. There is not a government in Christendom which is not growing weaker every day, so far as its strength lies in an appeal to physical force. The criminal code of most nations is daily shorn of some of its terrors. Where, as with us, the concurrence of so many minds is a prerequisite, the conviction of the guilty is often a matter of difficulty; and every guilty man who escapes is a missionary, going through society, and preaching the immunity of guilt wherever he goes. War will never again be waged to disburden the crowded prisons, or to relieve the weary executioner. The arts of civilization have so multiplied the harvests of the earth, that a general famine will not again lend its aid to free the community of its surplus members. Society at large has emerged from that barbarian and semi-barbarian state where pestilence formerly had its birth, and committed its ravages. These great outlets and sluice-ways, which, in former times, relieved nations of the dregs and refuse of their population, being now closed, whatever want or crime we engender, or suffer to exist, we must live with. If improvidence begets hunger, that hunger will break into our garners. If animal instincts are suffered to grow into licentious passions, those passions will find their way to our most secret chambers. We have no armed guard which can save our warehouses, our market-places, and our depositories of silver and gold, from spoilation by the hands of a mob. When the perjured witness or the forsworn juryman invades the temple of justice, the evil becomes too subtile for the police to seize. It is beyond legislative or judicial or executive power to redeem the sanctuaries of religion from hypocrisy and uncharitableness. In a word, the freedom of our institutions gives full play to all the passions of the human heart. The objects which excite and inflame those passions abound; and, as a fact, nearly or quite universal, there is intelligence sufficient to point out some sure way, lawful or unlawful, by which those passions can be gratified. Whatever children, then, we suffer to grow up amongst us, we must live with as men; and our children must be their contemporaries. They are to be our copartners in the relations of life, our equals at the polls, our rulers in legislative halls; the awarders of justice in our courts. However intolerable at home, they cannot be banished to any foreign land; however worthless, they will not be sent to die in camps, or to be slain in battle; however flagitious, but few of them will be sequestered from society by imprisonment, or doomed to expiate their offences with their lives.

In the history of the world, that period which opened with the war of the American Revolution, and with the adoption of the Constitution of the United States, forms a new era. Those events, it is true, did not change human nature; but they placed that nature in circumstances so different from any it had ever before occupied, that we must expect a new series of developments in human character and conduct. Theoretically, and, to a great extent, practically, the nation passed at once, from being governed by others, to self-government. Hereditary misrule was abolished; but power and opportunity for personal misrule were given in its stead. In the hour of exultation at the achievement of liberty, it was not considered that the evils of license may be more formidable than the evils of oppression, because a man may sink himself to a profounder depth of degradation than it is in the power of any other mortal to sink him, and because the slave of the vilest tyrant is less debased than the thrall of his own passions. Restraints of physical force were cast off; but no adequate measures were taken to supply their place with the restraints of moral force. In the absence of the latter, the former, degrading as they are, are still desirable,—as a strait-jacket for the maniac is better than the liberty by which he would inflict wounds or death upon himself. The question now arises,—and it is a question on whose decision the worth or worthlessness of our free institutions are suspended,—whether some more powerful agency cannot be put in requisition to impart a higher moral tone to the public mind; to enthrone the great ideas of justice, truth, benevolence, and reverence, in the breasts of the people, and give them a more authoritative sway over conduct than they have ever yet possessed. Of course, so great an object can be reached only by gradual approaches. Revolutions which change only the surface of society can be effected in a day; but revolutions working down among the primordial elements of human character, taking away ascendency from faculties which have long had control over the conduct of men, and transferring it to faculties which have long been in subjection,—such revolutions cannot be accomplished by one conclusive effort, though every fibre in the nation should be strained to the endeavor. Time is an essential element in their consummation; nor can they be effected without an extensive apparatus of means, efficiently worked. Yet such revolutions have taken place,—as when nations emerged from the barbarian into the classic and chivalrous or romantic ages, or when they passed from these into the commercial and philosophic periods. By a brief retrospect of the condition of the more civilized nations of ancient and modern times, it can be easily shown that such a change has already taken place on the subject of education itself. It is the mission of our age to carry this cause one step farther onward in its progress of development.

Among the ancients, physical education was deemed of paramount importance. A preparation of the masses for war was the grand, the almost exclusive, object of national concern. War being carried on, and battles decided, mainly by muscular strength and agility; by the distance and accuracy with which the javelin could be hurled, or the vigor and dexterity with which the falchion could be wielded,—the desire of physical celerity and force predominated among men. It was not the cultivation of the great heart of the nation, it was not even the development of the intellect of the masses, but it was the invigoration of the frame, the growth and the strengthening of the limbs, that constituted the object of national policy and ambition. Bodily hardihood, the power of physical endurance, the ability to make long marches unfatigued, and to fight hand-to-hand, for the longest period, unterrified, were the qualities which won the spoils and the plaudits of victory, and kindled to enthusiasm the aspirations of the emulous youth. Who can fail to see that the tendency of all this was, not only to weaken the intellectual nature, and to narrow its range of action, but to degrade and demoralize the spiritual affections? The man was sacrificed to the animal; his soul was deemed of less value than his sinews. As the nobler qualities of his nature sunk to the level of brute force, it happened, naturally, that the horse became as valuable as his rider; and the elephant that went out to battle was of more consequence than the dozen warriors whom he bore in the tower upon his back. During the middle ages, and until the introduction of fire-arms,—which, to a very great extent, neutralized the inequities of physical strength,—the great barbarian idea, that the body of man is the only part of him worth cultivating, retained unquestioned ascendency in regard to the masses of the people. The soul was not consciously excluded from culture; for it was not sufficiently thought of, as the object of culture, to raise the question. Even down to the present century, the rulers and aristocracy of England have always encouraged athletic sports among the people—wrestling, running, leaping, boxing —as a part of the national policy, because, as it was said, these exercises tended to invigorate the *breed*, and thus to make better soldiers and sailors; the very language which was used betraying the sentiment, that it was the animal, and not the spiritual, part of man which was the object of national concern. Nor even in our own times, nor in our own country, have philosophy and Christianity dispelled this fatal idea, —an idea which is proper to the savage and the heathen only, and which we have inherited from them. In all the nations of Europe, the regulations of military schools in regard to training the body for vigor and robustness, and the capability of endurance, are entirely different from those of the classical, medical, legal, or theological schools; and in the military academy of our own government, at West Point, the cadets are inured to exposure, and their bodies hardened by camp-duty; while in our colleges and higher schools there are no regulations which have the health of the student for their object. On the contrary, so far as the body is concerned, the latter classes of institutions provide for all the natural tendencies to ease and inactivity as carefully as though paleness and languor, muscular enervation and debility, were held to be constituents in national beauty.

The introduction of the Baconian philosophy wrought a great revolution in the education of mankind. Since that epoch, the cultivation of the intellect has received more general attention than ever before; and, just in proportion as the intellect has been developed, it has seen more clearly and appreciated more fully the advantages of its own development. In Prussia and a few of the smaller States of Continental Europe, the action of the intellect, for reasons too obvious to be mentioned, has taken more of a speculative turn. In Great Britain, it has been turned towards practical or utilitarian objects; and, in the United States, it has been pre-eminently so turned. The immense natural resources of our country would have stimulated to activity a less enterprising and a less energetic race than the Anglo-Saxon. But such glittering prizes, placed within the reach of such fervid natures and such capacious desires, turned every man into a competitor and an aspirant. The exuberance that overspread the almost interminable valleys of the West drew forth hosts of colonists to gather their varied harvests. The tide of emigration rolled on, and it still continues to roll, with a volume and a celerity never before known in any part of the world, or in any period of history. Unlike all other nations, we have had no fixed, but a rapidly-advancing frontier. The geographical information of yesterday has become obsolete to-day. The outposts of civilization have moved forward with such gigantic strides, that their marches are reckoned, not by leagues, but by degrees of longitude; and cities containing thirty or fifty thousand souls have sprung up before the relics of the primeval forests had decayed on the soil they had so lately shaded. In the space of half a century, vast wildernesses have been organized into Territories, and these Territories erected into States, to take their place in the great family of the confederacy, and to be heard by their representatives in the council-halls of the nation. But scarcely had the immigrant and the adventurer surveyed the richness of vegetation which covered the surface of the earth, before they discovered an equal vastness of mineral wealth beneath it,—wealth which had been laid up, of old, in subterranean chambers, no man yet knows how capacious. Thus every man, however poor his parentage, became the heir-apparent of a rich inheritance. And while millions were thus appropriating fortunes to themselves out of the great treasure-house of the West, other millions on the Atlantic seaboard, with equal enterprise and equal avidity, were amassing the means of refinement and luxury. In one section, where Nature had adapted the soil to the production of new and valuable staples, the planter seized the opportunity,—literally a golden one,— and soon filled the markets of the world with some of the cheapest and most indispensable necessaries of life. In another section, foreign commerce invited attention; and the hardy and fearless inhabitants went forth to the uttermost parts of the earth in quest of gain. They drew wealth from the bosom of every ocean that spans the globe; they visited every country, and searched out every port on its circumference, where wind and water could carry them, and brought home, for sustenance or for superfluity, the natural and artificial productions of every people and of every zone. Meantime, science and invention applied themselves to the mechanic arts. They found that Nature, in all her recesses, had hidden stores of power, surpassing the accumulated strength of the whole human race, though all its vigor could be concentrated in a single arm. They found that whoever would rightly apply to Nature, by a performance of the true scientific and mechanical conditions, for the privilege of using her agencies, should forthwith be invested with a power such as no Babylonian or Egyptian king, with all his myriads of slaves, could ever command. With the aid of a little hand-machinery, at the beginning, water and steam have been taught to construct machines; and out of their match-less perfection, when guided by a few intelligent minds, have come the endless variety, the prodigality and the cheapness, of modern manufactures. In the Northern States, too, one universal habit of personal industry, not confined to the middle-aged and the vigorous alone, but enlisting the services of all,—the old, the young, the decrepit, the bed-ridden, each according to his strength,—has never ceased to coin labor into gold; and from the confluence of these numberless streams, though individually small, the great ocean of common comfort and competence has been unfailingly replenished.

Gathered together from these numerous and prolific sources, individual opulence has increased; and the sum total or valuation of the nation's capital has doubled and redoubled with a rapidity to which the history of every other nation that has ever existed must acknowledge itself to be a stranger. This easy accumulation of wealth has inflamed the laudable desire of competence into a culpable ambi-tion for superfluous riches. To convert natural resources into the means of voluptuous enjoyments, to turn mineral wealth into metal-lic currency, to invent more productive machinery, to open new channels of intercommunication between the States, and to lengthen the prodigious inventory of capital invested in commerce, has spurred the energies and quickened the talent of a people, every one of whom is at liberty to choose his own employment, and to change it, when chosen, for any other that promises to be more lucrative.

Nor is this the only side on which hope has been stimulated and ambition aroused. Others of the most craving instincts of human nature have been called into fervid activity. Political ambition, the love of power,—whether it consists in the base passion of exercising authority over the will of others, or in the more expansive and generous desire of occupying a conspicuous place among our fellows by their consent,—these motives have acted upon a strong natural instinct in the hearts of all. The chief magistrate and the legislators of the nation, the chief magistrate and the legislators of the States, the numerous county, town, parochial, and district officers, are, with but few exceptions, elective; and therefore the possession of all such offices implies the confidence and the regard, of a majority at least of their respective constituencies. So, too, of a great proportion of the militia offices. In addition to all these, there are voluntary, civil, social, philanthropic, and corporate organizations, each presided over, and its affairs administered, by officers of its own election. Probably there are, at the present hour, in the United States, as many persons holding offices, bestowed upon them by the votes of others, and therefore indicative of some degree of respect and estimation, as existed through all the centuries of the Roman Republic when its dominion was co-extensive with the known world. Doubtless there are more such elective offices at this time, among the twenty millions of this country, than the two hundred millions of Europe, and far more than in all the world besides. Many of these offices are sources of emolument as well as of power, and hence they present to competitors the double motive of a desire of gain and a love of approbation. If most of these innumerable fountains of honor are too small to slake the thirst of aspirants, they are sufficient to excite it. They create desires that are often unappeasable,—desires that embroil towns, states, and the nation itself, in the fiercest contentions of party.

Now, it is too obvious to need remark, that the main tendency of institutions and of a state of society like those here depicted is to cultivate the intellect and to inflame the passions, rather than to teach humility and lowliness to the heart. Our civil and social condition holds out splendid rewards for the competitions of talent, rather than motives for the practice of virtue. It sharpens the perceptive faculties in comparing different objects of desire, it exercises the judgment in arranging means for the production of ends, it gives a grasp of thought and a power of combination which nothing else could so effectively impart; but, on the other hand, it tends not merely to the neglect of the moral nature, but to an invasion of its rights, to a disregard of its laws, and, in cases of conflict, to the silencing of its remonstrances and the denial of its sovereignty.

And has not experience proved what reason might have predicted? Within the last half-century, has not speculation, to a fearful extent, taken the place of honest industry? Has not the glare of wealth so dazzled the public eye as often to blind it to the fraudulent means by which the wealth itself had been procured? Have not men been honored for the offices of dignity and patronage they have held, rather than for the ever-enduring qualities of probity, fidelity, and intelligence, which alone are meritorious considerations for places of honor and power? In the moral price-current of the nation, has not intellect been rising, while virtue has been sinking, in value? Though the nation as a nation, and a very great majority of the States composing it, have performed all their pecuniary obligations, and preserved their reputation unsullied; yet have there not been great communities, acting through legislators whom they themselves had chosen, that have been guilty of such enormous breaches of plighted faith as would cause the expulsion of a robber from his brotherhood of bandits?

And who will say, even of the most favored portions of our country, that their advancement in moral excellence, in probity, in purity, and in the practical exemplification of the virtues of a Christian life, has kept pace with their progress in outward conveniences and embellishments? Can virtue recount as many triumphs in the moral world as intellect has won in the material? Can our advances towards perfection in the cultivation of private and domestic virtues, and in the feeling of brotherhood and kindness towards all the members of our households, bear comparison with the improvements in our dwellings, our furniture, or our equipages? Have our charities for the poor, the debased, the ignorant, been multiplied in proportion to our revenues? Have we subdued low vices, low indulgences, and selfish feelings? and have we fertilized the waste places in the human heart as extensively as we have converted the wilderness into plenteous harvest-fields, or enlisted the running waters in our service? In fine, have the mightier and swifter agencies which we have created or applied in the material world any parallel, in new spiritual instrumentalities, by which truth can be more rapidly diffused, by which the high places of iniquity can be brought low, or its crooked ways made straight?

Must it not be acknowledged, that, morally speaking, we stand in arrears to the age in which we live? and must not some new measures be adopted, by which, as philanthropists and Christians, we can redeem our forfeited obligations?

While, then, the legislator continues to denounce his penalties against such wicked desires as break into actual transgression, and while the judge continues to punish the small portion of offences that can be proved in court, the friends of education must do whatever can be done to diminish the terrible necessity of the penal law and the judicial condemnation.

THE PILGRIMS AND EDUCATION

From Tenth Annual Report (1846)

Mann's understanding of the colonial past was strikingly realistic yet reverent. In his interpretation of it he revealed how firm was the transition from it to the stirring and experimental days of his own reform age—an age which was being denounced by southern intellectual leaders as one which gave opportunities to crackpots, atheists, loose women, as well as other more evidently respectable but equally dangerous elements of society. Mann's vision of the Pilgrims and Puritans was, of course, infinitely truer than that which was projected by Arthur Miller in his play, The Crucible.

To write a history of popular education in Massachusetts would be a work of great interest, and of little difficulty. Such a history, however, seems not to have been contemplated, and, therefore, would not be warranted, by those resolves of the legislature under which the following pages are prepared. The resolves provide only for "the republication of so much of his (the late Secretary's) Tenth Annual Report, as, with the requisite additions and alterations, will exhibit a just and correct view of the common-school system of Massachusetts, and the provisions of law relating to it. An adequate idea of this "system," however, can hardly be obtained without a brief reference to its origin, and to those great fundamental principles which its authors and supporters seem rather to have tacitly assumed than to have fully expounded.

The Pilgrim Fathers who colonized Massachusetts Bay made a bolder innovation upon all pre-existing policy and usages than the world had ever known since the commencement of the Christian era. They adopted special and costly means to train up the whole body of the people to industry, to intelligence, to virtue, and to independent thought. The first entry in the public record-book of the town of Boston bears date, "1634, 7th month, day 1." The records of the public meetings for the residue of that year pertain to those obvious necessities that claimed the immediate attention of an infant settlement. But in the transactions of a public meeting, held on the 13th day of April, 1635, the following entry is found: "Likewise it was then generally agreed upon, that our brother Philemon Purmont [or Purment] shall be intreated to become scholemaster for the teaching and nourtering of children with us." Mr. Purmont was not expected to render his services gratuitously. Doubtless he received fees from parents; but the same records show, that a tract of thirty acres of land, at Muddy River, was assigned to him; and this grant, two years afterwards, was publicly confirmed. About the same time, an assignment was made of a "garden plott to Mr. Daniel Maude, schoolemaster, upon the condition of building thereon, if neede be." From this time forward, these golden threads are thickly inwoven in the texture of all the public records of Boston.

It is not unworthy of remark, that a word of beautiful significance, which is found in the first record on the subject of schools ever made on this continent, has now fallen wholly out of use. Mr. Purmont was entreated to become a "scholemaster," not merely for the "teaching," but for the "NOURTERING" of children. If, as is supposed, this word, now obsolete in this connection, implied the disposition and the power on the part of the teacher, as far as such an object can be accomplished by human instrumentality, to warm into birth, to foster into strength, and to advance into precedence and predominance, all kindly sympathies towards men, all elevated thoughts respecting the duties and the destiny of life, and a supreme reverence for the character and attributes of the Creator, then how many teachers have since been employed who have not NOURISHED the children committed to their care!

In 1642, the General Court of the colony, by a public act, enjoined upon the municipal authorities the duty of seeing that *every child* within their respective jurisdictions should be educated. Nor was the education which they contemplated either narrow or superficial. By the terms of the act, the selectmen of every town were required to "have a vigilant eye over their brethren and neighbors,— to see first that none of them shall suffer so much barbarism in any of their families, as not to endeavor to teach, by themselves or others, their children and apprentices, so much learning as may enable them perfectly to read the English tongue, and [obtain a] knowledge of the capital laws; upon penalty of twenty shillings for each neglect therein."

Such was the idea of "barbarism" entertained by the colonists of Massachusetts Bay more than two centuries ago. Tried by this standard, even at the present day, the regions of civilization become exceedingly narrow; and many a man who now blindly glories in the name and in the prerogatives of a republican citizen would, according to the better ideas of the Pilgrim Fathers, be known only as the "barbarian" father of "barbarian" children.

The same act further required that religious instruction should be given to all children; and also "that all parents and masters do breed and bring up their children and apprentices in some honest, lawful calling, labor, or employment, either in husbandry or some other trade profitable for themselves and the Commonwealth, if they will not or can not train them up in learning to fit them for higher employments."

Thus were recognized and embodied in a public statute the highest principles of political economy and of social well-being, the universal education of children, and the prevention of drones or non-producers among men.

By the same statute, the selectmen and magistrates were empowered to take children and servants from the custody of those parents and masters, who, "after admonition," "were still negligent of their duty in the particulars above mentioned," and to bind them out to such masters as they should deem worthy to supply the place of the unnatural parent,—boys until the age of twenty-one, and girls until that of eighteen.

The law of 1642 enjoined universal education; but it did not make education *free*, nor did it impose any penalty upon municipal corporations for neglecting to maintain a school. The spirit of the law, however, worked energetically in the hearts of the people; for in Gov. Winthrop's Journal ("History of New England," vol. ii. p. 215, Savage's edition), under date of 1645, we find the following: "Divers free schools were erected, as at Roxbury (for maintenance whereof every inhabitant bound some house or land for a yearly allowance forever) and at Boston, where they made an order to allow fifty pounds to the master, and an house and thirty pounds to an usher, who should also teach to read and write and cipher, and Indians' children were to be taught freely, and the charge to be by yearly contribution, either by voluntary allowance, or by rate of such as refused, &tc.; and this order was confirmed by the General Court. Other towns did the like, providing maintenance by several means."

It is probable, however, that some towns, owing to the sparseness of their population and the scantiness of their resources, found all the moneys in their treasury too little to pay the salary of a master;

and surrounded by dangers, as they were, from the ferocity of the aborigines and the inclemency of the climate, believed that not an eye could be spared from watching nor a hand from labor, even for so sacred a purpose as that of instruction; and therefore failed to sustain a school for the teaching and "nourtering" of their children. But, in all these privations and disabilities, the government of the colony saw no adequate excuse for neglecting the one thing needful. They saw and felt, that "if learning were to be buried in the graves of their fore-fathers, in Church and Commonwealth," then they had escaped from the house of bondage, and swum an ocean, and braved the terrors of the wilderness, in vain. In the year 1647, therefore, a law was passed making the support of schools compulsory, and education both universal and *free.*

By this law, every town containing fifty householders was required to appoint a teacher "to teach all such children as shall resort to him to write and read;" and every town containing one hundred families or householders was required to "set up a grammar school," whose master should be "able to instruct youth so far as they may be fitted for the university."

It is common to say that the act of 1647 *laid the foundation* of our present system of free schools; but the truth is, it not only laid the foundation of the present system, but, in some particulars, it laid a far broader foundation than has since been built upon, and reared a far higher superstructure than has since been sustained. Modern times have witnessed great improvements in the methods of instruction, and in the motives of discipline; but, in some respects, the ancient foundation has been narrowed, and the ancient superstructure lowered. The term "grammar school," in the old laws, always meant a school where the ancient languages were taught, and where youth could be "fitted for the university." Every town containing one hundred householders was required to keep such a school. Were such a law in force at the present time, there are not more than twelve towns in the Commonwealth which would be exempt from its requisitions. But the term "grammar school" has wholly lost its original meaning; and the number of towns and cities which are now required by law to maintain a school where the Greek and Latin languages are taught, and where youth can be fitted for college, does not exceed thirty. The contrast between our ancestors and ourselves in this respect is most humiliating. Their meanness in wealth was more than compensated by their grandeur of soul.

The institution of a free-school system on so broad a basis, and of such ample proportions, appears still more remarkable when we consider the period in the world's history at which it was originated, and the fewness and poverty of the people by whom it was maintained. In 1647, the entire population of the colony of Massachusetts Bay is supposed to have amounted only to twenty-one thousand souls. The scattered and feeble settlements were almost buried in the depths of the forest. The external resources of the people were small, their dwellings humble, and their rainment and subsistence scanty and homely. They had no enriching commerce; and the wonderful forces of Nature had not then, as now, become gratuitous producers of every human comfort and luxury. The whole valuation of all the colonial estates, both public and private, would hardly have been equal to the inventory of many a private citizen of the present day. The fierce eye of the savage was nightly seen glaring from the edge of the surrounding wilderness; and no defence or succor, save in their own brave natures, was at hand. Yet it was then, amid all these privations and dangers, that the Pilgrim Fathers conceived the magnificent idea, not only of a universal, but of a free education, for the whole people. To find the time and the means to reduce this grand conception to practice, they stinted themselves, amid all their poverty, to a still scantier pittance; amid their toils, they imposed upon themselves still more burdensome labors; and, amid their perils, they braved still greater dangers. Two divine ideas filled their great hearts,—their duty to God and to posterity. For the one, they built the church; for the other, they opened the school. Religion and knowledge,—two attributes of the same glorious and eternal truth, and that truth the only one on which immortal happiness can be securely founded!

It is impossible for us adequately to conceive the boldness of the measure which aimed at universal education through the establishment of free schools. As a fact, it had no precedent in the world's history; and, as a theory, it could have been refuted and silenced by a more formidable array of argument and experience than was ever marshalled against any other institution of human origin. But time has ratified its soundness. Two centuries of successful operation now proclaim it to be as wise as it was courageous, and as beneficent as it was disinterested. Every community in the civilized world awards it the meed of praise; and states at home, and nations abroad, in the order of their intelligence, are copying the bright example. What we call the enlightened nations of Christendom are approaching, by slow degrees, to the moral elevation which our ancestors reached at a single bound; and the tardy convictions of the one have been assimilating, through a period of two centuries, to the intuitions of the other.

The establishment of free schools was one of those grand mental and moral experiments whose effects could not be developed and made manifest in a single generation. But now, according to the manner in which human life is computed, we are the sixth generation from its founders; and have we not reason to be grateful both to God and man for its unnumbered blessings? The sincerity of our gratitude must be tested by our efforts to perpetuate and to improve what they established. The gratitude of the lips only is an unholy offering.

EXPENSES OF EDUCATION, AND OTHER EXPENSES

From Eleventh Annual Report (1847)

This is one of Mann's most varied reports. It included an inquiry into the views of practicing teachers of common-school education. Replies came from such notables as the Rev. Jacob Abbott (author of the famous Rollo stories) and Catherine E. Beecher, of the great Beecher clan. He enunciated basic principles by which "the desolating torrent of practical iniquity" could be stayed through education. He went on to assert his conviction that the materials for proper educational establishment were available, if they would but be sought, and, as in the matter of teachers, sustained with necessary funds. He went on to make comparisons of figures which revealed the emphases which society permitted in terms of its actual expenditures. They make absorbing reading, especially when compared with more modern budgets.

THE intrinsically noble profession of teaching has, most unfortunately, been surrounded by an atmosphere of repulsion rather than of attraction. Young men of talent are generally determined by two things in selecting an employment for life. The first of these is the natural tendency of the mind,—its predisposition towards one pursuit rather than towards another. In this way, Nature often predetermines what a man shall do; and, to make her purpose inevitable, she kneads it, as it were, into the stamina of his existence. She does not content herself with standing before his will, soliciting or tempting him to a particular course, but she stands behind the will, guiding and propelling it; so that from birth he seems to be projected towards his object like a well-aimed arrow to its mark. Those in whom the love of beautiful forms, colors, and proportions, predominates, are naturally won to the cultivation of the fine arts, or to some branch of the useful arts most congenial to the fine. Those who have a great fondness for botany and chemistry, and to whom physiological inquiries are especially grateful, become physicians. Persons enamoured of forensic contests, roused by their excitements, and panting for the *éclat* which their victories confer, betake themselves to the study of the law, and become advocates. The clerical profession is composed of men whose minds are deeply imbued and penetrated with the religious sentiment, and who ponder profoundly and devoutly upon the solemn concerns of an hereafter.* This constitutional or moral affinity for one sphere of employment rather than for another predetermines many minds in choosing the object of their pursuit for life. It is like the elective attractions of the chemist, existing beforehand, and only awaiting the contiguity of the related substances to make their secret affinities manifest.

But this natural tendency is often subjected to a disturbing or modifying force; and it yields to this force the more readily as it is itself less intense and dominant. All minds have a desire, more or less energetic, for pleasure, for wealth, for honor, or for some of that assemblage of rewards which obtains such willing allegiance from mankind. Hence the internal, inborn impulse is often diverted from the specific object to which it naturally points, and is lured away to another object, which, from some collateral or adventitious reason, promises a readier gratification.

There is also a class of minds of vigorous and varied capacities, which stand nearly balanced between different pursuits, and which, therefore, may be turned, by slight circumstances, in any one of many directions. They are like fountains of water rising on a table-land, whose channels may be so cut as to cover either of its slopes with fertility.

Now, the qualities which predispose their possessor to become the companion, guide, and teacher of children, are good sense, lively religious sensibilities, practical, unaffected benevolence, a genuine sympathy with the young, and that sunny, genial temperament which always sees its own cheerfulness reflected from the ever-open mirror of a child's face. The slightest exercise of good sense makes it apparent that any one year of childhood will exert a more decisive control over future destiny than any ten years afterwards. The religious and benevolent elements seize instinctively upon the promise made to those who train up children in the way they should go. The love of children casts a pleasing illusion over the mind in regard to every thing they do,—if, indeed, it be an illusion, and not a truth above the reach of the intellect,—elevating their puerile sports into dignity,

---

* This general remark must be taken with the exception of a few of the very worst men which any age ever produces. These become members of the clerical profession, because, under the mask of its sanctity, they hope to practise their iniquities with impunity.

hailing each step in their progress as though it were some grand discovery in science, and grieving over their youthful wanderings or backslidings with as deep a sorrow as is felt for the turpitude of a full-grown man, or for the heaven-defying sins of a nation. So that genial, joyous, ever-smiling temperament, which sees only rainbows where others see clouds, and which is delighted by the reflection of itself when coming from one child's face, will never tire of its labors when the same charming image perpetually comes back from the multiplying glasses of group after group of happy children,—ever-varying, but always beautiful.

Now, I think we have abundant reason to believe that a sufficient number of persons, bearing from the hand of Nature this distinctive image and superscription of a school-teacher, are born into the world with every generation. But the misfortune is, that when they arrive at years of discretion, and begin to survey the various fields of labor that lie open before them, they find that the noblest of them all, and the one, too, for which they have the greatest natural predilection, is neither honored by distinction nor rewarded by emolument. They see, that, if they enter it, many of their colleagues and associates will be persons with whom they have no congeniality of feeling, and who occupy a far less elevated position in the social scale than that to which their own aspirations point. If they go through the whole country, and question every man, they cannot find a single public-school teacher who has acquired wealth by the longest and the most devoted life of labor. They cannot find one who has been promoted to the presidency of a college, or to a professorship in it; nor one who has been elected or appointed to fill any distinguished civil station. Hence, in most cases, the adventitious circumstances which surround the object of their preference repel them from it. Or, if they enter the profession, it is only for a brief period, and for some collateral purpose; and, when their temporary end is gained, they sink it still lower by their avowed or well-understood reasons for abandoning it. Such is the literal history of hundreds and thousands who have shone or are now shining in other walks of life, but who would have shone with beams far more creative of human happiness had they not been struck from the sphere for which Nature pre-adapted them.

Look at the average rate of wages paid to teachers in some of the pattern States of the Union. In Maine, it is $15.40 per month to males, and $4.80 to females. In New Hampshire, it is $13.50 per month to males, and $5.65 to females. In Vermont, it is $12.00 per month to males, and $4.75 to females. In Connecticut, it is $16.00 per month to males, and $6.50 to females. In New York, it is $14.96 per month to males, and $6.69 to females. In Pennsylvania, it is $17.02 per month to males, and 10.09 to females. In Ohio, it is 15.42 per month to males, and $8.73 to females. In Indiana, it is 12.00 per month to males, and $6.00 to females. In Michigan, it is 12.71 per month for males, and $5.36 for females. Even in Massachusetts, it is only $24.51 per month to males, and $8.07 to females. All this is exclusive of board; but let it be compared with what is paid to cashiers of banks, to secretaries of insurance-companies, to engineers upon railroads, to superintendents in factories, to custom-house officers, navy agents, and so forth, and so forth, and it will then be seen what pecuniary temptations there are on every side, drawing enterprising and talented young men from the ranks of the teacher's profession.

Nor does the social estimation accorded to teachers much surpass the pecuniary value set upon their services. The nature of their calling debars them, almost universally, from political honors, which, throughout our whole country, have a factitious value so much above their real worth. Without entire faithlessness to their trust, they cannot engage in trade or commercial speculations. Modes of education have heretofore been so imperfect, that I do not know a single instance where a teacher has been transferred from his school to any of those departments of educated labor in which such liberal salaries are now given. And thus it is, that the profession at large, while it enjoys but a measured degree of public respect, seems shut out from all the paths that lead to fortune or to fame. No worldly prize is held up before it; and, in the present condition of mankind, how few there are who will work exclusively for the immortal reward! It supposes the possession only of very low faculties, to derive pleasure from singing the praises of a martyr; but to be the martyr one's self requires very high ones.

Hence is it, as was before said, that when the aspiring and highly-endowed youth of our country arrive at years of discretion, and begin to survey the varied employments which lie spread out before them, they find that the noblest of them all presents the fewest external attractions. Those whose natural or acquired ambition seeks for wealth, go into trade. The mechanical genius applies himself to the useful arts. The politically ambitious connect themselves with some one of those classes from which public officers are usually selected. Medicine attracts those who have the peculiar combination of tastes congenial to it. Those who ponder most upon the ways of God to men, minister in sacred things. Who, then, are left to fill the most important position known to social life? A few remain, whose natural tendencies in this direction are too vehement to be resisted or diverted; a somewhat larger number, who have no strong predilection for one sphere of exertion rather than for another, and to whom, under the circumstances peculiar to each, school-keeping is as eligible as any other employment: but many, very many, the great majority, engage in it, not for its own sake, but only to make it subservient to some ulterior object, or—with humiliation it is said—perhaps only to escape from manual labor.

The profession of school-keeping, then, as a profession, has never had an equal chance with its competitors. On the one hand, it has been resorted to by great numbers, whose only object was to make a little money out of it, and then abandon it; and, on the other, its true disciples, those who might have been and should have been its leaders and priesthood, have been lured and seduced away from it by the more splendid prizes of life.

Even though, therefore, the profession of school-keeping has not been crowded by learned and able men, devoting their energies and their lives to its beneficent labors, this fact wholly fails to prove that Nature does not produce, with each generation, a sufficient number of fit persons, who, under an equitable distribution or apportionment of honors and rewards for meritorious services, would be found pre-adapted for school-keeping, in the same way that Newton was for mathematics, or Pope for poetry, or Franklin for the infallibility of his common sense. Indeed, the proportion of good teachers whom we now have, notwithstanding all their discouragements against entering, and their seducements for leaving, the profession, seem demonstrative of the contrary.

Thus far, the argument has proceeded upon the basis that the required number of teachers, possessing the high grade of qualifications supposed, must equal the present number, such as these are. But it is almost too obvious to need mentioning, that if the qualifications of teachers were to be so greatly enhanced, and the term of the schools so materially lengthened, as is proposed, teaching would then really become a profession, and the same teachers would keep school through the year. Instead, therefore, of changing from male teachers in the winter to female in the summer, back again to males in the winter, and so on alternately,—the children of each school suffering under a new step-father or a new step-mother each half-year,—they would enjoy the vastly-improved system of continuous training under the same hands. This would diminish, by almost one-half, the required number of teachers for our schools; the poorer half would be discarded, the better half retained. Surely, under these circumstances, if a sufficient number of the very highest class of teachers could not be found, it would not be owing to any parsimony of Nature in withholding the endowments, but to our unpardonable niggardliness in not cultivating and employing them.

Feeling now authorized to assume that the first proposition has been satisfactorily established, it only remains to be considered, under this head, whether the community at large—the towns separately, or the towns and the State by joint contributions—can afford to make such compensation as shall attract to this field of labor the high order of teachers supposed, and shall requite them generously for their services.

To induce persons of the highest order of talent to become teachers, and to deter good teachers from abandoning the profession, its emoluments must bear some close analogy to those which the same persons could command in other employments. The case, too, as presented in the circular, and upon which the evidence has been obtained, supposes the schools to continue for ten months in each year. Although in many large towns the schools are now kept more than this portion of the year, yet their average length for the whole State is but eight months. The increased expense, then, both of the longer term and of the more liberal compensation, must be provided for. Can the community sustain this expense?

Let us suppose, for a moment, that ninety-nine per cent of our whole community should be temperate, honest, industrious, frugal people,—conscientious in feeling, and exemplary in conduct,—is it not certain that two grand pecuniary consequences would immediately follow; namely, a vast gain in productive power, and a vast saving in the criminal destruction and loss of property? Either of these sources of gain would more than defray the increased expenses of the system, which, according to the evidence I have obtained, would insure both. The current expenses last year, for the education of all the children in the State between the ages of four and sixteen, was $3.14, on an average, for each one. Look into the police courts of our cities in the morning, and especially on Monday morning, when the ghastly array of drunkards is marched in for trial. A case may not occupy ten minutes; and yet the fine, costs, and expenses would educate two children, for a year, in our public schools, at the present rate, or one child at double the present rate. The expenses incurred in punishing the smallest theft that is committed exceed the present cost of educating a child in our schools for a year. A knave who proposes to obtain goods by false pretences will hardly aim at making less than a thousand dollars by his speculation. There are more than one hundred and fifty towns in Massachusetts,—that is, about half the whole number in the State,—in each of which the annual appropriation for all its schools is less than one thousand dollars. A burglar or highway robber will seldom peril his life without the prospect of a prize which would educate five hundred or a thousand children for a year. An incendiary exhibits fire-works at an expense which would educate all the children of many a school-district in the State, from the age of four to that of sixteen; while the only reward he expects is that of stealing a few garments or trinkets during the conflagration. In a single city in the State, consisting of sixteen or seventeen thousand inhabitants, it was estimated by a most respectable and intelligent committee, that the cost of alcoholic drinks during the last year far exceeded the combined cost of all the schools and all the churches in it, although, for both religion and education, it is a highly liberal city. The police expenses alone of the city of New York are about half a million a year. But all these are but a part of the sluice-ways through which the hard-earned wealth of the people is wasted. What shall be said of those stock-swindlings and bank-failures whose capitals of hundreds of thousands of dollars are embezzled in "fair business transactions;" whose vaults, sworn to be full of specie or bullion, remind one, on inspection, not merely of a pecuniary, but of a philosophical, vacuum? what of those epidemic speculations in land (often Fairy-land, though void of both beauty and poetry), where fortunes change hands as rapidly as if dependent upon the throw of a gambler's dice? and what of those enormous peculations by government defaulters, where more money is ingulfed by one stupendous fraud than Massachusetts expends for the education of all her children in a year? All this devastation and loss the public bears with marvellous, with most criminal composure. The people at large stand by the wreck-covered shore, where so many millions are dashed in pieces and sunk, and seem not to recognize the destruction; and, what is infinitely worse, there are those who rejoice in the howl of the tempest and the shrieks of the sufferers, because they can grow rich by plundering only here and there a fragment of property from the dead or the defenceless. By charity, by direct taxes, by paying twenty or thirty per cent more for every article or necessity of life than it is equitably worth, by bad debts, by the occasional and involuntary contribution of a pocket-book, a watch, a horse, a carriage, a ship, or a cargo, to which the robber and the barrator help themselves by paying premiums for insurance, and in a hundred other ways, the honest and industrious part of the people not only support themselves, but supply the mighty current of wealth that goes to destruction through these flood-gates of iniquity. The people do not yet seem to see that all the cost of legislating against criminals; of judges and prosecuting officers, of jurors and witnesses, to convict them; of building houses of correction and jails and penitentiaries for restricting and punishing them,— is not a hundredth part of the grand total of expenditure incurred by private and social immoralities and crimes. The people do not yet seem to see that the intelligence and the morality which education can impart is that beneficent kind of insurance, which, by preventing losses, obviates the necessity of indemnifying for them; thus saving both premium and risk. What is ingulfed in the vortex of crime in each generation would build a palace of more than Oriental splendor in every school-district in the land, would endow it with a library beyond the ability of a life-time to read, would supply it with apparatus and laboratories for the illustration of every study and the exemplification of every art, and munificently requite the services of a teacher worthy to preside in such a sanctuary of intelligence and virtue.

But the prevention of all that havoc of worldly goods which is caused by vice transfers only one item from the loss to the profit side of the account. Were all idle, intemperate, predatory men to become industrious, sober, and honest, they would add vast sums to the inventory of the nation's wealth, instead of subtracting from it. Let any person take a single town, village, or neighborhood, and look at its inhabitants individually, with the question in his mind, how many of them are producers, and how many are non-producers,—that is, how many, either by the labor of the body or the labor of the mind, add value and dignity to life, and how many barely support themselves,— and I think he will often be surprised at the smallness of the number by whose talent and industry the storehouses of the earth are mainly filled, and all the complicated business of society is principally managed. Could we convert into co-workers for the benefit of mankind all those physical and spiritual powers of usefulness which are now antagonists or neutrals, the gain would be incalculable.

Add the above two items together,—namely, the saving of what the vicious now squander or destroy, and the wealth, which, as virtuous men, they would amass,—and the only difficulty presented would be to find in what manner so vast an amount could be beneficially disposed of.

But it is not to be disguised, whatever reforms may be instituted, that the cost of crime cannot, at once, be prevented. For a season, therefore, and until the expenses of education shall arrest and supersede the expenses of guilt, both must be borne. I wish to state the difficulty without extenuation. The question, then, is, Can both be temporarily borne?

The appropriations for which the towns voluntarily taxed themselves last year for the current expenses of the schools—that is, for the wages and board of teachers, and for fuel—were $662,870.57. Adding the income of the surplus revenue, when appropriated for the support of schools, it was $670,628.13. The valuation of the State I suppose to be not less than $450,000,000. Last year's tax, therefore, for the current expenses of the schools, was less than one mill and a half on the dollar,—less than one mill and a half on a thousand mills. Taking the average of the State, then, no man was obliged to pay more than one six hundred and sixty-sixth part of his property for this purpose; or, rather, such would have been the case had there been no poll-tax,—had the whole tax been levied upon property alone. At this rate, it would take six hundred and sixty-six years for all the property of the State to be *once* devoted to this purpose. And does not the portion of our worldly interests which is dependent upon public schools bear a greater ratio to the whole of those interests than one to six hundred and sixty-six? I need not argue this point; for who, out of an insane asylum, or even of the *curable* classes in it, will question the fact? Who will say that the importance of this interest, as compared with all the earthly interests of mankind, is not indefinitely greater than this? Who will say, that, to secure so precious an end as the diffusion of almost universal intelligence and virtue, and the suppression, with an equal degree of universality, of ignorance and vice, it would not be expedient to do as the Bishop of Landaff once proposed that the British nation should do, in an eventful crisis of its affairs,—vote away, by acclamation, one-half of all the wealth of the kingdom? But there is no need of carrying our feelings or our reason to this pitch of exultation. There is no need of any signal or unwonted sacrifice. There is no need of a devotion of life, as is done in battle. There is no need of perilling fortunes, as is done every day in trade. There is no need that any man in the community should lose one day from his life, or an hour from his sleep, or a comfort from his wardrobe or his table. Three times more than is now expended—that is, four and a half mills on every thousand mills of the property of the State, or only one part in two hundred and twenty-two, instead of one in six hundred and sixty-six—would defray every expense, and insure the result. Regarded merely as a commercial transaction,—a pecuniary enterprise, whose elements are dollars and cents alone,—there is not an intelligent capitalist in the State who would not, on the evidence here adduced, assume the whole of it, and pay a bonus for the privilege. When the State was convinced of the lucrativeness or general expediency of a railroad from Worcester to its western border; it bound itself, at a word, to the amount of five millions of dollars; and I suppose it to be now the opinion of every intelligent man in the Commonwealth, that, when the day of payment shall arrive, the road itself, in addition to all the collateral advantages which it will have conferred, will have paid for itself, and will then forever remain, not merely a monument of wisdom, but a reward for sagacity. Yet what is a railroad, though it does cut down the mountains and lift up the valleys, compared with an all-embracing agency of social and moral reform which shall abase the pride of power, and elevate the lowliness of misfortune? And those facilities for travel which supersede the tediousness of former journeyings and the labor of transportation—what are they, when compared with the prevention of that "lamentation, mourning, and woe" which come from the perpetration of crime? When the city of Boston was convinced of the necessity of having a supply of pure water from abroad for the use of its inhabitants, it voted three millions of dollars to obtain it; and he would be a bold man who would now propose a repeal of the ordinance, though all past expenditures could be refunded. Yet all the school-houses in Boston, which it has erected during the present century, are not worth a fourth part of this sum. For the supply of water, the city of New York lately incurred an expenditure of thirteen millions of dollars. Admitting, as I most cheerfully do, that the use of water pertains to the moral as well as to the ceremonial law, yet our cities have pollutions which water can never wash away,—

defilements which the baptism of a moral and Christian education alone can remove. There is not an appetite that allies man to the brutes, nor a passion for vain display which makes him more contemptible than any part of the irrational creation, which does not cost the country more, every year, than such a system as would, according to the evidence I have exhibited, redeem it, almost entirely, from its follies and its guilt. Consider a single factitious habit of our people, which no one will pretend adds any degree to the health, or length of the life, or decency to the manners, of the nation: I mean the smoking of tobacco. It is said, on good authority, that the *annual* expenditure in the country for the support of this habit is ten millions of dollars; and if we reflect that this sum, averaged upon all the people, would be only half a dollar apiece, the estimate seems by no means extravagant. Yet this is far more than is paid to the teachers of all the public schools in the whole United States.

Were nations to embark in the cause of education for the redemption of mankind, as they have in that of war for their destruction, the darkest chapters in the history of earthly calamities would soon be brought to a close. But, where units have been grudged for education, millions have been lavished for war. While, for the one purpose, mankind have refused to part with superfluities, for the other they have not only impoverished themselves, but levied burdensome taxes upon posterity. The vast national debts of Europe originated in war; and, but for the scourge of mankind, they never would have existed. The amount of money now owed by the different European nations, is said, on good authority, to be $6,387,000,000. Of this inconceivable sum, the share of Great Britain is about $4,000,000,000 (in round numbers, 800,000,000 pounds sterling); of France, $780,000,000; of Russia and Austria, $300,000,000 each; of Prussia, $100,000,000; and the debts of the minor powers increase this sum to $6,387,000,000. The national debt of Great Britain now amounts to more than $140 for every man, woman, and child in the three kingdoms. Allowing six persons to each family, it will average more than $850 to every household,—a sum which would be deemed by thousands and tens of thousands of families in that country to be a handsome competence, nay, wealth itself, if it were owing *to* instead of *from* them.

It is estimated, that, during the twenty-two years preceding the general peace of 1815, the unimaginable sum of 6,250,000,000 pounds sterling, or $30,000,000,000, had been expended in war by nations calling themselves *Christian*,—an amount of wealth many fold greater than has ever been expended, for the same purpose, by all the nations on the globe whom we call *savage*, since the commencement of the Christian era. The earth itself could not be pawned for so vast a sum as this, were there any pawn-broker's office which would accept such a pledge. Were it to be set up at auction, in the presence of fierce competitors for the purchase, it would not sell for enough to pay its war-bills for a single century. The war-estimates of the British Government, even for the current year of peace, are $85,000,000; and the annual interest on the national debt incurred by war is at least $120,000,000 more, or more than $200,000,000 for a common, and, on the whole, a very favorable year. Well might Christ, in the Beatitudes, pronounce his emphatic benediction upon the "peace-makers."

We have emulated, in this country, the same gigantic scale of expenditure for the same purpose. Since the organization of the Federal Government, in 1789, the expense of our military and naval establishments and equipments, in round numbers, is $700,000,000. Two of our ships of the line have cost more than $2,000,000. The value of the arms accumulated at one time at the Arsenal in Springfield, in this State, was $2,000,000. The Military Academy at West Point has cost more than $4,000,000. In our town-meetings, and in our school-district-meetings, wealthy and substantial men oppose the grant of $15 for a school-library, and of $30 for both library and apparatus; while at West Point they spend $50 in a single lesson at target-firing; and the government keeps a hundred horses, and grooms and black-smiths to take care of them, as an indispensable part of the *apparatus* of the academy. The pupils at our normal schools, who are preparing to become teachers, must maintain themselves: the cadets at the academy receive $28 a month, during their entire term, as a compensation for being educated at the public expense. Adding bounties and pensions to wages and rations, I suppose the cost of a common foot-soldier in the army cannot be less than $250 a year. The average cost of female teachers for the public schools of Massachusetts last year was only $13.60 a month, inclusive of board, or at a rate which would give $163.20 for the year; but the average length of the schools was but eight months: so that the cost of *two* common soldiers is nearly that of *five* female teachers. The annual salary of a colonel of dragoons in the United-States army is $2,206; of a brigadier-general, $2,958; of a major-general, $4,512; that of a captain of a ship of the line, when in service, $4,500; and, even when off duty, it is $2,500. There are but seven towns in Massachusetts where any teacher of a public school receives so high a salary as $1,000; and, in four of these towns, one teacher only receives this sum.

Had my purpose been simply to show the pecuniary ability of the people at large to give the most generous compensation to such a company of accomplished, high-minded, noble teachers as would lift the race, at once, out of the pit of vice and ignorance and super-stition as safely and as tenderly as a mother bears her infant in her arms,—had my purpose been merely to show this pecuniary ability, then I have already said too much. But my design was, not merely to carry conviction to the minds of those who would contest this fact, but to make the denial of it ridiculous.

So far as higher mental and moral attributes in teachers will be required, reasons have been offered to show that Nature, or the common course of Providence, supplies an abundance of intellectual power and of moral capability; but that, through our present misuse or mal-administration of these noble qualities, they are either lost by neglect of culture, or diverted to less worthy pursuits. There is no more iron in the world now than there ever was; we have only discovered how to use it more advantageously,—for steamboats, for railroads, for machinery, and a thousand mechanical purposes: and thus, in point or mere pecuniary value, we have given it the first rank among the precious metals. There is no more water flowing down our streams now then there was centuries ago; but we have just found out how to make it saw timber, grind wheat, and make cloth: and already it does a thousand times more work than all our twenty millions of people could do by their own unassisted strength, should every man vie with his neighbor in the severity of his toil and in the amount of his productions. There are no more individual particles of electricity in the air or in the earth to-day than there always have been. Forever, since creation, there has been an inconceivable host of these particles,—a multitude deriding all human power of computation,—which have careered round the earth by laws of their own, each one being as distinct from all the rest, and having as separate and independent an existence, as one wild horse upon the prairies has from another. Long ago, science learned how to catch and confine these natural racers; but it was not until our day that she discovered how to take them,—one, ten, a hundred, or a thousand,—and despatch them as messengers to distant cities; to make them the common carriers of intelligence, whom no pursuers can overtake, no bribe can corrupt, nor robbers despoil. Thus it is with the capacities of the human mind. By the bounty of Providence, they may be employed and made sufficient for the greatest work of reform. It is through our blindness and perversity that they are not yet used to achieve their sublime purposes. Like the iron, like the gravity of falling water, like the electric coursers, they, too, have the power of conferring unimaginable blessings upon the race; but as yet they have only been very partially enlisted in the highest services of humanity.

END POVERTY THROUGH EDUCATION

From Twelfth Annual Report (1848)

The year 1848 was the revolutionary year, throughout Europe. It was an appropriate year for Mann to emphasize the revolutionary potential in education: its capacity for uplifting humanity, for obliterating conditions which bred despair, vengefulness, human waste. Mann's diagnoses and prescriptions need little commentary today.

ANOTHER cardinal object which the government of Massachusetts, and all the influential men in the State, should propose to themselves, is the physical well-being of all the people,—the sufficiency, comfort, competence, of every individual in regard to food, raiment, and shelter. And these necessaries and conveniences of life should be obtained by each individual for himself, or by each family for themselves, rather than accepted from the hand of charity or extorted by poor-laws. It is not averred that this most desirable result can, in all instances, be obtained; but it is, nevertheless, the end to be aimed at. True statesmanship and true political economy, not less than true philanthropy, present this perfect theory as the goal, to be more and more closely approximated by our imperfect practice. The desire to achieve such a result cannot be regarded as an unreasonable ambition; for, though all mankind were well fed, well clothed, and well housed, they might still be but half civilized.

Poverty is a public as well as a private evil. There is no physical law necessitating its existence. The earth contains abundant resources for ten times—doubtless for twenty times—its present inhabitants. Cold, hunger, and nakedness are not, like death, an inevitable lot. There are many single States in this Union which could supply an abundance of edible products for the inhabitants of the thirty States that compose it. There are single States capable of raising a sufficient quantity of cotton to clothe the whole nation; and there are other States having sufficient factories and machinery to manufacture it. The coal-fields of Pennsylvania are sufficiently abundant to keep every house in the land at the temperature of sixty-five degrees for centuries to come. Were there to be a competition, on the one hand, to supply wool for every conceivable fabric, and, on the other, to wear out these fabrics as fast as possible, the single State of New York would beat the whole country. There is, indeed, no assignable limit to the capacities of the earth for producing whatever is necessary for the sustenance, comfort, and improvement of the race. Indigence, therefore, and the miseries and degradations incident to indigence, seem to be no part of the eternal ordinances of Heaven. The bounty of God is not brought into question or suspicion by its existence; for man who suffers it might have avoided it. Even the wealth which the world now has on hand is more than sufficient to supply all the rational wants of every individual in it. Privations and sufferings exist, not from the smallness of its sum, but from the inequality of its distribution. Poverty is set over against profusion. In some, all healthy appetite is cloyed and sickened by repletion; while in others, the stomach seems to be a supernumerary organ in the system, or, like the human eye or human lungs before birth, is waiting to be transferred to some other region, where its functions may come into use. One gorgeous palace absorbs all the labor and expense that might have made a thousand hovels comfortable. That one man may ride in carriages of Oriental luxury, hundreds of other men are turned into beasts of burden. To supply a superfluous wardrobe for the gratification of one man's pride, a thousand women and children shiver with cold; and, for every flash of the diamonds that royalty wears, there is a tear of distress in the poor man's dwelling. Not one Lazarus, but a hundred, sit at the gate of Dives. Tantalus is no fiction. The ancient one might have been fabulous; but the modern ones are terrible realities. Millions are perishing in the midst of superfluities.

According to the European theory, men are divided into classes,—some toil to earn, others seize and enjoy. According to the Massachusetts theory, all are to have an equal chance for earning, and equal security in the enjoyment of what they earn. The latter tends to equality of condition; the former, to the grossest inequalities. Tried by any Christian standard of morals, or even by any of the better sort of heathen standards, can any one hesitate, for a moment, in declaring which of the two will produce the greater amount of human welfare, and which, therefore, is the more comfortable to the divine will? The European theory is blind to what constitutes the highest glory as well as the highest duty of a State. Its advocates and admirers are forgetful of that which should be their highest ambition, and proud of that which constitutes their shame. How can any one possessed of the

attributes of humanity look with satisfaction upon the splendid treasures, the golden regalia, deposited in the Tower of London or in
Windsor Palace, each "an India in itself," while thousands around
are dying of starvation, or have been made criminals by the combined
forces of temptation and neglect? The present condition of Ireland
cancels all the glories of the British crown. The brilliant conception
which symbolizes the nationality of Great Britain as a superb temple,
whose massive and grand proportions are upheld and adorned by the
four hundred and thirty Corinthian columns of the aristocracy, is
turned into a loathing and a scorn when we behold the five millions
of paupers that cower and shiver at its base. The galleries and fountains
of Versailles, the Louvre of Paris, her Notre Dame, and her Madeleine,
though multiplied by thousands in number and in brilliancy, would
be no atonement for the hundred thousand Parisian *ouvriers* without
bread and without work. The galleries of painting and of sculpture
at Rome, at Munich, or at Dresden, which body forth the divinest
ideals ever executed or ever conceived, are but an abomination in the
sight of Heaven and of all good men, while actual, living beings—
beings that have hearts to palpitate, and nerves to agonize, and
affections to be crushed or corrupted—are experimenting all around
them upon the capacities of human nature for suffering and for sin.
Where standards like these exist, and are upheld by council and by
court, by fashion and by law, *Christianity is yet to be discovered*;
at least, it is yet to be applied in practice to the social condition of men.
    Our ambition as a State should trace itself to a different origin,
and propose to itself a different object. Its flame should be lighted
at the skies. Its radiance and its warmth should reach the darkest
and the coldest abodes of men. It should seek the solution of such
problems as these: To what extent can competence displace pauperism?
How nearly can we free ourselves from the low-minded and the vicious,
not by their expatriation, but by their elevation? To what extent can
the resources and powers of Nature be converted into human welfare,
the peaceful arts of life be advanced, and the vast treasures of human
talent and genius be developed? How much of suffering, in all its
forms, can be relieved? or, what is better than relief, how much can be
prevented? Cannot the classes of crimes be lessened, and the number
of criminals in each class be diminished? Our exemplars, both for
public and for private imitation, should be the parables of the lost
sheep and of the lost piece of silver. When we have spread competence
through all the abodes of poverty, when we have substituted knowl-

edge for ignorance in the minds of the whole people, when we have reformed the vicious and reclaimed the criminal, then may we invite all neighboring nations to behold the spectacle, and say to them, in the conscious elation of virtue, "Rejoice with me," for I have found that which is lost. Until that day shall arrive, our duties will not be wholly fulfilled, and our ambition will have new honors to win.

But is it not true that Massachusetts, in some respects, instead of adhering more and more closely to her own theory, is becoming emulous of the baneful examples of Europe? The distance between the two extremes of society is lengthening, instead of being abridged. With every generation, fortunes increase on the one hand, and some new privation is added to poverty on the other. We are verging towards those extremes of opulence and of penury, each of which unhumanizes the human mind. A perpetual struggle for the bare necessaries of life, without the ability to obtain them, makes men wolfish. Avarice, on the other hand, sees, in all the victims of misery around it, not objects for pity and succor, but only crude materials to be worked up into more money.

I suppose it to be the universal sentiment of all those who mingle any ingredient of benevolence with their notions on political economy, that vast and overshadowing private fortunes are among the greatest dangers to which the happiness of the people in a republic can be subjected. Such fortunes would create a feudalism of a new kind, but one more oppressive and unrelenting than that of the middle ages. The feudal lords in England and on the Continent never held their retainers in a more abject condition of servitude than the great majority of foreign manufacturers and capitalists hold their operatives and laborers at the present day. The means employed are different; but the similarity in results is striking. What force did then, money does now. The villein of the middle ages had no spot of earth on which he could live, unless one were granted to him by his lord. The operative or laborer of the present day has no employment, and therefore no bread, unless the capitalist will accept his services. The vassal had no shelter but such as his master provided for him. Not one in five thousand of English operatives or farm-laborers is able to build or own even a hovel; and therefore they must accept such shelter as capital offers them. The baron prescribed his own terms to his retainers: those terms were peremptory, and the serf must submit or perish. The British manufacturer or farmer prescribes the rate of wages he will give to his work-people; he reduces these wages under whatever pretext he pleases; and they, too, have no alternative but submission or starvation. In some respects, indeed, the condition of the modern dependant is more forlorn than that of the corresponding serf class in former times. Some attributes of the patriarchal relation did spring up between the lord and his lieges to soften the harsh relations sub-sisting between them. Hence came some oversight of the condition of children, some relief in sickness, some protection and support in the decrepitude of age. But only in instances comparatively few have kindly offices smoothed the rugged relation between British capital and British labor. The children of the work-people are abandoned to their fate; and notwithstanding the privations they suffer, and the dangers they threaten, no power in the realm has yet been able to secure them an education; and when the adult laborer is prostrated by sickness, or eventually worn out by toil and age, the poor-house, which has all along been his destination, becomes his destiny.

Now, two or three things will doubtless be admitted to be true, beyond all controversy, in regard to Massachusetts. By its industrial condition, and its business operations, it is exposed, far beyond any other State in the Union, to the fatal extremes of overgrown wealth and desperate poverty. Its population is far more dense than that of any other State. It is four or five times more dense than the average of all the other States taken together; and density of population has always been one of the proximate causes of social inequality. According to population and territorial extent, there is far more capital in Massa-chusetts—capital which is movable, and instantaneously available—than in any other State in the Union; and probably both these quali-fications respecting population and territory could be omitted without endangering the truth of the assertion. It has been recently stated in a very respectable public journal, on the authority of a writer con-versant with the subject, that from the last of June, 1846, to the first of August, 1848, the amount of money invested by the citizens of Massachusetts "in manufacturing cities, railroads, and other improve-ments," is "fifty-seven millions of dollars, of which more than fifty has been paid in and expended." The dividends to be received by citizens of Massachusetts from June, 1848, to April, 1849, are estimated by the same writer at ten millions, and the annual increase of capital a "little short of twenty-two millions." If this be so, are we not in danger of neutralizing and domesticating among ourselves those hideous evils which are always engendered between capital and labor, when all the capital is in the hands of one class, and all the labor is thrown upon another?

Now, surely nothing but universal education can counterwork this tendency to the domination of capital and the servility of labor. If one class possesses all the wealth and the education, while the residue of society is ignorant and poor, it matters not by what name the relation between them may be called: the latter, in fact and in truth, will be the servile dependants and subjects of the former. But, if edution be equally diffused, it will draw property after it by the strongest of all attractions; for such a thing never did happen, and never can happen, as that an intelligent and practical body of men should be permanently poor. Property and labor in different classes are essentially antagonistic; but property and labor in the same class are essentially fraternal. The people of Massachusetts have, in some degree, appreciated the truth, that the unexampled prosperity of the State—its comfort, its competence, its general intelligence and virtue—is attributable to the education, more or less perfect, which all its people have received: but are they sensible of a fact equally important; namely, that it is to this same education that two-thirds of the people are indebted for not being to-day the vassals of as severe a tyranny, in the form of capital, as the lower classes of Europe are bound to in the form of brute force?

Education, then, beyond all other devices of human origin, is the great equalizer of the conditions of men,—the balance-wheel of the social machinery. I do not here mean that it so elevates the moral nature as to make men disdain and abhor the oppression of their fellow-men. This idea pertains to another of its attributes. But I mean that it gives each man the independence and the means by which he can resist the selfishness of other men. It does better than to disarm the poor of their hostility towards the rich: it prevents being poor. Agrarianism is the revenge of poverty against wealth. The wanton destruction of the property of others—the burning of hay-ricks and corn-ricks, the demolition of machinery because it supersedes hand-labor, the sprinkling of vitriol on rich dresses—is only agrarianism run mad. Education prevents both the revenge and the madness. On the other hand, a fellow-feeling for one's class or caste is the common instinct of hearts not wholly sunk in selfish regards for person or for family. The spread of education, by enlarging the cultivated class or caste, will open a wider area over which the social feelings will expand; and, if this education should be universal and complete, it would do more than all things else to obliterate distinctions in society.

The main idea set forth in the creeds of some political reformers, or revolutionizers, is, that some people are poor *because* others are rich. This idea supposes a fixed amount of property in the community, which by fraud or force, or arbitrary law, is unequally divided among men; and the problem presented for solution is, how to transfer a portion of this property from those who are supposed to have too much to those who feel and know that they have too little. At this point, both their theory and their expectation of reform stop. But the beneficent power of education would not be exhausted, even though it should peaceably abolish all the miseries that spring from the co-existence, side by side, of enormous wealth and squalid want. It has a higher function. Beyond the power of diffusing old wealth, it has the prerogative of creating new. It is a thousand times more lucrative than fraud, and adds a thousand-fold more to a nation's resources than the most successful conquests. Knaves and robbers can obtain only what was before possessed by others. But education creates or develops new treasures,—treasures not before possessed or dreamed of by any one.

Had mankind been endowed with only the instincts and faculties of the brute creation, there are hundreds of the irrational tribes to which they would have been inferior, and of which they would have been the prey. Did they, with other animals, roam a common forest, how many of their fellow-tenants of the wood would overcome them by superior force, or outstrip them by greater fleetness, or circumvent them by a sharper cunning! There are but few of the irrational tribes whose bodies are not better provided with the means of defence or attack than is the body of a man. The claws and canine teeth of the the lion and of the whole tiger family, the beak and talons of the eagle and the vulture, the speed of the deer and of other timid races, are means of assault or of escape far superior to any we possess; and all the power which we have, like so many of the reptile and insect classes, of secreting a deadly venom, either for protection or for aggression, has relation to moral venom, and not to physical.

In a few lines, nowhere surpassed in philosophic strength and beauty, Pope groups together the remarkable qualities of several different races of animals,—the strength of one class, the genial covering of another, the fleetness of a third. He brings vividly to our recollection the lynx's vision of excelling keenness, the sagacity of the

hound that reads a name or a sign in the last vanishing odor of a
footprint, the exquisite fineness of the spider's touch, and that chemical
nicety by which the bee discriminates between honey and poison in
the same flower-cup. He then closes with an interrogatory, which has
human reason both for its subject and its object:—

> "The powers of all subdued by thee alone:
> *Is not thy reason all these powers in one?*"

When Pope, now a little more than a century ago, mingled these
beauties with his didactic strains, he had no conception, the world at
that time had no conception, of other powers and properties, infinitely more energetic and more exhaustless than all which the animal
races possess, to which the reason of man is an equivalent. It was
not then known that God had endued the earth and the elements
with energies and activities as much superior to those which animals
or men possess as the bulk and frame of the earth itself exceeds their
diminutive proportions. It was not then known that the earth is a great
reservoir of powers, and that any man is free to use any quantity of
them if he will but possess himself of the key of knowledge,—the only
key, but the infallible one, by which to unlock their gates. At that
time, if a philosopher wished to operate a mechanical toy, he could
lift or pump a few gallons of water for a moving-power: but it was
not understood that Nature, by the process of evaporation and conden-
sation, is constantly lifting up into the sky, and pouring back upon the
earth, all the mass of waters that flow in all the rivers of the world;
and that, in order to perform the work of the world, the weight of all
these waters might be used again and again in each one of their
perpetual circuits.* The power-press and the power-loom, the steamboat and the locomotive, the paper-machine and the telegraph, were
not then known. All these instruments of human comfort and ag-
grandizement, and others almost innumerable, similar to them, are
operated by the energies and the velocities of Nature; and, had Pope
grouped together all the splendid profusion and prodigality of her
powers, he might still have appealed to man, and said,—

> *"Is not thy reason all these powers in one?"*

To the weight of waters, the velocity of winds, the expansive force
of heat, and other kindred agencies, any man may go, and he may

---

* The waters of the Blackstone River, which flows partly in Massachusetts,
and partly in Rhode Island, are used for driving mills, twenty-five times over,
in a distance of less than forty miles.

draw from them as much as he pleases without money and without price: or rather, I should say, any educated man may go; for Nature flouts and scorns, and seems to abhor, an ignorant man. She drowns him, and consumes him, and tears him to pieces, if he but ventures to profane with his touch her divinely-wrought machinery.

Now, these powers of Nature, by being enlisted in the service of man ADD to the wealth of the world,—unlike robbery or slavery or agrarianism, which aim only at the appropriation, by one man or one class, of the wealth belonging to another man or class. One man, with a Foudrinier, will make more paper in a twelvemonth than all Egypt could have made in a hundred years during the reign of the Ptolemies. One man, with a power-press, will print books faster than a million of scribes could copy them before the invention of printing. One man, with an iron-foundry, will make more utensils or machinery than Tubal-Cain could have made had he worked diligently till this time.* And so in all the departments of mechanical labor, in the whole circle of useful arts. These powers of Nature are able to give to all the inhabitants of the earth, not merely shelter, covering, and food, but all the means of refinement, embellishment, and mental improvement. In the most strict and literal sense, they are bounties which God gives for proficiency in knowledge.

The above ideas are beginning to be pretty well understood by all men of respectable intelligence. I have adverted to them, not so much on their own account, as by way of introduction or preface to two or three considerations, which certainly are not understood, or not appreciated, as they deserve to be.

It is a remarkable fact, that human progress, even in regard to the worldly interests of the race, did not begin with those improvements which are most closely allied to material prosperity. One would have supposed, beforehand, that improvements would commence with the near rather than with the remote. Yet mankind had made great advances in astronomy, in geometry, and other mathematical sciences; in the writing of history, in oratory, and in poetry: it is supposed by many to have reached the highest point of yet attained perfection in painting and in sculpture, and in those kinds of architecture which

---

* In 1740, the whole amount of iron made in England and Wales was seventeen thousand tons; in 1840, it was more than a million tons, notwithstanding all that had been manufactured and accumulated in the intervening century. What would a Jewish or a Roman artificer have said to an annual product of a million tons of iron?

may be called regal or religious, centuries before the great mechanical discoveries and inventions which now bless the world were brought to light. And the question has often forced itself upon reflecting minds, why there was this preposterousness, this inversion of what would appear to be the natural order of progress. Why was it, for instance, that men should have learned the courses of the stars, and the revolutions of the planets, before they found out how to make a good wagon-wheel? Why was it that they built the Parthenon and the Colosseum before they knew how to construct a comfortable, healthful dwelling-house? Why did they construct the Roman aqueducts before they constructed a saw-mill? Or why did they achieve the noblest models in eloquence, in poetry, and in the drama, before they invented movable types? I think we have now arrived at a point where we can unriddle this enigma. *The labor of the world has been performed by ignorant men,* by classes doomed to ignorance from sire to son, by the bondmen and bond-women of the Jews, by the helots of Sparta, by the captives who passed under the Roman yoke, and by the villeins and serfs and slaves of more modern times. The masters—the aristocratic or patrician orders—not only disdained labor for themselves and their children, which was one fatal mistake, but they supposed that knowledge was of no use to a laborer, which was a mistake still more fatal. Hence, ignorance, for almost six thousand years, has gone on plying its animal muscles, and dropping its bloody sweat, and never discovered any way, nor dreamed that there was any way, by which it might accomplish many times more work with many times less labor. And yet nothing is more true than that an ignorant man will toil all his life long, moving to and fro within an inch of some great discovery, and will never see it. All the elements of a great discovery may fall into his hands, or be thrust into his face; but his eyes will be too blind to behold it. If he is a slave, what motive has he to behold it? Its greater profitableness will not redound to his benefit; for another stands ready to seize all the gain. Its abridgment of labor will not conduce to his ease; for other toils await him. But the moment an intelligent man applies himself to labor, and labors for his own benefit or for that of his family, he begins to inquire whether the same task cannot be performed with less expenditure of strength, or a greater task with an equal expenditure. He makes his wits save his bones. He finds it to be easier to think than to work; nay, that it is easier both to think and work than to work without thinking. He foresees a prize as the reward of successful effort; and this stimulates his brain to deep contrivance, as well as his arms to rapid motion. Taking, for illustration, the result of an experiment which has been actually made, let us suppose this intelligent laborer to be employed in moving blocks of squared granite, each weighing 1080 pounds. To move such a block along the floor of a roughly-chiselled quarry requires a force equal to 758 pounds. An ignorant man, therefore, must employ and pay several assistants, or he can never move such a block an inch. But to draw the same block over a floor of planks will require a force of only 652 pounds. The expense of one assistant, therefore, might be dispensed with. Placed on a platform of wood, and drawn over the same floor, a draught of 606 pounds would be sufficient. By soaping the two surfaces of the wood, the requisite force would be reduced to 182 pounds. Placed on rollers three inches in diameter, a force equal to 34 pounds would be sufficient. Substituting a wooden for a stone floor, and the requisite force is 28 pounds. With the same rollers on a wooden platform, 22 pounds only would be required. And now, by the invention and use of locomotives and railroads, a traction or draught of between *three* and *four* pounds is found to be sufficient to move a body weighing 1080 pounds. Thus the amount of force necessary to remove the body is reduced about two hundred times. Now, take away from these steps the single element of intelligence, and each improvement would have been impossible. The ignorant man would never have discovered how nearly synonymous are freight and friction.

If a savage will learn how to swim, he can fasten a dozen pounds' weight to his back, and transport it across a narrow river or other body of water of moderate width. If he will invent an axe, or other instrument, by which to cut down a tree, he can use the tree for a float, and one of its limbs for a paddle, and can thus transport many times the former weight many times the former distance. Hollowing out this log, he will increase what may be called its tonnage, or rather its *poundage*; and, by sharpening its ends, it will cleave the water both more easily and more swiftly. Fastening several trees together, he makes a raft, and thus increases the buoyant power of his embryo water-craft. Turning up the ends of small poles, or using knees of timber instead of straight pieces, and grooving them together, or filling up the interstices between them in some other way, so as to make them water-tight, he brings his rude raft literally into *ship-shape*. Improving upon hull below and rigging above, he makes a proud merchantman, to be wafted by the winds from continent to

continent. But even this does not content the adventurous naval arch-
itect. He frames iron arms for his ship; and, for oars, affixes iron
wheels, capable of swift revolution, and stronger than the strong sea.
Into iron-walled cavities in her bosom he puts iron organs of massive
structure and strength, and of cohesion insoluble by fire. Within these
he kindles a small volcano; and then, like a sentient and rational existence, this wonderful creation of his hands cleaves oceans, breasts
tides, defies tempests, and bears its living and jubilant freight around
the globe. Now, take away intelligence from the ship-builder, and the
steamship—that miracle of human art—falls back into a floating log;
the log itself is lost; and the savage swimmer, bearing his dozen pounds
on his back, alone remains.

And so it is, not in one department only, but in the whole circle
of human labors. The annihilation of the sun would no more certainly
be followed by darkness than the extinction of human intelligence
would plunge the race at once into the weakness and helplessness of
barbarism. To have created such beings as we are, and to have placed
them in this world without the light of the sun, would be no more
cruel than for a government to suffer its laboring classes to grow up
without knowledge.

In this fact, then, we find a solution of the problem that so long
embarrassed inquirers. The reason why the mechanical and useful
arts,—those arts which have done so much to civilize mankind, and
which have given comforts and luxuries to the common laborer of the
present day, such as kings and queens could not command three
centuries ago,—the reason why these arts made no progress, and until
recently, indeed, can hardly be said to have had any thing more
than a beginning, is, that the labor of the world was performed by
ignorant men. As soon as some degree of intelligence dawned upon
the workman, then a corresponding degree of improvement in his
work followed. At first, this intelligence was confined to a very small
number, and therefore improvements were few; and they followed
each other only after long intervals. They uniformly began in the
nations and among the classes where there was most intelligence.
The middle classes of England, and the people of Holland and Scotland, have done a hundred times more than all the Eastern hemisphere
besides. What single improvement in art, or discovery in science, has
ever originated in Spain, or throughout the vast empire of the Russias?
But just in proportion as intelligence—that is, education—has quickened and stimulated a greater and a greater number of minds, just

in the same proportion have inventions and discoveries increased in their wonderfulness, and in the rapidity of their succession. The progression has been rather geometrical than arithmetical. By the laws of Nature, it must be so. If, among ten well-educated children, the chance is that at least one of them will originate some new and useful processes in the arts, or will discover some new scientific principle, or some new application of one, then, among a hundred such well-educated children, there is a moral certainty that there will be more than ten such originators or discoverers of new utilities; for the action of the mind is like the action of fire. One billet of wood will hardly burn alone, though dry as suns and north-west winds can make it, and though placed in the range of a current of air; ten such billets will burn well together; but a hundred will create a heat fifty times as intense as ten, will make a current of air to fan their own flame, and consume even greenness itself.

For the creation of wealth, then,—for the existence of a wealthy people and a wealthy nation,—intelligence is the grand condition. The number of improvers will increase as the intellectual constituency, if I may so call it, increases. In former times, and in most parts of the world even at the present day, not one man in a million has ever had such a development of mind as made it possible for him to become a contributor to art or science. Let this development precede, and contributions, numberless, and of inestimable value, will be sure to follow. That political economy, therefore, which busies itself about capital and labor, supply and demand, interest and rents, favorable balances of trade, but leaves out of account the element of a widespread mental development, is nought but stupendous folly. The greatest of all the arts in political economy is to change a consumer into a producer; and the next greatest is to increase the producer's producing power,—an end to be directly attained by increasing his intelligence. For mere delving, an ignorant man is but little better than a swine, whom he so much resembles in his appetites, and surpasses in his powers of mischief.

3.

The Educational Debate

MANNERS

Manners are the root, laws only the trunk and branches. Manners are the archetypes of laws. Manners are laws in their infancy; laws are manners fully grown,—or, manners are children, which, when grown up, become laws.

DUTY OF THE TEACHER

When the teacher fails to meet the intellectual wants of a child, it is the case of asking for bread and receiving a stone; but when he fails to meet its moral wants, it is giving a serpent.

THE EXTENT OF OUR KNOWLEDGE

It is said that we are an educated people; and there is a sense in which this declaration is true. Such an assertion, however, supposes a comparison. . . . Compared with many, and even with most on the earth, the result would be in our favor; but compared with what we may be, and should be, our present inferiority is unspeakable.

HASTE IN TEACHING

In trying to teach children a great deal in a short time, they are treated not as though the race they were to run was for life, but simply a three-mile heat.

REASON IN TEACHING

It was the sin of Pharaoh to make the children of Israel write composition without ideas—that is, to make bricks without straw.

TEACHERS AND CHILDREN:
EXTRACTS FROM THE *COMMON SCHOOL JOURNAL*
(1839-1848)

Mann, in the great years of his secretaryship, wrote incessantly on educational topics, and his editorial essays, letters, and other papers trace the course of his crusade. Some of his writings belong to history, rather than to us. But even such writings include stories and observations which continue to illuminate modern educational discourse. Thus, one may ask how "corny" is his recollection of "an aged and distinguished clergyman" who had been relating an anecdote of brilliant point but, Mann tells us, fraudulent purpose. Mann described the general laughter the tale provoked, and the rebuke given the speaker by his nine or ten year old daughter, who asked meekly: "But father, was that honest?" Her instinct, Mann observed, reached what all his philosophy and his Christianity had failed to discover.

In the following pages, Mann appears in all his strength, meeting the problems confronting the pioneer educator with force, resourcefulness, and vivid illustration. He pleads the cause of the child; describes the many benefits which will accrue to individual and Commonwealth; emphasizes that purposes, however sincere, however desirable, can never be attained unless effective methods are forged to meet and master actual conditions. He draws on history, precedent, homely example and metaphor to make his points, as he discusses the principles of education, or hails the opening of the first Normal School as marking an epoch in human affairs.

"WORDS, WORDS, WORDS"

On the subject of teaching words, without a knowledge of the things they signify, we have an earnest and sincere appeal to prefer, in behalf of that younger portion of our community, known by the name of *"The Spelling Book Public."*

In Scotland, the Spelling Book is called the *Spell Book*, and we ought to adopt that appellation here, for, as it is often used with us, it does cast a spell over the faculties of children, which, generally, they do not break for years;—and oftentimes, we believe, never. If any two things on earth should be put together and kept together, one would suppose that it should be the idea of a thing and the name of that thing. The spelling book, however, is a most artful and elaborate contrivance, by which words are separated from their meanings, so that the words can be transferred into the mind of the pupil, without permitting any glimmer of the meaning to accompany them. A spelling book is a collection of signs without the things signified;— of words without sense;—a dictionary without definitions. It is a place where words are shut up and impounded so that their significations cannot get at them. The very notion of language is that it is a vehicle of thought and feeling, from mind to mind. Without the thought and feeling the vehicle goes empty. Pretending to carry freight, it carries no freight. To become familiar with things and their properties, without any knowledge of the names by which they are called, would be the part of beings, who had intelligence, but no faculty of speech; but to learn names, without the things or properties signified, is surely the part of beings, who have speech, but no intelligence. Who does not know that he can get ideas both of a man and his name or of a thing and its name, together, tenfold easier than apart. When I see a person whose appearance interests me, or when I see any new work of art, or when I enter a strange town; my first inquiry is, what is the name. That is the point of time when the name becomes important to me, and therefore, it is the point, when I can acquire its pronunciation and its orthography and so connect them together by association in my mind, that they will always reappear together, afterwards, as an identity. When names and things are only mechanically fastened, instead of being chemically combined, why should they not get jostled and jumbled so that the right idea shall come accompanied by the wrong name; or the right name shall associate the wrong idea; or, what is more probable, shall associate no idea at all? In the first two cases, the result is error; in the last, nonsense.

In teaching children words, in the earlier stages of education, the objects they designate should, as far as possible, be presented. Where the object is familiar to the child, but is not or cannot be present or in sight, then, let it be referred to, so that there shall be in the mind of the child a conscious union of the name and object, as in case of the words *river, boat, moon,* etc. If the object itself cannot be exhibited, and is not familiar, so as to be referred to, then some representation or model of it should be presented. But let a preference always be given to the object itself, or to the recollection of it, when known. In the school of Pestalozzi, a series of engravings was prepared, representing a variety of objects, whose names, structure and use, the children were to learn. One day the master having presented to his class the engraving of a ladder, a lively little boy exclaimed, "But there is a real ladder in the court-yard; why not talk about that rather than the picture?" "The engraving is here," said the master, "and it is more convenient to talk about what is before your eyes, than to go into the yard to talk about the other." The boy's remark, thus eluded, was for that time disregarded. Soon after, the engraving of a window formed the subject of examination. "But why," exclaimed the same little objector, "why talk of this picture of a window, when there is a real window in the room, and there is no need to go into the court-yard for it?" In the evening both circumstances were mentioned to Pestalozzi. "The boy is right," said he, "the reality is better than the counterfeit;—put away the engravings and let the class be instructed in real objects." This was the origin of a better mode of instruction, suggested by the wants and the pleasures of an active mind. Put away the engravings, we respond, where the real objects can be had or referred to. If it be impractical to exhibit the real object, as it is to show a ship to an inland child, then present the picture, or what is better, a model.

If one wished to prepare a boy to work upon a farm, or to be a salesman in a store, would he shut him up in a closet, giving him a list of names of all the farming utensils and seeds and products; or a list of all the commodities in a trader's invoice, and when he had learned these, send him to his place of destination as one acquainted with the objects, the materials, with which he is to be occupied? If one wished to make a boy personally acquainted with the business community of the city of Boston, would he give him a bare list of their names, unaccompanied by a single suggestion as to person, occupation or character;—would he have a city Directory expressly prepared, which would contain no designation of residence or employments, but exhibit a mere bald catalogue of names from A to Z, and when, after much anguish of spirit, he had learned to spell and pronounce all the names, send him forth into the marts and exchanges of the city as one acquainted with its people and ready to transact business with them? Or, would he not rather take him to the resorts of business, and when he and the merchants or mechanics stood face to face, acquaint him with the name, occupation, etc., of each; so that name, person, and employment might be mingled into one conception;—as, in making blue paper, the manufacturer stirs the color into the pulp, so that when the paper is made, the color cannot be removed without destroying the substance? If the person or thing cannot be exhibited, the absence should be supplied, as far as possible, by some visible representation, or some description.

Again, the things, the relations, of art, of science, of business, are to the mind of a child, what the nutriment of food is to his body; and the mind will be enervated, if fed on the names of things, as much as the body would be emaciated, if fed upon the names of food. Yet, formerly, it was the almost universal practice,— and we fear it is now nearly so,—to keep children two or three years in the spelling book, where the mind's eye is averted from the objects, qualities, and relations of existing things, and fastened upon a few marks, of themselves wholly uninteresting.

Who has ever looked at a child, above the age of nine months, without witnessing his eager curiosity to gaze at and handle the objects within his reach. He loves to play with a bright shovel and tongs, to pull the dishes from the table by the corner of the cloth, to disperse the contents of a work-basket, because these are something. There is substance, color, motion, in them. What an imagination it is, which turns a stick into a horse; and makes a little girl dress and undress a doll to prepare it for going to visit or to bed. But what is there in the alphabet or in monosyllables, to stimulate this curiosity or to gratify it? The senseless combinations of letters into *ba, be, bi, bo, bu,* deaden this curiosity. And after it has been pretty effectually extinguished, so that, by the further aid of the spelling book, the child can perform the feat of speaking without thinking,—as circus horses are taught to trot without advancing,—then let him be carried into reading lessons, where there are but few words he has ever seen or heard before, and where the subject is wholly beyond the reach of his previous attainments, and if by this process, the very faculty of thought be not subjugated, it must be because the child is incorrigibly strong-minded. These are the most efficient means of stultification, and if they do not succeed, the experiment must be given up.

The gorges and marshy places in the Alps and Pyrenees produce a race of idiots, known, technically, by the name of *Cretins.* These beings are divided by physiologists into three classes. The Cretins of the first degree are mere blank idiots. But the Cretins of the third degree have great facility in acquiring languages. They can be taught so as to translate the words of one language into those of another, though without the slightest comprehension of the meaning of either; and what is more remarkable, they will, so far as the rhyme is concerned, make good poetry. If words are taught to children for years, during the most active part of their life, without any of the ideas they are intended to convey, ought we to be surprised, if much of our public speaking and popular literature should be the production of Cretins of the third degree?

First and chiefest, in reading, let the lesson be understood; its words, its phrases, its connections; its object, if it have any object; if not, it is not proper for a reading lesson. Every word and sentence to which no meaning is attached is an enemy, lying in ambush. Keep the videttes of the mind out, to discover that enemy. If the name *Socrates* or *Rome* occur, see that the pupil knows who Socrates, what Rome was; and that he do not suppose the former to be a city and the latter a man. In reading the chapters, giving an account of St. Paul's shipwreck, let every place, which is named, be exhibited upon the map. In reading the account of the discovery of America by Columbus, see that the mind of every child goes back to "Friday the third day of August, in the year one thousand four hundred and ninety-two," and starts with the great discoverer, from Palos in Spain, "a little before sunrise, in presence of a vast crowd of spectators." Let them accompany the three ships as they proceed out of port and sail directly to the Canary islands; show them where the Canaries are; see that they comprehend the thrilling incidents of the voyage; that they sympathize with the noble commander; that they get a notion of the length of time, which was occupied in sailing through a distance, which could now be passed over in a steamboat in twelve days. Make them perceive the perils and dejection of the crew, the shout of *Land!* from the mast-head, and the Thanksgiving for its discovery. The whole scene of debarkation;—the manning, arming and rowing of the boats; the flying of the colors; the warlike music; the multitude of wondering savages upon the shore, gazing, with all the gestures of astonishment, as the boats approach the land; the landing of Columbus, grasping in his hand a naked sword, (which has not yet ceased to be the terrible emblem of the Indian's fate); his men kneeling down and kissing the ground, which they had despaired of ever beholding again;—all this can be presented to the minds of the children, just as vividly as though it had been witnessed by themselves, like the last militia training. Let this be once understandingly read, and the children will no more forget it, than a country Miss will forget the first time she went to Boston to spend a pocket-full of money. Yet we have known the first class in a school read this animating description without any more knowledge of what was in the book, than the book had of what was in them. When the celebrated phrenologist, Mr. George Combe, came from Edinburgh to this country in order to deliver lectures in all the principal cities of the United States, the Edinburgh Phrenological Society loaned him a variety of skulls of people of different nations and characters, to illustrate the different conformations of human heads. These skulls have crossed the Atlantic, they are now travelling from city to city, through this country, and when they have visited the principal places, they will take passage to Edinburgh, and be deposited again upon the shelves of the Phrenological Society. How many of the children in our schools are travelling over the varied beauties of the lessons in their reading books, and will know as little, at the end of the season, where they have been, as Mr. Combe's collection of travelling skulls will know of the United States, when they get back to Edinburgh?

TO TEACHERS

Few persons ever addressed a more influential or powerful body of men, than we now do, in saying a few words to the twenty-four or twenty-five hundred Male Teachers, at the present time engaged in our winter schools. They are the governors of men, in a far more extended sense, than those legislators, who, with state and ceremony, convene in the Halls of a metropolis, to enact and promulgate laws. They are more than rulers, for he who *forms*, is greater than he who *commands*. While other men arrogate wisdom and profess an ability to foresee and predict future events, the teachers, by their influences upon the children, are not uttering prediction, but preparing *fulfilment* and predetermining of what nature the future events shall be;—for events will grow out of the condition of the mind, and they are producing that condition. It is not to be supposed that these teachers have assumed so vast a responsibility, without looking inward upon themselves and asking the questions, "By what motives have I been influenced in undertaking this great work?" "Am I competent to its skilful performance?" "Have I a clear, distinct, living conception of what a man, formed in the image of God, should be; of the various excellences, he should possess; of the innumerable vices and weaknesses, from which he should be free; and can I take the uncultivated souls of children and form them into such men?" "Do I know enough of the nature of the human faculties, in their number and variety, to determine in what order of precedence or priority they should be ranged, so that in any contest between rival faculties, the higher and better shall not be sacrificed to the lower;—do I know to what point each one of the faculties should grow, so that the character may not be impoverished by deficiency, and at what point each one should stop, so as not to become rank and disproportionate,— and do I know by what processes and means such a wonderful work is to be accomplished?" Questions like these, or more solemn than these, will arise in the mind of every teacher, who is not incapable of moralizing upon the highest duties of life; and they will give a devotedness and a sincerity to his purposes, and an energy and a success to his efforts, which can come from no other source.

These are general views, indispensable to be taken, yet not comprising a hundreth part of that which is to be done. As soon as we regard the situation of the teacher in its practical aspects, we must descend into details.

The teacher's duties are not confined to the schoolroom. He has duties, almost as important, out of it, as in it. It has been well said respecting clergymen, that the relation and the intercourse, which they hold with other people, during the six week-days, determines the question, whether or not they shall do them any good on the seventh. And the relation, which the teacher holds to the parents in the district, goes far towards measuring the usefulness he can confer upon their children in the school. During the very first weeks of the school, there should not only be a good understanding, but a friendly intercourse, established between the teacher and the parents. This, it is the duty of the parents to proffer. Their welfare and the welfare of their children require it. Common hospitality requires it. Is it not barbarian, to allow any man, who is fit to keep a school, to come into a district and remain there for months, without any tender of civilities to him? The parents, then, should seek acquaintance and proffer hospitality. But if they are neglectful of this obvious duty of common politeness, still the teacher is not to keep his term through, in ignorance of the people among whom he lives. He has a right, always, to call upon the prudential-committee man. Through him, he may seek acquaintance with others, make himself interesting to them by inquiring into the progress of their children, commending their conduct, when it is commendable, asking advice and assistance in reforming them, when it is not. Parents love to have their children made the theme of conversation. Some of them would stop in the middle of a Thanksgiving dinner to enjoy that luxury. When a stranger evinces a sincere, generous, disinterested interest in the welfare of children, there are few hearts so selfish, as not to throw open their iron doors and bid him a hearty welcome. The teacher can approach the parents through this avenue. Many occasions will occur, when the teacher and parents will be thrown, as by change, into each other's presence,—in the street, at meeting, at a friend's house, or elsewhere. The teacher must seize upon these occasions, show that he is interested in his work, listen to their wonderful stories about the prodigies they send to school, stay by them, walk with them, do anything but *drink* or *smoke*, to prolong the interview and excite their interest in the school. This is a great affair, and worthy of great efforts. It is the teacher's duty, day after day, to toil in his school; week after week, if we may use a sailor's phrase, to pull at the rope, but what a difference it would make in the draught, should every parent in the district take hold and pull with him. Were all to take hold with him as one man, how easy as well as swiftly they could raise up the children out of the dark depths of ignorance and error. But what can one poor teacher do, tugging alone, if half the parents pull at the wrong end of the rope, or, in their listlessness, jump on to increase the weight to be raised. In some of the old towns in Essex county, records are now to be found in the town books of annual grants of money made by the town to the clergyman for *dining the schoolmaster.* On Saturdays, the schoolmaster was invited to dine with the clergyman. The town judged that honor to be due to the office, and, in order that the purse of the clergyman might not suffer, it paid the scot. Let it be remembered, too, that, in those days, the office of clergyman meant something. Its power and majesty might be compared with that of a Roman pontiff, rather than with the free familiarity of the present day. In point of honor and distinction, seven dinners per week would not now be an equivalent for that one service.

We have said that the teacher ought to seek the acquaintance of the parents of the school children. But this is for an important object, and not for its own sake. For yet a long time, in this State, the school-master must be a school-missionary; and the object of his mission must be to increase an interest in the school-system, and to improve the fixtures, the appurtenances, and all the arrangements of the schools. If the schoolhouse is bad, the teacher can not only explain its imperfections, but he can point out their consequences upon the health and mental activity, the proficiency, the tempers and dispositions even, of the pupils. After making himself thoroughly acquainted with the form, size, structure, accommodations, and benefits of a good schoolhouse, he can exhibit and illustrate these qualities and advantages, in such a manner that no sensible and humane man, in the district, can shut his eyes to the truth and repel conviction. Conversations with the inhabitants of a district, during a single winter, not obtrusively and dogmatically, but judiciously and in a conciliatory manner, sought and carried on, would result in many instances in the destruction of an old house and the erection of a new one. In such discussions, he may be certain, that, in nine cases out of ten, he will have all the children and their mothers on his side, and any cause, blessed with their advocacy, will ultimately prevail. Could the attention of the parents once be steadily fixed upon the condition of their schoolhouses, could they be brought to realize their unfitness for the important purposes to which they are devoted, could they be made to contrast them with their meetinghouses, their own houses, and even with their own barns, two out of every three in the State would not survive, in their present condition, for a single twelvemonth. This very winter, schoolmasters can do much towards the accomplishment of so desirable an object,—towards getting a new house for themselves or their successors, the next. There is no inconsistency in their doing every thing to preserve the schoolhouse, while they are in it, from trespass and injury, and at the same time plotting its speedy destruction. Hence, contrary to the geometrical axiom, the greater does not contain the less.

Besides securing the affection of his pupils and making the schoolroom a place of delight to them, the teacher can do much in another way to secure regularity and punctuality, in their attendance at school. An immense point is gained by enlisting the desires of the children in favor of attendance. If the school, for any reason, is odious or even unattractive to them, they will not only avail themselves of every permission to stay away, but they will fabricate a thousand excuses for deserting it. They will have some work to do, on one day; they will desire to make or receive a visit, on another; they will lose a book, on a third, and all parts of their bodies will take turns in aching, as an excuse for abandoning the school. Not so, when the children love the school;—the work will be done in the morning or evening, though they have to rise an hour earlier or sit up an hour later to accomplish it; the visits will be postponed or shortened, and the aches will be suppressed or forgotten. But if the desire of the children to attend is secured, still inconsiderate parents may interfere to disappoint it. This opens another field for the teacher's labor and skill. He must visit the parents and explain to them the untold and unspeakable mischiefs of absence and tardiness; how it wastes time, deadens exertion, interrupts classes, and bafflles all attempts at system and uniformity of movement, in the school. In one of the old arithmetical books, we remember there was a question like this:—"If a frog be at the bottom of a well, thirty feet deep, and he hops up three feet every day, but falls back two feet every night, how long will it take him to get out?" Whether this was put into the arithmetic to explain the slow progress made by tardy and irregular scholars, we know not; but it is an apt illustration; for they, like the frog, will accomplish no more in twenty-eight days than they might do in ten. Perhaps the parent of the delinquent children is a lawyer or a trader;—let the teacher ask him, what would become of his clients or customers, should he absent himself from his office or store, every other day, or even for half the mornings and afternoons. Perhaps the parent is a miller or manufacturer;—let his attention be turned to the loss of permitting his head of water to run off while his wheels are standing motionless, just as the term of the school is wasting away, while his children are deriving no benefit from it. Perhaps he is a blacksmith;—let the teacher ask him, how long it would take to weld two pieces of iron together, if, as soon as they became about half hot enough for the union, he were to pull them out and cool them, again and again and again. Yet this is just what they do to their children, for as soon as their minds get a little warmth and engagedness in their studies, they keep them at home until they get cold again. In this way, let the teacher convince, or coax or shame every parent, who fails to act like a parent, into the conduct of a parent.

There is another copious source of benefit to his school, which the teacher can open. Parents are incredibly negligent about the condition of things in the school-room. Many, after they leave it as scholars, never enter it again, as citizens, nor as fathers and mothers. They seem not only destitute of all interest in it, but absolutely shy of it. If they have any other interest, they look after it; travel miles to learn how it prospers, or hold regular correspondence with agents who have the charge of it. But, except when their children get punished in the school, they seem not to know of its existence; when, had they attended to its prosperity as they ought, in nine cases out of ten, it would have superseded the necessity of punishment. At one of the Common-School Conventions held last fall, a gentleman made the following brief and pertinent statement. "A neighbor of mine," said he, "last week met me in the road, near my house, and asked me to take a walk with him. Not being engaged and feeling socially disposed, I consented. We proceeded a little way, when he struck off from the road and took me across fields, not less than two or three miles, when I found his errand was to see if a neat creature, which he had put there, three or four days before, to be pastured, had water. Finding all things right, he seemed well satisfied, and we returned. A day or two after, I was in the city. There I met a man walking in great haste, with whom I had some business. I stopped to address him on the business, when he said he must go to another part of the city, and requested me to walk with him and converse as we went along. I did so. He took me from street to street, until I almost lost my breath, when we arrived at a tavern,—to the stable of which he immediately repaired, *to see if his horse was feeding, or whether, through negligence or fraudulence, the hostler had taken no care of him.* "And how is it," said he, "that men are so careful to see that their cattle and horses have water and hay, but suffer their children to go to school, through a whole winter, without asking whether they are fed either intellectually or morally, with any thing better than the east wind?" Now this indifference about visiting the school, or this repugnance to do so, the teacher must overcome. Let him explain to the parents of any school district of ordinary size, that if the heads of each family would spend but *six hours* in the school, during a whole winter's term, making two or three visits only, the school would be visited nearly every day. In a common district, no man is so industrious, no man is so engaged in business; rarely is any family ever so sick, or so far off, that they cannot, with entire convenience, spend *six hours*, during an entire winter, in visiting the school. If a few hours are wanted for any other purpose, or even half a day or a whole one, to go to an auction, or a militia muster, or a cattle show, they are easily found. Let the teacher urge this upon them, explain to them the utility of a visit to him, and its utility to themselves, in the effect it would have upon their children, and let him *compel them to come in.* The visitation of schools, by parents, has been objected to by some. "It may lead," say they, "to familiarity, to interference, to embarrassment." There is very little danger of this. If the teacher is what he should be, they will discover, that, though they can aid him by their presence, they cannot improve his processes. But should any one be disposed to visit the school too frequently,—

to make the schoolhouse a lounge,—let the teacher still treat him with perfect civility, but let him be requested to wedge himself into some one of the narrow, cramp-giving seats provided for the children, so hard, sharp-edged, pillory-like, as to stop the blood from circulating to his lower extremities, and he will avoid the house, ever afterwards, as much as if it were the "long, low, suspicious, black schooner," that frightened our coasts, some months ago.

Finally, let the teachers in every town form an association for mutual improvement. At weekly meetings, let them discuss any and all questions, which pertain to the great cause of Education;—the practicability and advantages of a union of school districts; the construction of schoolhouses; the processes and modes of instruction; the benefits of a globe and other apparatus, and of a district-school library. The teachers cannot be expected to furnish apparatus for the school, but there is one thing that every Yankee-born teacher can do. When there is no blackboard in the school-room and the prudential-committee man refuses or declines to supply one, the teacher, if he can find a pine board, a fore-plane and a pot of black paint, can make one.

By such exertions in the cause, and by an interchange of ideas with his associates in the same field of employment, every teacher will find his head grow clearer, and his heart will warm to the noble work in which he is engaged.

THE CONDITION OF THE CHILDREN OF LABORERS ON PUBLIC WORKS

Our country in general, and the State of Massachusetts in particular, owe a vast economical debt to that class of people, whose labor has been mainly instrumental in rearing the great material structures of which we so often boast. It is by the toil of that people, that these instruments of prosperity have been brought into being. In looking at the creative cause, their muscle bears a closer relation to the work, than our capital. They have materially changed the surface of the earth for our accommodation, and profit, and delight; building piers and wharves for our commerce, turning the bed of the ocean into dry land for the enlargement of our cities, cutting down the mountain and upheaving the valley, to smooth a pathway, by which distant and alien people might hold communion with each other. Were all considerations of social and Christian duty out of the question, an equitable and fair-minded people ought to blush, to receive such substantial benefits, without any other requital, than just enough food and clothing for the laborers, to enable them to enlarge and prolong the benefits they are conferring. Allowing it to be ever so true, in point of fact, it would still be a low and unworthy view of the case, to regard them as ignorant, poor, and destitute of some of the elements of civilization, that belong to the age, and therefore to treat them as though their condition were remediless, or to refer the obligation of improvement to themselves. The only noble and worthy view is that which regards them as fellow-beings, capable of advancement, and suffering from the want of such aids, as it is in our power to render. It is impossible for us to pay them *in kind*; but there is a compensation, elevating both to the giver and the receiver, which we have the ability to bestow; there is a medium of payment, which we richly possess, and which they most of all need. We can confer the blessings of education upon their children. And the impulse of duty to do so may lawfully derive additional energy from the reflection, that every wise and humane measure, adopted for their welfare, directly promotes our own security. For, it must be manifest to every fore-casting mind, that the children of this people will soon possess the rights of men, whether they possess the characters of men or not. There is a certainty about their future political and social powers, while there is a contingency, depending upon the education they receive, whether those powers shall be exercised for weal or woe. The idea of Burke, that education was the best preventive police, is a very just idea, and for his time, it was a very advanced one;—but, though a just idea, it is a very narrow one, because it is the noble office of education to do good positively, by refining the purest and elevating the highest blessings, as well as to do good negatively, by warding off evils. In that thought, Burke only declares, that education can save to the government the fees of jailers and hangmen, the expense of chains and halters;—he does not say, that education can convert the very materials, which go to make the felon and the traitor, into the strength and ornament of the State. It is obvious, that there may be people, who, from the very circumstances and condition of their birth, and therefore without fault of their own, may be so profoundly immersed in ignorance, as not to know how ignorant they are, and who, there-fore, feel no discontent under their privations, nor any aspirings after a more elevated existence. But for men, who have felt the enduring satisfactions of knowledge, who know the pleasure it confers, the pain it averts;—for such men to stand around their ignorant fellow-beings, and lift no hand to raise them from their debasement,—what is it, but for those who chance to be awake, to stand around the dwelling of their neighbors who are asleep, when that dwelling is on fire, and make no effort to extinguish the flames, nor to raise any cry of alarm, audible to the unconscious sleepers?

... There is another consideration pertaining to this subject, which we cannot express with half the energy that we feel. The children of the Irish are not infrequently brought into association with those of our native population, either at school, at work, or at play. On these occasions, the former are often treated with indignity and contempt by the latter. A garb less respectable, manners, in some respects, less proper, are made the subjects of scoff and ridicule. How unmanly, how ungenerous, how unjust, is this! No tattered garments, though rag is flapping farewell to rag,—no coarseness of manners, though it descend to the very sty,—is half so shameful or so degrading, as the sneer with which pride insults misfortune. Children or men proclaim their own reproach, when their dress is better than their manners. Let parents and teachers see to this. Kindness and sympathy are due to those, whom circumstances have placed in an inferior condition; and the greater that inferiority, the greater should the kindness and sympathy be. Children should be early imbued, on this as well as on all other subjects, with the feelings, which they ought spontaneously to exercise when they become men; and no ignorance or rusticity is so disgraceful, as airs of superiority over those, who have enjoyed no opportunity for learning, and whose manners are the misfortune of birth, and not of their own choosing.

MANAGEMENT OF DISOBEDIENT CHILDREN

The management of disobedient children is one of the most difficult of duties, whether in school or at home. In this branch of government, ignorance and bad temper run into mistakes, as certainly as water will run down hill. They cannot proceed rightly. It requires all possible prudence, calmness, consideration, judgment, wisely to govern a refractory child. It is a common saying, that anger should never be manifested towards the young or the insane. This, though true, is but a feeble expression of the truth. Feelings of wrath, madness, are as absurd and incongruous, in the management of a disobedient child, as they would be in a surgeon, when amputating a limb or couching an eye. Suppose we were to witness an operation upon the human eye, and the oculist, as he approached his work, should begin to redden in the face and tremble in the joints, to feel all the emotions and to put on the natural language of wrath; and should then spring upon his patient, like a panther, and strike his knife into the eyeball, at hazard;—should we call this *Couching*, or *Gouging?* But are the moral sensibilities of a child less delicate in their texture, than the corporeal senses? Does the body require a finer touch and a nicer skill, than the soul? Is less knowledge and discretion necessary, in him who seeks to influence the invisible and immortal spirit, than in him who operates on the visible and material frame? Is the husk more delicately wrought than the kernel? No; as much more exquisite as the painting is, than the frame, or the jewel, than the casket, so much more excellent is the soul, than the body it inhabits; and he, who does not approach it in this faith, wants one of the essential prerequisites for acting upon it wisely. Firstly, then, let teachers discipline their own feelings to the holy work they have undertaken.

Teachers have their severest trials with disobedient children. To instruct the beautiful, the affectionate, the intelligent, the grateful, is unalloyed delight. A school, composed entirely of such, would not be earth, but elysium. But to take an awkward, gawky, unclean, ill-dressed, ill-mannered, ill-tempered child, and to work up an interest in it, to love it, to caress it, to perform a full measure of duty to it;—this draws upon all the resources of conscience, virtue, and religion. Yet, in the eye of true benevolence, of Christian duty, this class of children presents the dearest of objects,—the first to be attended to, the last to be forgotten. They are at an immeasurable distance from the "Image," to whose similitude they are to be brought, and their restoration to the "Divine likeness" is a work, only inferior, in quality and in difficulty, to an act of original creation. For such a great work, great efforts are requisite. A band of the highest motives must be summoned for the task. The teacher must stand, like an angel, by the wanderer, and reclaim his wayward steps. Love is one of the most potent agencies, with children who have never known the luxury of being loved. Perhaps the child has inherited a defective organization from vicious parents. We know that God has implanted hereditary tendencies in the constitutions of men, in order to furnish to parents a motive for obedience to his laws, and to punish those who transgress them, not only in their own persons, but in their love for their offspring. The liability to deteriorate goes with the capacity to improve.

But, when a child suffers under this hereditary curse, is it a reason why the teacher should inflict upon it the further curse of severity or unkindness? Perhaps the child has been badly governed, at home, or at some previous school; has suffered under the cruelty of rigor, or the cruelty of indulgence. Can a humane and just teacher say, that this calamity should be the very means of bringing down upon it another calamity? Rather, with every benevolent mind, does not this constitute the highest claim to compassion? It should inspire greater tenderness. It is a title to good will, not a forfeiture of it.

The motive of interest, also, coincides with the motive of duty. If the teacher truly consults his own ease and comfort, he will treat the less amiable children, in his school, with great kindness and regard; because, by this course of conduct, he will save himself from a vast amount of labor and vexation, in the end. When he knows that wounds actually exist, the true question of policy, with him, is, whether it is better even for himself, to inflame and aggravate, or to soothe and heal them. At a Common School convention in Hampden county, we heard the Rev. Dr. Cooley relate an anecdote, strikingly illustrative of this principle. He said, that, many years ago, a young man went into a district, to keep school, and, before he had been there a week, many persons came to see him, and kindly told him, that there was one boy in school, whom it would be necessary to whip, every day; leading him to infer that such was the custom of the school and that the inference of injustice towards the boy would be drawn, whenever he should escape, not when he should suffer. The teacher saw the affair in a different light. He treated the boy with signal kindness and attention. At first, this novel course seemed to bewilder him. He could not divine its meaning. But, when the persevering kindness of the teacher begot a kindred sentiment of kindness in the pupil, his very nature seemed transformed. Old impulses died. A new creation of motives supplied their place. Never was there a more diligent, obedient, and successful pupil; and, *now*, said the reverend gentleman, in concluding his narrative, that boy is the Chief Justice of a neighboring State. The relator of this story, though he modestly kept back the fact, was himself the actor. If the Romans justly bestowed a civic crown upon a soldier, who had saved the life of a fellow-soldier, in battle, what honors are too great for the teacher, who has thus rescued a child from ruin?

One great error, in the management of untoward children, consists in expecting too much from them, at once, and immediately. Time is an important element in the process of weakening and subduing bad principles of action as well as in the growing and strengthening of good ones. All actions proceed from some internal faculty or propensity; and it is not in accordance with the course of Nature, to expect that an overgrown and over-active propensity can be reduced to its natural size and vigor, in a day. Whenever a child has yielded to an impulse to do wrong, but has been induced, by expostulation or discipline, to do right, the peculiar circumstances, under which he was tempted to the wrong, should be avoided, if possible, until the resolution to do right has had time to be confirmed; that is, those faculties or sentiments of his nature, from whose ascendency we hope improvement and reform, must have time to grow, and to become superior to their antagonists, if we expect they will prevail over them. . . .

Are not great mistakes committed in the government of children, by acting upon the supposition, that they can grow strong in virtuous resolutions, *in a single day?* This, it is true, would save the teacher all further trouble. But, if all our active affections, whether good or bad, are the result of growth, then opportunity must be allowed for the seeds to germinate, after they have been sown. Everybody knows, how tenacious of life the Lombardy poplar is. Its twigs, cut off and stuck into a sand-bank, will throw off roots, and grow. We once knew a boy, who cut off a great number of these twigs, and set them out in the garden, that they might grow and form an arbor;—but, every morning, for a fortnight, he regularly pulled them all up, to see if the roots had started. At the end of the fortnight, he gave up in despair; *and so did the twigs.* The boy's conduct is necessarily imitated by all those parents and teachers, who think they can take out a wrong inclination from a child's mind, and substitute a right one, by a single act, just as they can take one weight from a scale and supply its place with another. If, however, all good purposes in the mind are the result of growth, the seed must first be sown, and then all those circumstances attended to, which will warm, and foster, and nourish it.

We have space and time, at present, but for one more idea. No parent or teacher should ever issue a command, without the highest degree of certainty, that it will be obeyed. To command a child to do, or to abstain from doing, what, under the circumstances, he will probably refuse to do or to abstain from doing, is as false to duty, as it would be in a general to engage, voluntarily, in a battle, when he was exposed to certain defeat. In directing a child to carry a burden, we consider his age, his size, his strength. None but a tyrant would command him to bear a weight, beneath which he could not stand. This principle applies to moral efforts, with far greater force, than it does to physical. Where the moral sense is weak, and the selfish propensities strong, we must begin, in regard to the former, with the lightest conceivable duties. Present no temptation to the child, which he has not strength to overcome. Let the temptation be increased, only as the power of resistance is strengthened. In this way, the capacity of a child to resist only the weakest seductions may grow, until his soul is clad in moral mail against the most powerful temptations. But, alas! who, in the present state of the public mind, on the subject of education, has wisdom and skill, sufficient for these things?

THE LAW, THE CLERGY, AND THE SCHOOLS

The Massachusetts Legislature, for 1842, passed the following Resolves:—

"*Resolves concerning Normal Schools and School District Libraries.*

"1. *Resolved*, That the sum of six thousand dollars, annually, for three years, be, and the same is hereby, appropriated to the support of Normal Schools, under the direction of the Board of Education. And His Excellency the Governor is hereby authorized, from time to time, to draw his warrant on the treasury for the same, on the application of said Board.

"2. *Resolved*, That the sum of fifteen dollars, to be taken from the school fund, be, and the same is, hereby appropriated to every school district in the Commonwealth, to be expended in books for a School District Library, and that the Treasurer pay said sum, for said purpose, to the order of the mayor of every city, and the selectmen of every town, for each and every school district within the same, which shall have produced evidence of having raised and appropriated fifteen dollars or more for the same object.

"Approved March 3, 1842."

Though occupying but an inch or two of space upon the statute-book, yet these Resolves are eventful of the fate of all coming time. They are intrinsically of greater importance than volumes or centuries of common legislation. Unlike the laws designed to act upon the material interests of the race, whose effects are turned aside by new developments of human action, and become obsolete by the lapse of time, these brief and simple provisions will be found to possess an inherent, perennial efficiency,—to be endued with a living spirit, ever-renewing and ever-expanding, which will work outward until it reaches all contemporaries, and onward until it blesses all posterity. To the tide of beneficence which these acts will send forth, there will be no refluent wave. It will widen and roll onward, until it covers the furthest shores of the earth, and passes the confines where time is merged in eternity.

We are not mad, but speak forth the words of truth and soberness. This simultaneous provision for the qualification of teachers for our Common Schools, and for the diffusion over the whole State of the means of knowledge,—the dissuasives against vice and the incitements to virtue,—will make Massachusetts an illuminated,—nay, more, —a self-luminous spot upon the earth's surface. Though our Commonwealth possesses but a handbreath of territory, and seems thrust aside into an obscure corner of the Union, yet the provision which it has now so nobly made for the culture of all its children, will be a lever lifting up to a sublime moral height, where it will fill a wide and conspicuous space in the world's eye, for generations to come. In numbers, in natural resources, whether of the sky above or of the earth beneath, we are insignificant,—over-shadowed and lost in the vastness that surrounds us;—but in the means of creating intellectual riches, of diffusing that moral serenity and grandeur which are purer and sweeter than all the balm and fragrance that sky or earth can exhale, where is the State that has done so much and so wisely,— where the State that has prepared such a precious and glorious boon as a heritage for its children, as will arise from the brief and simple, but sublime enactments we have cited!

Our anticipations on this subject are not conjecture or vagary. The spiritual world, not less than the material, is governed by fixed and immutable laws; and they who prepare the means, predestinate the ends. It is as certain that good seed sown in a moral soil, will ere long yield an abundant harvest, as that the seasons will revolve, or corn will grow. In both spheres of action, material and spiritual, we are in the universe of the same all-wise and true Creator; and every law of His universe which He has made us capable of discovering or understanding, is a covenant of promise, that if we will obey it we shall have our reward. And hence it is that efficient and comprehensive provisions for the education and training of the young, possess a higher character than prediction or prophecy. They are creative *fiats.* They do not simply declare or prognosticate honors and blessings for the future, but they cause and oblige the future to shower down honors and blessings upon the race.

The considerations which lead us to attach such an inappreciable value to the legislative measures we have recorded, are few and simple; and the occasion is worthy of giving them a brief exposition. Mankind are rapidly passing through a transition state. The idea and feeling that the world was made, and life given, for the happiness of all, and not for the ambition, or pride, or luxury, of one, or of a few, are pouring in, like a resistless tide, upon the minds of men, and are effecting a universal revolution in human affairs. Governments, laws, social usages, are rapidly dissolving, and recombining in new forms. The axiom which holds the highest welfare of all recipients of human existence to be the end and aim of that existence, is the theoretical foundation of all the governments of this Union; it has already modified all the old despotisms of Europe, and has obtained a foothold on the hitherto inaccessible shores of Asia and Africa, and the islands of the sea. A new phrase,—the people,—is becoming incorporated into all languages and laws; and the correlative idea of human rights is evolving, and casting off old institutions and customs, as the expanding body bursts and casts away the narrow and worn-out garments of childhood. A juster and holier tribunal is installed over the actions of men. Glory and infamy are hereafter to be awarded on new principles, and for new actions. The code of moral jurisprudence is to be administered in a different spirit. No future historian will assign the rank and honors of a god to the demon who has inflicted the greatest woes upon men. The flames of burning cities are no longer to be gazed at as the effulgence which radiates from a conqueror's brow; but they are to be regarded as—what in truth they are—the unquenchable fire in which his character shall suffer perdition. The splendid palaces of royal robbers will hereafter be looked upon with loathing and abhorrence,—as a concentration of human tears and blood,—and that government will be deemed faithless to one of its highest trusts which endows institutions to cultivate genius and knowledge in a few, while it spurns the millions from its protecting care. The contrast will not redound to the honor, but to the infamy, of any state or kingdom which displays a few gems of art or intellect amid the ebon blackness of national ignorance.

This change in the fortunes of the race is now going on. We occupy the point of transition. It is a change which may be hastened and made peaceful by wisdom; it may be postponed for centuries, and crowded with social and national calamity at every point, by folly or guilt, and even by injudicious benevolence. Our want, then,—nay, the world's desideratum,—is a generation of sober, wise, good men, to prepare for coming events, to adjust society to the new relations it is to fill, to remove the old, and to substitute a new social edifice, without overwhelming the present occupants in its ruins.

It is said, indeed, that the future will be a reproduction of the past, because human nature is everywhere the same. The adage is true, but not the inference derived from it. What is this identity? Human nature consists of capacities so manifold and diverse, that the same being is susceptible of the most opposite destinies. So also are the same people. Because human nature is the same, does it follow that there was no difference between Washington and Arnold; or that there is no difference between cannibals and civilized men? The sphere of human action is immeasurably wide. We may rise to the sublimest heights of wisdom and virtue, or we may plunge to unfathomable depths of infamy and wretchedness, without bringing doubt or question upon the fact of our common nature. Human nature occupies the vast intermediate space between the angel and the demon. It may ascend to the one; it may fall to the other. It may select and occupy any spot in this immense ascending and descending scale.

The grand fact, then, that human nature is always the same, though incontestable, is by no means so important as that other equally incontestable fact, that this same identical human nature can be made to yield the most opposite results, both as to the character of the individual, and the fate of the community;—not here and there an individual, we do not mean, or here and there a community, but as to all individuals and all communities.

The question then is, What measures should be adopted to give scope, expansion, and supremacy, to the better susceptibilities of human nature, and to clamp down, as with triple bands of iron and brass, the passions and propensities which heretofore have made such havoc of the world's welfare? We answer, The two legislative provisions above quoted, will be more efficient for the accomplishment of this work than the united force of all existing agencies. Let us, for a moment, compare the efficiency of the proposed measures with the great instrumentalities upon which society now relies, whether for the promotion of good, or the repression of evil.

One of the weapons put into the hands of the sovereign State by which to keep down the insurgent forces of violence and fraud, is the institution of the judiciary. To establish and maintain a system of judicature, the profoundest intellects of the community are culled, the vast machinery of courts, witnesses, jurors, and executive officers, is kept in motion, at an enormous expense; and an awful power over personal freedom, and life, and death, is deposited in the hands of judges. The whole plan and scheme of this institution is, not to preserve innocence, but to wait until it is depraved, and then punish it;—not to promote industry and economy, but, when idleness and prodigality have stimulated to thefts or robberies, to thrust the criminal into a dungeon for years or for life;—not to instil the idea and feeling that life is a sacred thing, but, when one has been murderously taken, then to take another in retribution. These are the dread prerogatives with which the courts are invested. Fines, chains, death, are the emoluments with which the criminal tribunals of the State assuage the anguish of social wounds. The courts, as courts, take no note of early exposure to temptation;—they interpose no advice or guidance to the inexperienced;—they administer no word of kindness, or expostulation, or warning, to incipient criminality;—they stretch forth no hand to rescue, or even to beckon backward the wayward steps of youth just diverging into paths whose end is ruin;—but they sit silently by, they wait for the smallest leprous spot to spread until it covers the whole surface, and then their first appliances are the knife, the cautery, or the halter. The whole function of criminal tribunals is, not reclaiming, but avenging,—not the early extermination of the vice, but the late and terrible extermination of its victim,—not prevention by foresight and guidance, but expiation by bondage or blood.

And again, whom and what does the judiciary reach? They aim only at the *actions* of men, as contradistinguished from *thoughts* and *motives*. The members of society may commit, daily, *in their hearts*, all the crimes prohibited in the decalogue; they may corrupt the moral atmosphere until it reeks with pestilence; but if they perpetrate no overt act in contravention of existing laws, the power of the courts does not attach to the case, and they may persevere with impunity. Officially, the courts know nothing of human thoughts in their hiding-places, where they nourish their strength in secret, and plan their desecrations of the laws of God and man. The courts lie by,—in ambush, as it were,—till the theft is committed, till the robber has despoiled, till the libellous shaft has pierced the heart of its victim, till the innocent are murdered; and then, and only then, after the mischief is done and suffered, have they eyes or ears to see the deed and hear the wrong. Though they inflict vengeance and retribution on the guilty, yet they have no power to recompense the injured or restore life to the dead. Nay, more,—even the law may be broken, all the sanctities of life may be profaned, and sacrilege or blasphemy be wantonly committed; but if the culprit have the ingenuity to avoid suspicion, or the skill to elude pursuit, or the chicanery to baffle proof, or the strength to break from the executioner's clutch, he is safe, and the joy of the escape and the pride of triumph stimulate him to new zeal in his career of villainy.

Criminal jurisdiction, also, is local. It is confined to acts committed within its own territory, whether state or national. A man may be guilty of the most heinous offences in Great Britain, or in Canada, and if he can escape across the ocean, or the line, and come upon our ground, he is secure. Our law is not only ignorant of his guilt, but affords him protection against his pursuer. And so of criminals here, who escape to other countries. It is, therefore, not only blind to all that passes in the hearts of men, but beyond its own territorial jurisdiction, all is blankness and nonentity.

How small, therefore,—we might almost say how insignificant,— a portion of those acts which constitute human happiness or misery, in the sight of men,—which make up human innocence or guilt, in the sight of God,—comes under the cognizance of legal tribunals! It almost seems a mockery to refer to the courts as having any capacity to advance the work of civilization, or to restore to the heart of man the defaced image of his Maker.

Let us look at another, and one which is regarded as the principal, instrumentality for the reformation of mankind;—we mean the institution of the clergy or church. This is an instrumentality sustained and worked at an immense cost of time, and talent, and wealth; yet, in the first place, one half, at least, of the whole community, lies *outside* of its reforming influences. One half of mankind hear nothing and see nothing of the stated ministrations of the church. Conceding, then, to these ministrations the fullest efficacy, within their limited circle, yet they do not inspire hope or allay fear, in regard to the multitudes who are beyond the circumference of their action.

Again, the church addresses itself principally to men, to adults, to those whose habits of thinking and acting are established, who have made their choice among the objects of life, have commenced the race in pursuit of them, and have already acquired such momentum and headway, that they can hardly be arrested by secondary causes. The clergy, as clergy, do but little to guide the stream of infant thought and feeling as it gushes clear from the spring, at a time when the

direction of its channel might be turned by a motion of the hand;—
custom and stipulation do not make it a part of their duty to watch
sedulously over the fountain of infancy and childhood, and save its
waters from pollution; but they wait until the tiny current of youth
swells into the river of wild and passionate manhood, and becomes
wide, and deep, and foul with earthly stains; and it is then, when
its vast volume sweeps rapid and headlong to the cataract, that they
strive to arrest its impetuous course, and to filter out the impurities
from its multitudinous waters.

Nor is it unworthy of notice, in this connection, that by tradition
and the common usages of the age,—or by some force equivalent to a
law,— our spiritual guides address but a small part of the various
faculties of the human mind. They speak only *from* one set of faculties
in their own minds, and *to* one set only in the minds of their hearers;
and thus, without any fault of their own, but in accordance with the
practice of the times, they sometimes leave a feeling of want or
incompleteness, which seeks for relief elsewhere, and often, in improper
gratifications. The many-toned soul is not satisfied, when the performer
strikes but a few of the numerous strings which make its music. This
circumstance is not mentioned either in complaint or disparagement
of those who labor in the vineyard of the Lord, but only to show
that their agency, powerful and indispensable as it is, does not
supersede the necessity of something still more pervading and comprehensive, and beginning further back in the formation of human
character.

The only instrumentality left is that of Public Schools. This
institution, like the law, takes cognizance of outward actions. Like the
church, it enters into the sanctuary of the soul, and inquires there what
are its motives, affections, purposes,—whether they flow out into action,
or are indulged only in the secret recesses of thought. But it possesses
two grand, fundamental attributes, peculiar to itself. One of its points
of superiority, as a means of reclaiming the world, consists in its
universality. It may be made co-extensive with our territory,—finding
its way where less diffusible influences do not penetrate, searching
out every dark spot in the land, and filling it with light. And,
secondly, its action is upon childhood. Every effort made here prop-
agates its influence over the whole life. Impulses given in the cradle
reach to the grave. The words spoken in the ear of infancy do not
die. Their echoes come back at each successive turn in the journey
of life; they are heard in old age, and in the depths of the soul, even

though the outward ear may have become too dead for the thunder to awaken.

The time of childhood, too, is valueless, or of little comparative value. Its six days are not worth one day of the parent for labor. Its mind, also, is not preoccupied. It is not burdened with the necessity of providing for subsistence. It looks but a little way into the doubtful future, and what it sees, it sees with the eye of hope, and not of fear. Hence the mind is open, receptive, watching, and eager to catch whatever is thrown to it; and the seed of good instructions sown in it, at this period, is not choked with the cares of the world, and the deceitfulness of riches, and the lusts of other things entering in, and thus made unfruitful.

In these circumstances, then, lies the superiority of schools over all other human agencies. But without good teachers, there cannot be good schools; and we have as little right to expect good teachers without adopting adequate means to prepare them, as we have to expect beautiful gardens and cultivated fields to spring up spontaneously in the wilderness. At this point, therefore, the inestimable value of the first Resolve we have quoted, opens upon us at once in all its beauty and amplitude. It provides the means of preparing good teachers, and thus of placing our hopes of human improvement upon solid grounds of fact and reason.

In unfolding the utility of this measure, we must pass by the various considerations that lie upon the surface, and are obvious to all, and invite the attention of our readers to a single point that is not so apparent, yet one of invaluable and indispensable importance in the great work by which civilization is to be extended outward and onward until it shall reach and bless the neglected and miserable portion of our fellow-beings now alive, and prepare a better world for the reception of the millions who are to come after us.

In all the towns in our Commonwealth,—in the small and obscure, and perhaps still more in cities and in other populous places,—there are many children,—orphans, or those who, in the curse of vicious parentage, suffer a worse evil than orphanage,—children doomed to incessant drudgery, and who, from the straitened circumstances of the household, from awkwardness of manners, or indigence in dress, never emerge from their solitude and obscurity, and therefore necessarily grow up with all the coarseness, narrowness, prejudices, and bad manners, almost inseparable from spending the years of non-age in entire seclusion from the world. This is a true picture of the condition of many children in every town in the State. Although there may be a few exceptions, in regard to *sons*, as to the effects which these misfortunes of birth and parentage tend to produce, yet there are scarcely any such exceptions in regard to *daughters*. At the age of sixteen or eighteen, a vigorous-minded boy may break away from the dark hovel where his eyes first saw the light, and go abroad in quest of better fortunes; but there is hardly any such option in regard to girls. As a rule, they will remain at home, until, perhaps, the relation of marriage is entered into with some individual of fortunes similar to their own, when it will become their turn to rear up children after the model which was furnished in their own degraded and degrading birthplace.

Now, in the common course of events, and without the instrumentality of schools, this class of children, during the whole period of their minority, would never be brought into communication or acquaintance with a single educated, intelligent, benevolent individual, —with one who loves children with a wise and forecasting love,— with one whose manners are refined, whose tastes and sentiments are pure and elevating,—who can display the beauty and excellence of knowledge, and win others to obtain what they cannot fail to admire. The most which this class of children would be likely to see of any educated men, would be when the clergyman should make his brief annual parochial call, or when the physician should be summoned to administer to diseases brought on by ignorance or improper indulgences, or when they should be carried before the courts to answer for offences which their untaught and unchastened passions had prompted them to commit. But let the company of well-educated, well-trained, devoted teachers be sent into the school districts of the Commonwealth, to hold intercourse and communion with these children, week after week and month after month,—let their qualities of knowledge, dignity, kindness, purity, and refinement, be brought to act upon the ignorance, vulgarity, squalidness, and obscenity, of these neglected and perverted beings,—and how inexpressibly beautiful it would be to see the latter gradually enlightened, purified, and humanized, by the benignant influences of the former,—to see them casting off not only the foul *exuvioe* of the surface, but the deeper impurities of the soul! By wise precepts, by patterns and examples of what is good and great in human character, how many of them may be led to admire, to reverence, and then to imitate! O, how beautiful and divine the work by which the jungles of a society that calls itself civilized, can be cleared from the harpies, the wild beasts, and the foul creeping things which now dwell therein! This is the work of civilization and Christianity; and it is time that those who call upon us to send our wealth to other lands should bestow a thought upon the barbarism and heathenism around their own doors. It is time that the current of public sentiment should be changed on another point, and that the honor and glory of a people should be held to consist in the *general prevalence* of virtue and intelligence, rather than in the production of a few splendid examples of genius and knowledge. In the great march of society, it is rather our duty to bring up the rear than to push forward the van; and it will be to the ever-enduring and ever-expanding renown of the Legislature of Massachusetts for 1842 that they have adopted and acted upon this broad principle of philanthropy more completely and efficiently than any other body that ever held in its hands the destinies of mankind.

As to the Resolve for establishing a Library in every school district in the State, it was a fit accompaniment of the preceding. Without the other, each would have been incomplete. Without sound instruction in the schools, the benefits of the library would have been, to a great extent, lost; and without the library, the key of knowledge would have been given, while the treasures which it was designed to unlock would have been withheld. Hence each was the supplement of the other; and it is impossible for any finite mind to comprehend the blessings their united action will diffuse. By means of the library, the great and good men of ancient and modern times,—poets, orators, statesmen, philosophers, sages, and divines, will come and take up their abode in every secluded nook and corner of our land, and sit down by the fireside in the humblest and lowliest dwelling, and offer to take the young by the hand, and lead them to a knowledge and contemplation of this glorious universe,—the handiwork of God,— into which they have been brought, and to unfold the marvels of their own physical structure, and the profounder and more awful mysteries of their spiritual being, and to display before them the heavenly beauty of truth, and justice, and benevolence, and moral intrepidity, and to instil into their young hearts some conceptions of the adorable character of their Creator. How many youth will such a library save who would otherwise be ruined; how many it will fill with intelligence who would otherwise grope in perpetual darkness, and, under the cravings of an unsatisfied mind, become misanthropes, or the pests of society! If ever an act was done, for which a Legislature might indulge a feeling,—not of pride, but a far nobler and purer feeling than pride,—a consciousness that a great deed has been performed, and is no longer subject to chance, whose blessed influences cannot be defeated, but will go on, and make the whole future wiser, better, and happier, than it would otherwise have been,—if ever any body of men were authorized to indulge this feeling, it is the Legislature of Massachusetts for 1842.

REMARKS AT THE DEDICATION OF THE BRIDGEWATER STATE NORMAL SCHOOLHOUSE.

(August 19, 1846.)

MR. PRESIDENT:— Among all the lights and shadows that have ever crossed my path, this day's radiance is the brightest. Two years ago, I would have been willing to compromise for ten year's work, as hard as any I had ever performed, to have been insured that, at the end of that period, I should see what our eyes this day behold. We now witness the completion of a new and beautiful Normal Schoolhouse for the State Normal School at Bridgewater. One fortnight from tomorrow, another house, as beautiful as this, is to be dedicated at Westfield, for the State Normal School at that place. West Newton was already provided for by private munificence. Each Normal School then will occupy a house, neat, commodious, and well adapted to its wants; and the principals of the schools will be relieved from the annoyance of keeping a Normal School in an *ab*-Normal house.

I shall not even avert to the painful causes which have hastened this most desirable consummation,—since what was meant for evil has resulted in so much good. Let me, however, say to you, as the moral of this result, that it strengthens in my own mind what I have always felt; and I hope it will strengthen, or create, in all *your* minds, a repugnance to that sickly and cowardly sentiment of the poet, which made him long

> "For a lodge in some vast wilderness,
>   Some boundless contiguity of shade,
>   Where rumor of oppression and deceit,
>   Of unsuccessful wars,
>   Might never reach him more."

There is oppression in the world which almost crushes the life out of humanity. There is deceit, which not only ensnares the unwary, but almost abolishes the security, and confidence, and delight, which rational and social beings ought to enjoy in their intercourse with each other. There are wars, and the question whether they are right or wrong tortures the good man a thousand times more than any successes or defeats of either belligerent. But the feeling which springs up spontaneously in my mind, and which I hope springs up spontaneously in your minds, my friends, in view of the errors, and calamities, and iniquities of the race, is *not* to flee from the world, but to remain in it; *not* to hie away to forest solitudes or hermit cells, but to confront selfishness, and wickedness, and ignorance, at whatever personal peril, and to subdue and extirpate them, or to die in the attempt. Had it not been for a feeling like this among your friends, and the friends of the sacred cause of education in which you have enlisted, you well know that the Normal Schools of Massachusetts would have been put down, and that this day never would have shone to gladden our hearts and to reward our toils and sacrifices. Let no man who knows not what has been suffered, what has been borne and forborne, to bring to pass the present event, accuse me of an extravagance of joy.

Mr. President: I consider this event as marking an era in the progress of education,—which, as we all know, is the progress of civilization,—on this western continent and throughout the world. It is the completion of the first Normal Schoolhouse ever erected in Massachusetts,—in the Union,—in this hemisphere. It belongs to that class of events which may happen once, but are incapable of being repeated.

I believe Normal Schools to be a new instrumentality in the advancement of the race. I believe that, without them, Free Schools themselves would be shorn of their strength and their healing power, and would at length become mere charity schools, and thus die out in fact and in form. Neither the art of printing, nor the trial by jury, nor a free press, nor free suffrage, can long exist, to any beneficial and salutary purpose, without schools for the training of teachers; for, if the character and qualifications of teachers be allowed to degenerate, the Free Schools will become pauper schools, and the pauper schools will produce pauper souls, and the free press will become a false and licentious press, and ignorant voters will become venal voters, and through the medium and guise of republican forms, an oligarchy of profligate and flagitious men will govern the land; nay, the universal diffusion and ultimate triumph of all-glorious Christianity itself must await the time when knowledge shall be diffused among men through the instrumentality of good schools. Coiled up in this institution, as in a spring, there is vigor, whose uncoiling may wheel the spheres.

But this occasion brings to mind the past history of these schools, not less than it awakens our hopes and convinces our judgment respecting their future success.

I hold, sir, in my hand, a paper, which contains the origin, the source, the *punctum saliens*, of the Normal Schools of Massachusetts.[1] It will be observed that this note refers to a conversation held on the evening previous to its date. The time, the spot, the words of that conversation can never be erased from my soul. This day, triumphant over the past, auspicious for the future, then rose to my sight. By the auroral light of hope, I saw company after company go forth from the bosom of these institutions, like angel ministers, to spread abroad, over waste spiritual realms, the power of knowledge and the delights of virtue. Thank God, the enemies who have since risen up to oppose and malign us, did not cast their hideous shadows across that beautiful scene.

The proposition made to the Legislature was accepted, almost without opposition, in both branches; and on the third day of July, 1839, the first Normal School, consisting of only *three* pupils, was opened at Lexington, under the care of a gentleman who now sits before me,—Mr. Cyrus Pierce, of Nantucket,—then of island, but now of continental fame. I say that, though the average number of Mr. Pierce's school is now from sixty to eighty; and though this school, at the present term, consists of one hundred pupils, yet the first term of the first school opened with *three* pupils only. The truth is, though it may seem a paradox to say so, the Normal Schools had to come to prepare a way for themselves, and to show, by practical demonstration, what they were able to accomplish. Like Christianity itself, had they waited till the world at large called for them, or was ready to receive them, they would never have come.

In September, 1839, two other Normal Schools were established, one at Barre, in the county of Worcester, since removed to Westfield,

---

[1] Here Mr. Mann read a note from the Hon. Edmund Dwight, dated March 10th, 1838, authorizing him, Mr. Mann, to say to the Legislature, that the sum of ten thousand dollars would be given by an individual for the preparation of teachers of Common Schools, provided the Legislature would give an equal sum. The reading was received with great applause.

in the county of Hampden; and the other at this place, whose only removal has been a constant moving onwards and upwards, to higher and higher degrees of prosperity and usefulness.

In tracing down the history of these schools to the present time, I prefer to bring into view, rather the agencies that have helped, than the obstacles which have opposed them. I say, then, that I believe Massachusetts to have been the only State in the Union, where Normal Schools could have been established; or where, if established, they would have been allowed to continue. At the time they were established, five or six thousand teachers were annually engaged in our Common Schools; and probably nearly as many more were looking forward to the same occupation. These incumbents and expectants, together with their families and circles of relatives and acquaintances, would probably have constituted the greater portion of active influence on school affairs in the State; and had they, as a body, yielded to the invidious appeals that were made to them by a few agents and emissaries of evil, they might have extinguished the Normal Schools, as a whirlwind puts out a taper. I honor the great body of Common School teachers in Massachusetts, for the magnanimity they have displayed on this subject. I know that many of them have said, almost in so many words, and what is nobler, they have acted as they have said:—"We are conscious of our deficiencies; we are grateful for any means that will supply them,—nay, we are ready to retire from our places when better teachers can be found to fill them. We deserve, it is true, our daily bread from school-keeping, but it is better that our bodies should be pinched with hunger than that the souls of children should starve for want of mental nourishment; and we should be unworthy of the husks which the swine do eat, if we could prefer our own emolument or comfort to the intellectual and moral culture of the rising generation. We give you our hand and heart for the glorious work of improving the schools of Massachusetts, while we scorn the baseness of men who would appeal to our love of gain, or of ease, to seduce us from the path of duty." This statement does no more than justice to the noble conduct of the great body of teachers in Massachusetts. To be sure, there always have been some who have opposed the Normal Schools, and who will, probably, continue to oppose them as long as they live, lest they themselves should be superseded by a class of competent teachers. These are they who would arrest education where it is; because they cannot keep up with it, or overtake it in its onward progress. But the wheels of education are rolling on, and they who will not go with them must go under them.

The Normal Schools were supposed by some to stand in an antagonistic relation to academies and select schools; and some teachers of academies and select schools have opposed them. They declare that they can make as good teachers as Normal Schools can. But, sir, academies and select schools have existed in this State in great numbers, for more than half a century. A generation of school teachers does not last, at the extent, more than three or four years; so that a dozen generations of teachers have passed through our Public Schools within the last fifty years. Now, if the academies and high schools can supply an adequate number of school teachers, why have they not done it? We have waited half a century for them. Let them not complain to us, because we are unwilling to wait half a century more. Academies are good in their place; colleges are good in their place. Both have done invaluable service to the cause of education. The standard of intelligence is vastly higher now, than it would have been without their aid; but they have not provided a sufficiency of competent teachers; and if they perform their appropriate duties hereafter, as they have done heretofore, they cannot supply them; and I cannot forbear, Mr. President, to express my firm conviction, that if the work is to be left in their hands, we never can have a supply of competent teachers for our Common Schools, without a perpetual Pentecost of miraculous endowments.

But if any teacher of an academy had a right to be jealous of the Normal Schools, it was a gentleman now before me, who, at the time when the Bridgewater Normal School came into his town, and planted itself by the path which led to his door, and offered to teach gratuitously such of the young men and women attending his school, as had proposed to become teachers of Common Schools, instead of opposing it, acted with a high and magnanimous regard to the great interests of humanity. So far from opposing, he gave his voice, his vote, and his purse, for the establishment of the school, whose benefits, you, my young friends, have since enjoyed. (Great applause.) Don't applaud yet, for I have better things to tell of him than this. In the winter session of the Legislature of 1840, it is well known that a powerful attack was made, in the House of Representatives, upon the Board of Education, the Normal Schools, and all the improvements which had then been commenced, and which have since produced such beneficent and abundant fruits. It was proposed to abolish the

Board of Education, and go back to the condition of things in 1837. It was proposed to abolish the Normal Schools, and to throw back with indignity, into the hands of Mr. Dwight, the money he had given for their support.

That attack combined all the elements of opposition which selfishness and intolerance had created,—whether latent or patent. It availed itself of the argument of expense. It appealed invidiously to the pride of teachers. It menaced Prussian despotism as the natural consequence of imitating Prussia in preparing teachers for schools. It fomented political partisanship. It invoked religious bigotry. It united them all into one phalanx, animated by various motives, but intent upon a single object. The gentleman to whom I have referred was then a member of the House of Representatives, and Chairman of the Committee on Education, and he, in company with Mr. Thomas A. Greene, of New Bedford, made a minority report, and during the debate which followed, he defended the Board of Education so ably, and vindicated the necessity of Normal Schools and other improvements so convincingly, that their adversaries were foiled, and these institutions were saved. The gentleman to whom I refer is the Hon. JOHN A. SHAW, now Superintendent of schools in New Orleans. . . .

I have, my young friends, former and present pupils of the school, but a single word more to say to you on this occasion. It is a word of caution and admonition. You have enjoyed, or are enjoying, advantages superior to most of those engaged in our Common Schools. Never pride yourselves upon these advantages. Think of them often, but always as motives to greater diligence and exertion, not as points of superiority. As you go forth, after having enjoyed the bounty of the State, you will probably be subjected to a rigid examination. Submit to it without complaint. More will sometimes be demanded of you than is reasonable. Bear it meekly, and exhaust your time and strength in performing your duties, rather than in vindicating your rights. Be silent, even when you are misrepresented. Turn aside when opposed, rather than confront opposition with resistance. Bear and forbear, not defending yourselves, so much as trusting to your works to defend you. Yet, in counselling you thus, I would not be understood to be a total non-resistant;—a perfectly passive, non-elastic sand-bag, in society; but I would not have you resist until the blow be aimed, not so much at you, as, through you, at the sacred cause of human improvement, in which you are engaged,—a point at which forbearance would be allied to crime.

To the young ladies who are here,—teachers and those who are preparing themselves to become teachers,—I would say, that, if there be any human being whom I ever envied, it is they. As I have seen them go, day after day, and month after month, with inexhaustible cheerfulness and gentleness, to their obscure, unobserved, and I might almost say, unrequited labors, I have thought that I would rather fill their place, than be one in the proudest triumphal procession that ever received the acclamations of a city, though I myself were the crowned victor of the ceremonies. May Heaven forgive them for the only sin which, as I hope, they ever commit,—that of tempting me to break commandment, by coveting the blissfulness and purity of their quiet and secluded virtues.

DUTIES OF SCHOOL COMMITTEES: I

... We deem this a fit opportunity to say a few words to our co-laborers and friends, the school committees of Massachusetts. We wish to address them on a few topics of public duty, acknowledged to be not only important, but paramount,—namely, the means of improving the young, of advancing the welfare of the state and of the race. Precious interests are at stake. An eventful struggle is going on between good and evil. The world need reforming. We have emerged from barbarism, and call ourselves civilized; but our civilization needs civilizing. If mankind cannot be made better than they now are, it is matter for infinite regret that Noah's ark had not sprung a leak, and foundered, with all its passengers, when the waters were at the deepest. It is thought, by those who know most on the subject, that school committees, and others engaged in the sacred cause of education, are more worthy than any other class of men, to be considered as the pilots, who are directing the course of the bark that contains all the precious interests of mankind, and steering it either for its rescue or its ruin. . . .

Consider, in the first place, what our schools would be, if candidates for teaching were subjected to no test, in regard to their fitness or qualification. It is almost an analogous case, to consider what our currency would be if there were no assayer of the mint to expose adulterated coin, or no counterfeit detecters to prevent the circulation of spurious notes. The motives to fraud are almost as strong in the one case as in the other. As a general rule,—almost a universal one,— are not the ignorant and incompetent more self-esteeming, more exorbitant, more clamorous, than those whom culture has made, or has even begun to make, conscious of their deficiencies? Modesty and self-diffidence have no place to stand upon, until a man begins to know his deficiencies. A perfectly ignorant man, like an animal, does not know that there is any thing lying outside of his own narrow circle of knowledge. And hence it is, that really intelligent men act under a class of restraints whose obligations the ignorant never feel.

The difference in regard to mortal attributes is still more striking. Suppose a candidate for teaching to be actuated by no higher motive than how he can get his bread and butter most easily; or how he can spend a winter most comfortably, and with least exposure to the inclemencies of the season; or how, in the shortest time, he can obtain the most money to help forward some other plan; or by what means, for the coming three months, he can work the least, and have the most time for frolic and laughter;—for the period of three months is as much of the future as many ever embrace in their plan of life;—and suppose, with such low aims, such sordid or ignoble motives, a school is sought for the ensuing season, will such a seeker ever be restrained from taking any school, by a sense of his unfitness for its requirements? Will he not be ready to attempt to teach any thing which childish or parental folly may desire, without any reference to the scholar's benefit in learning, or his own capacity for teaching? And, on the other hand, will he not be equally ready to strike any study from the list, however important it may be, if either his own incapacity to teach it, or the child's whimsical disinclination to study it, shall so counsel? Will not such a teacher, too, manage and govern the school with reference to his own personal ease or caprice, rather than on those eternal principles of benevolence and justice which lie under the whole length of existence?

In the first struggle of competition between the unprincipled and the well-principled, the former have an advantage. The honest can use none but honest means. To the dishonest, all means which will subserve their purpose are equally welcome. In the long-run, to be sure, integrity and high-mindedness are sure to prevail over knavish arts; but in the first encounter, and before the latter can be exposed, they have a temporary advantage. Now, this temporary advantage may be all that a man needs to secure a temporary place; and, as a general rule, the office of teacher is only temporary.

Most emphatically, then, is not this a case for an arbiter? Who is to secure the prize to the most deserving, if not some umpire who can investigate the merits of the respective claimants or candidates and who means honestly to decide upon their contending titles to it? This umpirage the school committee must execute. Their station, therefore, requires,—

1. INTEGRITY.—A school committee man is exposed to many temptations. His personal friends, or the relatives of his friends, may be candidates for the post of teacher. Perhaps a son or a daughter of one who has conferred personal favors upon himself is an applicant, and a refusal will be taken as ingratitude. Pecuniary considerations, means of support, perhaps subsistence itself, may be at stake. A committee man is a physician, and recoils from giving offence to a family circle, among whom he has a lucrative practice. Or he is a lawyer, and knows how easy it is for an old client to pass by his door to seek counsel from the office of another. Or he is a clergman, and knows that the imaginations of some of his people are already beginning to luxuriate in the greener pastures of another shepherd. Or he is ambitious of filling some municipal office, and understands that paradoxical law of the ballot-box,—more extraordinary than the hydrostatical one,— by which a single vote may be made to balance, and even to turn the scale against, all the rest. Or,—for even our virtues may become our tempters,—he is kind-hearted, and cherishes peace with all mankind, and therefore is seduced to make a small present good balance a great future evil. Now, against the weight of such perilous motives as these, what, but the poise of integrity, can maintain the equilibrium of the mind?

2. A school committee man should have SOUND COMMON SENSE. An individual of strong natural sense, and conversant with men and with affairs, is often able to form a correct and almost intuitive judgment He has a natural sagacity, which is a more unerring guide to truth than any formal logic ever can be. For all logical disquisitions, true premises are as necessary as true processes. If the premises be not true, while the processes are so, the result must be infallibly wrong. A man arguing from wrong premises has but one chance of arriving at correct conclusions; and that is, by making a mistake. As truth, however, is only one, while error is infinite, the chances are as infinity to one, that his mistake, if he makes one, will lead him, not to truth, but to some other error than the one towards which his logical processes pointed. But a man of sound sense, and practical acquaintance with men, often forms a just and quick estimate of character, and can predict such results as grow out of demeanor, temperament, and

disposition, with a high degree of certainty. Now, it is this kind of intelligence and judgment which a school committee man should bring to the discharge of his duty, when about to sit in judgment on the fitness or unfitness of a candidate.

3. A committee man should have a general acquaintance with ALL THE FUNDAMENTAL PRINCIPLES OF EDUCATION, and with the branches of study to be taught in the school. At least, there should always be some members upon the board who are familiar with the studies to be taught, and with the best modes of teaching them. But how can a man, who is unacquainted with the best rules and authorities for the pronunciation of words, decide upon the accuracy or inaccuracy of a candidate's pronunciation; or examine a school, and rectify the errors in enunciation which the pupils may commit? He may expatiate, as once did a committee man, before a school, upon "the infinite value of *pro-noun-sa-tion*;" but his oral teachings, however true, can never rectify the mis-teachings of his example.

If a committee man is ignorant, the examination must necessarily be a *sham*, in which the dignity of the office cannot preserve the officer from contempt.

If a committee man feels officially obliged to ask some questions, and yet is ignorant of the appropriate questions, or classes of questions, to be asked, he is necessitated to ask inappropriate ones; for no others are left for him;—he must ask such questions as furnish no test of the capacity or incapacity, the fitness or the unfitness, of the candidate.

We have known a case where the only question put to the candidate was, "How much do two and three make?" Would not an intelligent teacher feel that the whole subject was burlesqued, and himself insulted, by such an examinaton?

All the qualifications above enumerated are indispensable in a school committee, and the obligations they involve must be discharged before the opening of the school. Other qualifications and duties, not less important, come into requisition after the school has been commenced; but we must defer our remarks upon these until a subsequent number.

DUTIES OF SCHOOL COMMITTEES: II

In our last, we endeavored to set forth the importance of one class of the duties of school committee men,—those which relate to the examination of teachers.

Every teacher must be examined. Any Committee that approves or appoints a school teacher, without subjecting him to a previous examination by themselves,—personally, and not by proxy,—violates a solemn trust. And still further may it be said, that if any teacher fails through a want of literary qualifications, or any other deficiency, or through any privation or perversity, in manner or in temper, which the most rigid and scrutinizing examination could have exposed, such failure reflects hardly less disgrace upon the committee than upon the delinquent himself. For whatever might have been prevented by their vigilance or fidelity, they are responsible. . . .

So far, we have counselled not only thoroughness, but even some degree of rigor, on the part of the committee. While a candidate is suing for a school, the committee are to take nothing in his favor for granted,—to assume nothing in his behalf on trust. Every applicant must make out affirmatively a clear case of fitness. The attribute which the committee are to exercise is not that of charity, but justice. They are to act under the sentiment of fear, rather than of hope. They are to consider all the rising generation of the town as gathered around them, claiming their protection, cowering beneath the shield which it is their duty to uphold; and they are to look with jealousy upon one who seeks to be installed over those children, and to administer to them the bread and water of life. They are not to commit trusts so precious and enduring to any man, until they *know* whether he be a false shepherd or a true one; whether he has come to fatten upon the flock, or to feed it.

But when the committee, with the full approval of reason and conscience, have given to the candidate a certificate of qualification, the relation between them changes at once and entirely. From one of distrust, it becomes one of confidence. From one of jealousy and fear, it becomes one of favor and hope. Before, all presumptions were against the candidate; now, all are in his favor. While he was a suitor for the school, the committee were bound to be rigorous, exacting, and suspiciously viligant; but now, when he has wooed, and won, and wedded it, nothing but some very grave cause should alienate affection, or can justify the extreme measure of divorce.

As soon as the committee have given their certificate of approval,

the teacher, in a very comprehensive sense, is *their* teacher. They have
adopted him, they have chosen him as one of their agents to carry out a
great work for which they are accountable; and hence, in a most extensive sense, they are officially and personally responsible for his success.

Among the new duties, growing out of the new relation between
the committee and the newly-constituted and freshly-commissioned
teacher,—a relation which the committee themselves have assented to
and established,—is that,

1. Of propitiating, in his behalf, the good-will of the district in
which he is to keep school.

It often happens that there are prejudices on the part of one,
two, or a few families, against a teacher whom the committee have
felt bound, on a consideration of all the circumstances, to approve.
Between such families and the teacher, the committee should be
meditators. Suppose that, in order to have an interview with one or
more malcontents, for the purpose of disarming them of their hostility,
or of disabusing them of their prejudices, or of conciliating their
good will in behalf of the teacher, the members of the committee
should be obliged to ride an extra mile or two, or to prolong their
absence from home till a later hour,—are any such trifling and
transient inconveniences to countervail, for a moment, the vast gain
of a harmonious opening of the school, and of a voluntary and cordial
cooperation of *all* the parents in promoting its welfare? Suppose it
should even require a special visit, on the part of some member of the
committee, to allay the groundless animosities of some individual
or family against the proposed teacher, or to avert the spontaneous
injustice of partisans or sectarians, or to conciliate the charitable interpretations of those who seem to have been born with a supernumerary
instinct for grumbling and querulousness,—cannot the committee do
as much as this to secure the acquisition of so great a good?

But, in most cases, no great extra trouble will need to be taken
in order to secure these important objects. The common occasions
and chances of life will generally bring the committee in contact with
such of their townsmen as may need these special appeals. If the
committee have the desire and purpose to do so important a work,
if their minds are full of it, there will be no lack of opportunity.
"Where there is a will, there is a way," says the proverb. In ninety-
nine cases in a hundred, if there be any failure, it will be for want of
the *will*, not the *way*.

2. The duty of visiting the schools, at least as often as the law

requires, and of availing themselves of every such occasion to impress upon the minds of the children the necessity and the utility of good conduct, obedience to the teacher, and diligence in study, is so obviously within the narrowest definition of a school committee man's indispensable obligations, that it requires but a small amount of intellect to see it, and of conscience to feel it.

3. School committees are to keep an ever-open eye and ear for the first symptoms of discontent. They must extinguish difficulties while yet they are but sparks, and not wait till they have become a conflagration. If the fireman dozes even for a minute after the alarm-bell has sounded, of if he fails to take the shortest way, or make the quickest speed, to the scene of danger, the flames, in the mean time, may have reached a height which it will mock his efforts to subdue; or, at least, for every moment of delay, the loss and the peril may be immensely aggravated. So it is in regard to school strifes. They are emphatically like the letting out of water. At the beginning, they may be stayed; but no geometrical reduplications, or law of accelerated velocities of falling bodies, can adequately illustrate the swiftly-accumulating mischiefs of delay, when dissatisfaction against a teacher begins to prevail in a neighborhood, or insubordination in the school. When, therefore, the anxious ears of the committee shall hear the faintest note of alarm, they should be on the spot at once, and silence the whisper, that it may not grow into a whirlwind.

4. As we do not propose to go over the entire ground of the duties of committee men,—such as making annual reports, returns etc., we shall take up, at this time, but one topic more.

It sometimes happens that the board is not unanimous in granting to an applicant a certificate of approval. The legal power resides in a majority; and, if they so please, they may exercise it without any invasion of the minority's rights. Perhaps it may be inexpedient for a bare majority of one, or of half a one, to go counter to the convictions of their colleagues;—still they unquestionably have the *legal* power to do so. In such cases,—especially if the opposition has been pointed and strong,—the dissenting members of the committee are under a great temptation to be resigned, should the incumbent, whose appointment they opposed, fail of success. His failure would be their justification,—a proof of their superior foresight. It would be retroactive, and vindicate their previous opposition. A small mind could not forego such an occasion of triumph. An unprincipled mind might not only rejoice at such an occasion, but seek to produce it, that it might rejoice. Here, then, is a case which demands, not merely the fulfillment of an abstract duty, but the exercise of magnanimity, of all the high and generous attributes of our nature. While the question of appointment was pending, opposition to the candidate may have been not only lawful, but laudable; but when that question has been authoritatively settled, those who opposed the applicant are no less bound to be his friends, than those through whose advocacy or votes he prevailed. Having the certificate of the committee, he is entitled to the assistance and defence of the committee, in their collective capacity; and the very remembrance of the opposition, which failed to reject him, should be consigned to oblivion. Other great and paramount interests have now become involved,—the welfare of the children, the mischiefs of breaking up the school, a probable feud in the neighborhood, a possible schism in the committee itself. The case supposed, therefore, is one for the exercise of generous and noble sentiments, and generous and noble-minded men who will not fail to improve it.

PRACTICE *AGAINST* THEORY. THEORY *AND* PRACTICE.

Nature has placed the natural eye of men in the front side of the head. False education, or natural perversity, has twisted round the mental eye of some men, so that it looks out at the back side of the head. Hence there are two parties in the world,—the Forward-looking, and the Backward-looking; or the Progressives and the Retrogressives.

It seems to us that there is a great significancy in the arrangement of nature. The eyes of man look forward, that they may see where they are to go; because Progress is the law of the universe. Arts, science, government, have reached their present stage, from the rudest beginnings, by successive and numberless improvements. The present copiousness of written languages has grown out of a few alphabetic characters. Architecture may be traced gradually up, from a hollow tree, or cross-poles stuck in the earth, to its present magnificence and granite solidity. The multiplied uses of steam power, on land and river and ocean, originated in seeing the lid of a tea-kettle thrown off by the boiling of the water within. Even the earth itself, though made by Omnipotence, was not made in a day. The geologists tell us, that it took countless ages to prepare it for vegetation; and other cycles of countless ages to prepare it for the successive races of animals; and others still, to prepare it for the residence of man. To better the condition of all things around us is the moral law, as well as the physical.

A generation that does not leave the world and society better than it found them, has proved false to its mission. It is the unprofitable servant, who, with talents bestowed, makes no return of talents acquired; and whose just penalty is "outer darkness." And so, with each individual. All are bound to add something to the common welfare. This necessitates progress; and for safe progress,—in order that men may see in what direction they should go, that they may go in the most direct path, that they may not stumble,—for these purposes, men have their eyes in the front side of their heads.

It is true that, at the top of the spinal column, all men have the *atlas*, or ring of bone, on which the head is supported; and that, jutting up into the centre or hollow o f the *atlas*, is the *dentatus*, or tooth-like bone; and that, by means of this curious apparatus, the whole head can be swung round to one side or the other, as on a pivot, so as to command a view of the whole space behind us, should any indications of approaching danger in that direction be given. But it by no means follows from this, that man's rear is his natural field of vision.

If, by any sudden jerk, the head is thrown backwards with violence, the *dentatus* may be forced out of the *atlas*, which, in popular language, is *breaking the neck*. That is what usually takes place when criminals are executed by being hanged. Bigotry, however, when it can take its victims while they are young, has the art of so *suppling* the muscles, and twisting the head round more and more, by skilfully applied violence, as, at last, to make it face backwards, without breaking the neck. This last circumstance is a pity.

The Retrogressives look out of the back side of their head. Their natural, but now perverted instinct of advancement, urges them backwards, as it does other people forwards. They labor to restore the past. Some of them would go back further than others; but this is a difference of no consequence; for all would go back from the point where they happened to be; and this involves an infinite series of retrogradations. Though anyone should now flatter himself that he would be satisfied could he realize the institutions of Egypt; yet, were these secured, the same instinct would still hurry him on beyond Egypt, with as much vehemence as ever. In the lowest deep, a lower deep would still invite him to sink.

The retrogressive impulse, often, perhaps generally, exhibits itself in the form of stand-still, or opposition to all progress. As the universe is moving forward, if one moves backward at precisely the same pace, he appears to be stationary. It is only when one moves back faster than the sublime order of things advances, that he appears, in Hibernian phrase, to advance backwards. A man upon a tread-mill just maintains his position, when his own motion balances that of the wheel he steps on.

All nations and all interests, have their backward-looking or retrogressive class. In India, these are the Brahmins; in England, the tories; in the Fejee Islands, the cannibals. Religion has them; government has them; education has them.

In the department of education, and within a few years past, the retrogressive or stationary spirit has developed itself pretty vigorously, in some parts of Massachusetts, and in some other sections of the country. Until within a few years, indeed, there was not advancement enough anywhere in this country to provoke it to action. The great watchword under which the party has rallied, is that which we have placed first at the head of this article,—PRACTICE AGAINST THEORY. Under this *Slogan,* or war-cry, new things have been denounced as *Theoretic,* and old things have been defended as *Practical.* The advocates of new methods have been stigmatized as innovators, theorists, visionaries, dreamers, and so forth; while the defenders of antiquated notions and abuses, have been styled Practical men, in token of honor; and their most doughty champions have been advanced to posts of distinction. Facts and arguments, emanating from the friends of improvement and reform, have been set aside by the shortest of all arguments,—the despised Nazareth from which they come.

We propose to say a few words on this subject, which, as we hope, may serve to reconcile extremes, to moderate the views of ultraists, and to bring whatever of educational zeal and talent there may be amongst us, into more harmonious and co-operative action, in favor of the abiding and precious interests of education. In these remarks, we take for our text the second part of the title at the head of this article,—THEORY AND PRACTICE.

With deference to wiser men, we hold it as an axiom, that there is no such thing as intelligent practice which does not originate in theory; and no such thing as established or credible theory, which has not been ratified by practice. *All intelligent action includes both theory* AND *practice.* The blind mole, as he runs along his covered furrow in the earth, is a perfect prototype of the merely practical man; the miller that flies a second time into the candle's blaze, after having his legs and wings once scorched there, is a perfect prototype of the merely theoretic man. The first is impervious to all ideas of any thing better than he now does or knows; the second grows no wiser by experience. The epithet *Practical*, therefore, in the sense which excludes theory, or speculation, is a highly derogatory term; and the man who assumes it in this sense, dictates his own title as plainly as Dogberry did.

Every intelligent man, in every voluntary action he performs, has a theory. He has a purpose; he has an idea of the nature or properties of the object he wishes to affect, or effect; and he has a conception or notion that certain ways are better than other ways for accomplishing his design. *This is Theory.* It is the mind going before the hand, and directing its movements with reference to a desired result. If it stops there, then there is no test to show whether it is sound theory, or unsound; and hence the necessity of practice also.

The etymological meaning of the word theory, is, *to see* or *to contemplate.* Professor Olmsted says, "a *theory* is founded on inferences drawn from principles which have been established on independent evidence;" and in this, he distinguishes it from an *hypothesis*, which he defines to be "a proposition assumed, to account for certain phenomena, which has no other evidence of its truth than that it affords a satisfactory explanation of those phenomena." Yet men are often constrained to act on hypotheses merely,—a far less safe guide than theory.

What mechanician would ever invent a valuable machine, unless he first proposed to himself a certain improvement to be effected, and then, *mentally*, arranged every band, wheel, cog and pin, deemed necessary to its successful working. If he makes wheels *practically only*, that is, only as he has been taught to make them, there will be no improvement to the end of time; if he makes them at random, the doctrine of chances will show that no life is long enough to make even two that will fit and play together.

Columbus had a theory, that by sailing west he should discover land. O no! said his *practical* contemporaries; if there were land there, do you think the world would have existed more than five thousand years, and nobody would have discovered it; and so they quoted texts of Scriptures against him, from the Psalms and from the Hebrews, with passages from Lactantius and St. Augustine, as glibly as Solomon is now quoted to prove that every child must be whipped. Away, they said, you visionary, dreamer, enthusiast; you are more fit for a monastery's door-keeper than to undertake a voyage of discovery.

Dr. Franklin had a theory that the lightning which comes from the clouds, and the electricity which can be excited by rubbing silk against glass, or flannel against sealing-wax, were the same substance. He subjected that theory to experiment, and, to the inexpressible honor and welfare of mankind, he proved it to be a true one. Without the pre-existing theory, would he ever have sent up his kite, or used the key to catch the spark that was to illumine and bless the world?

What a splendid illustration of the value of theory has recently been given to the world, in the department of astronomy. The motion of the planet Uranus was found to deviate from what would be given it, by all the known bodies of the solar system. Here was a problem. What was the cause of this deviation? A young French astronomer began to theorize. He said, perchance there is a body beyond, far away in the depths of space, which no telescope has yet reached, that may cause these fluctuations. If so, said he, let us ascertain the amount of all known deviations of Uranus, and see what kind of a body would be adequate to cause them. By immense labor, working in the faith of his theory,—or perhaps, in this instance, working in the faith of a mere hypothesis,—the computations were made. It was found that a body of a given mass, and moving along a given curve, would explain the deviations observed. A telescope was directed to that part of the heavens occupied by the *theoretical* disturbing body, and there, at the first inspection, it was found,—a monument of the value of theory, coëval with the heavens where it shines.

Yet, both in the case of Columbus, and in the case of Leverrier, practice was necessary in order to verify the theory, and even to rectify some subordinate and incidental points into which the theory ran. Land was discovered, though it was not the East Indies, nor the territories of the Grand Khan. A planet was found, though it was but half as far off and half as large, as was anticipated. Here we see that theory and practice are each imperfect without the other; and we learn the value of both when united.

The intemperate man says to the physiologist, I cannot work without the stimulus of ardent spirits. Abstinence is a theory. I stand upon centuries of experience; you upon a theoretical idea or phantasm.

The hereditary tyrant declares Free Government to be a theory. Men are born to be governed, says he, as a horse to be bitted; just as the same tyrannical spirit, in a narrow sphere, says, every child must be flogged. So they scoff at, as theoretic, all idea and effort of making men or children capable of self-government.

On the other hand, it is said that the Chinese laws forbid

anatomists to dissect the human body. But all physicians and surgeons must proceed upon a theory. So the Chinese have invented a theory of human organization; they have filled it out with such minuteness, and they follow it with so much fidelity, that curable ailments become fatal ones, under the hand of the practitioner. Such are the abuses of theory divorced from practice, and of practice divorced from theory.

Our doctrine then is, that all plans for reform and improvement which appear to the eye of reason to be safe and useful, or which have been successfully tried elsewhere, are entitled to a fair trial among ourselves; and if they be found to pass this ordeal successfully, they should be adopted. In so difficult and delicate a work as education, we would introduce no new measure until it is commended by reason, nor consider it as established, until actual trial has proved its usefulness. Our creed condemns the credulity that blindly adopts, as much as it does the arrogance or the stupidity that blindly rejects. And we would go one step further, and say, that while we advocate progress, not only as the destiny but as the blessing of the race, we also hold that in all innovations, or tentative processes, it is better to be too cautious than too courageous. Like a careful engineer upon a railroad, we would slacken speed when rounding a curve.

Still the great idea perpetually recurs, and it cannot be barred out of any rational mind, that the whole history of human advancement and civilization is nothing but a history of innovations upon the then existing state of practice and belief; and yet there has always been a party clamorous and strenuous to hang up their opaque screen before the vision of the seers, to exclude the coming light.

But this blind resistance to improvement contradicts the noblest instincts of the race. It tends to beget its opposite. The fanaticism of reform is only the raging of the accumulated waters caused by the obstructions which an ultra conservatism has thrown across the stream of improvement; and revolution itself is but the sudden overwhelming and sweeping away of the impediments to progress, that should have been seasonably removed. The French Revolution was a frightful spectacle of a too rapid effort at reform. The present condition of Ireland is a spectacle still more frightful, of an inflexible conservatism. Progress is the beneficent law of the race. We cannot be circumscribed within the range of our fathers' ideas, any more than we can use their old implements. The manhood of the race cannot be confined within the swaddling-bands of its infancy.

In the end, too, we may add, the party of Progress is sure to triumph. More or less rapidly, the new opinion supplants the old. Conservative age dies; hopeful youth succeeds to its powers. Not only so, but youth always out-numbers age; for the ranks of life become thinner at every stage of its march. The law of advancement is just as certain as that men wish to better their condition. The highest interests of individuals and of communities can consist in nothing but in their embracing more and more truth in their belief, and more and more wisdom in their practice. Hence whenever sufficiently enlightened on any subject to see their own deficiencies, and to devise means for supplying them, the intelligence of men will adopt what ignorance and prejudice had before discarded.

MIND AND BODY, THE FREE MAN AND THE SLAVE.

It was not the design of Providence that the work of the world should be performed by muscular strength. God has filled the earth and imbued the elements with energies of greater power than all the inhabitants of a thousand planets like ours. Whence come our necessaries and our luxuries,—those comforts and appliances that make the difference between a houseless wandering tribe of Indians in the far West, and a New England village? They do not come wholly or principally from the original, unassisted strength of the human arm, but from the employment, through intelligence and skill, of those great natural forces with which the bountiful Creator has filled every part of the material Universe. Caloric, gravitation, expansibility, compressibility, electricity, chemical affinities and repulsions, spontaneous velocities,—these are the mighty agents which the intellect of man harnesses to the car of improvement. The application of water and wind and stream to the propulsion of machinery, and to the transportation of men and merchandise from place to place, has added ten thousand fold to the actual products of human industry. How small the wheel which the stoutest laborer can turn, and how soon will he be weary. Compare this with a wheel driving a thousand spindles or looms, which a stream of water can turn, and never tire. A locomotive will take five hundred men, and bear them on their journey hundreds of miles in a day. Look at these same five hundred men, starting from the same point, and attempting the same distance, with all the pedestrian's or the equestrian's toil and tardiness. The cotton mills of Massachusetts will turn out more cloth in one day than could have been manufactured by all the inhabitants of the Eastern continent during the tenth century. On an element which in ancient times was supposed to be exclusively within the control of the gods, and where it was deemed impious for human power to intrude, even there the gigantic forces of nature, which human science and skill have enlisted in their service, confront and overcome the raging of the elements,—breasting tempests and tides, escaping reefs and lee-shores, and careering triumphant around the globe. The velocity of winds, the weight of waters, and the rage of steam, are powers, each one of which is infinitely stronger than all the strength of all the nations and races of mankind, were it all gathered into a single arm. And all these energies are given us on one condition,—the condition of intelligence,—that is, of education.

Had God intended that the work of the world should be done by human bones and sinews, He would have given us an arm as solid and strong as the shaft of a steam engine; and enabled us to stand, day and night, and turn the crank of a steamship while sailing to Liverpool or Calcutta. Had God designed the human muscles to do the work of the world, then, instead of the ingredients of gunpowder or gun cotton, and the expansive force of heat, he would have given us hands which could take a granite quarry and break its solid acres into suitable and symmetrical blocks, as easily as we now open an orange. Had He intended us for bearing burdens, He would have given us Atlantean shoulders, by which we could carry the vast freights of rail-car and steamship, as a porter carries his pack. He would have given us lungs by which we could blow fleets before us; and wings to sweep over ocean wastes. But instead of iron arms, and Atlantean shoulders, and the lungs of Boreas, He has given us a mind, a soul, a capacity of acquiring knowledge, and thus of appropriating all these energies of nature to our own use. Instead of a telescopic and microscopic eye, He has given us power to invent the telescope and the microscope. Instead of ten thousand fingers, He has given us genius inventive of the power loom and the printing press. Without a cultivated intellect, man is among the weakest of all the dynamical forces of nature; with a cultivated intellect, he commands them all.

And now, what does the slave-maker do? He abolishes this mighty power of the intellect, and uses only the weak, degraded, half animated forces of the human limbs. A thousand slaves may stand by a river, and to them it is only an object of fear or of superstition. An intelligent man surpasses the ancient idea of a river-god; he stands by the Penobscot, the Kennebec, the Merrimack, or the Connecticut; he commands each to do more work than could be performed by a hundred thousand men,—to saw timber, to make cloth, to grind corn,—and they obey. Ignorant slaves stand upon a coal mine, and to them it is only a worthless part of the inanimate earth. An intelligent man uses the same mine to print a million books. Slaves will seek to obtain the same crop from the same field, year after year, though the *pabulum* of that crop is exhausted; the intelligent man, with his chemist's eye, sees not only the minutest atoms of the earth, but the imponderable gases that permeate it, and he is rewarded with a luxuriant harvest.

Nor are these advantages confined to those departments of nature where her mightiest forces are brought into requisition. In accomplishing whatever requires delicacy and precision, nature is as much more perfect than man, as she is more powerful in whatever requires strength. Whether in great or in small operations, all the improvements in the mechanical and the useful arts come as directly from intelligence, as a bird comes out of a shell, or the beautiful colors of a flower out of sunshine. The slave-worker is forever prying at the short end of Nature's lever; and using the back, instead of the edge, of her finest instruments.

The most abundant proof exists, derived from all departments of human industry, that uneducated labor is comparatively unprofitable labor. I have before me the statements of a number of the most intelligent gentlemen in Massachusetts, affirming this fact as the result of an experience extending over many years. In Massachusetts we have no native-born child wholly without school instruction; but the degrees of attainment, of mental development, are various. Half a dozen years ago, the Massachusetts Board of Education obtained statements from large numbers of our master manufacturers, authenticated from the books of their respective establishments, and covering a series of years; the result of which was, that increased wages were found in connection with increased intelligence, just as certainly as increased heat raises the mercury in the thermometer. Foreigners, and those coming from the other States who made their marks when they receipted their bills, earned the least; these who had a moderate or limited education, occupied a middle ground on the pay-roll; while the intelligent young women who worked in the mills in winter, and taught schools in summer, crowned the list. The larger capital in the form of intelligence, yielded the larger interest in the form of wages. This inquiry was not confined to manufactures, but was extended to other departments of business, where the results of labor could be made the subject of exact measurement.

This is universally so. The mechanic sees it when he compares the work of a stupid with that of an awakened mind. The traveller sees it, when he passes from an educated into an uneducated nation. There are countries in Europe, lying side by side, where, without compass or chart, without bound or landmark, I could run the line of demarcation between the two, by the broad, legible characters which ignorance has written on roads, fields, houses, and the persons of men, women, and children on one side, and which knowledge has inscribed on the other.

STUDYING INSECTS AND STUDYING CHILDREN.

The importance of any man's work is to be determined by the value of the materials on which he works. Judged by this standard, let us compare the calling of the teacher with some of the other avocations or professions among men.

To ascertain the infinite difference which exists between different created substances, we must classify and compare them. First, there is the unorganized and insentient. Rising in the scale, we come to the organized and animate, but unconscious. Higher still, we find the conscious, but irrational and ephemeral. Last, and unsurpassable, there is the animate, sentient, conscious, rational and immortal.

Of the first class, pleasure and pain cannot be affirmed. The quantity of most organized insentient substances is so great, as hardly to admit the idea of addition or diminution, of gain or loss. All the chemists who have ever lived, or who ever will live might try their experiments upon water, and they could not use up the ocean, or a single river that flows into it. All agriculturalists might experiment upon soils, and they could not consume the land; all masons or mineralogists, and they could not exhaust the deposit in the granite-ribbed mountains and hills. Gold, precious stones, pearls, crystals, diamonds, are rarer, and the pride and taste of mankind have given them an artificial or constructive value; and though all these substances are incapable of feeling, yet it is held to be only a dictate of common sense, to demand some more skill in the lapidary than in the macadamizer; in him who burnishes and chases gold than in the paver of streets. But the moment we cross the line which divides unorganized from organized substances, we know by the new agencies which we discover at work around us, that we have entered a higher sphere. Here, each act of ours not only produces its own effect, but it sets other forces at work also. We may take a drop of water, and freeze, or boil, or evaporate it, or analyze it into gases, and we have not changed its elements at all. We have not altered the nature of its ingredients. There remains still just as much oxygen and hydrogen as before. It is still a part of the earth, and annihilation has not come near it. But if we take a nut or seed of tree or vegetable, and seethe, or pulverize, or macerate it, or subtilize it over a fire, its principle of life is extinguished forever. Though the chemical elements remain, it is transferred from the organic and animate to the inorganic and lifeless class of substances. So, if the seed be allowed to germinate, and, either through carelessness or ignorance, we wound the germ or shoot, it will bear the scar through all its days; and even if the vital parts should grow over and conceal the wound, there will still be a spot of unsoundness within, through which disease may make a successful attack upon it, or through whose weakness the tempest may prove too strong. Hence the unconcern with which the delver leaves his trench, or the street paver his rubble-stone, compared with the circumspection and anxiety, with which the gardener or florist watches his young plants and flowers. All these must be guarded from frost, from violence, from insects, from drought, from disease, lest a single night's remissness, or even lest some act done to them in kindness, should destroy all hope of the bloom, fragrance and nutriment they were made capable of yielding. A single stroke inflicted upon a young germ, by a rude or a heedless hand, may destroy forever the honeyed flower in which the humming-bird might have revelled; or the towering oak in which the eagle might have brooded its young.

But from the bounteousness of the All-good, a higher form of life may be superadded to mere organic existence. There may be sentient life,—life capable of pain and pleasure; life instinct with fear and hope. Touch not heedlessly the nerves that tingle with pain or thrill with joy. Deal gently with the heart that palpitates with delight or throbs with agony. The animal, however low, ranks above the vegetable, however high. Not in the vast forests that belt the mountains, or cover half a continent with shade; not in all the luxuriant grasses that overspread pampas and prairies; not in all the flowers of hill-side or river margin, where the lost rainbows are found; not in all this profusion and magnificence, has the Deity so richly displayed His goodness and His power, as in the creation of the tiniest insect that opens its joyous eye to the light, that finds its paradise in a sunbeam, that glows with affection for its mate, that burns with love for its offspring. The one is matter, grand and beautiful, but dead. The other is animated by a conscious spark from the sun-source of life. And how extensive and persevering the investigations bestowed upon lower forms of animated existence! What profound sciences have been built upon their structure and habits,—the sciences that treat of insects, of reptiles, of fishes, of birds, of quadrupeds. The learned in these sciences win renown, are crowned with honors, leave celebrated names for the admiration of posterity. Yet the life which the naturalist observes is ephemeral. Insect, reptile, fish, bird, quadruped, live, each within the narrowest range of relations. They are not inwrapt in the all-comprehending bonds of country and of kind. Though their races and their tribes may date back myriads of ages before our race began; yet, for the better guidance of their life, they have no necessity for groping backwards in antiquarian or antediluvian researches. They are guided, at least mainly, by instincts; and instincts are the practical deductions of infinite reason, transferred, ready made and perfect, to creatures which we call irrational. To them, instinct is a perpetual revelation which needs neither rabbi, nor priest, nor commentator to explain it, and, therefore, it is never mystified or darkened by imposture or ignorance. Their natures are so slowly progressive, if progressive at all, that education can rarely raise them from the sphere in which they were born, or the want of education depress them below it. Of all the lower orders of animals, there is not one that depends upon the domestication and training of other animals for its own use; not one which, like man, can construct a machine so many thousand times more powerful than itself, not one that can conceive of a past eternity to be explored, or foresee a future one to be provided for. Their progeny do not depend for happiness upon transmitted wisdom, nor for knowledge upon transmitted lore. They gleam out from darkness, sparkle for a moment, and then vanish,—lustrous particles of the spray thrown up by the eternal rolling of the great ocean of life.

But compared with all these, who shall undertake to estimate the value of that race of beings who have been created in the image of God; whose capabilities of happiness, eye hath not seen, nor ear heard, neither hath it entered into the heart of man to conceive; whose susceptibilities of misery are countless in number and unlimited in degree,—disease, fear, bereavement, madness, remorse, despair, perdition;—whose relations on earth are so comprehensive and indissoluble, that the fate of millions, both of contemporaries and of posterity, is often determined by the will of one man; and whose existence is as eternal as that of the Being who created them; an existence, too, necessitated, by an inward and organic law, to move forward, in some direction, forever,—not in a circular line, but in a spiral one,—forever ascending to loftier heights of blessedness, or descending to lower depths of misery; and, to crown all, whose influence upon others, whether for good or for evil, accumulating and redoubling forever and ever, depends more upon the education it receives than upon all things else! When we come to this class of beings, in its infancy so yielding and impressible, in its manhood so impassive and resistant, and in its futurity so imperishable and priceless; by what standard shall we measure the value of each influence that affects it; where are the golden balances that can weigh it; where the strong-voiced archangel that can utter it!

And yet we affirm, there is not one of the subordinate departments of nature, whether the conscious but irrational, the organic but unconscious, or even the inorganic and insensate, for whose study and mastership greater emoluments are not paid, more social consideration awarded, and a higher grade of dignity universally conceded, than to that Art of Arts and Science of Sciences, by which the youthful mind is fashioned and trained for life and for futurity. Our colleges have professorships for teaching all the sciences that relate to animals, to metals and to minerals, but no professorship for expounding the science of education. All Christendom cannot show a school where the plants of immortal growth are as carefully tended, where the times and seasons for supplying nourishment and protection are as heedfully observed, where weeds and noxious influences are as industriously extirpated, as from those botanical gardens where no conscious life exists. Would that there were, somewhere upon the earth, one conservatory of children, as interesting to the possessors of wealth and the lovers of beauty, as a conservatory of flowers.

Scientific men devote themselves to studying the instincts and habits of the winged tribes. When will they deem it as honorable to devote themselves to the education of a race of beings, who will soon unfold a wing by which they will sweep through the upper or the nether worlds? To show how much more precious is a bug than a child, let us advert to a fact which has recently happened within the knowledge of the whole scientific community. Doubtless our readers generally know, that an entomological survey of the State of New York was made a few years ago by order of its Legislature. Whether represented at the seat of government or not, a law provided that all the tribes of insects should be recorded; and they were recorded as carefully as the twelve tribes of Israel. But it sometimes happened that the scientific insect-commissioner, in turning up a stone, or stripping a piece of bark from a decayed tree, or examining a weasel's back, found a living polypod, which he did not know whether to class with fleas, in the order *Suctoria*, or with mosquitoes in the order *Diptera*, or in some other. In all such trying emergencies, it is said that the insect was carefully "done up in lavender," incased in a box, sent several hundred miles to an officer in one of our colleges, to have its legs scientifically counted, its mandibles and bronchiæ examined, its capability or incapability of metamorphosis determined, and its name, its species, and its order ascertained; and then to be returned, as carefully as were the remains of Napoleon from St. Helena; and, at last, to be *pinned up*, in a cabinet immortality, at the capitol of the state. For examining these specimens, naming them, and assigning them a place among their kindred, it is said that a dollar was paid for each decision,—not by the bug, but by the State of New York.

But in the mean time, what measures are taken, what eminent professional talent is employed, what generous emoluments are bestowed, for investigating and expounding the laws of growth and influence, by which thousands of children are developed into the order *Beezlebub;* into the genus *atheist or bigot*; and into the species, *drunkard, thief, robber, murderer, lyncher.* In our streets, in our bar-rooms, at some of our firesides, and in some of our schools, there are metamorphoses going on every day, by which innocent and guileless children are turned into Ishmaelites, and Cains, and Judases. Is gnat, or grub, or larva, worth more than a human soul? Are bugs the principals, and sons and daughters incidents? Shall the resources of science be exhausted upon the former, while chance and accident, darkness and chaos, reign over the latter? And yet, throughout the scientific world, does not Ehrenberg stand higher than Fellenberg; and while, in the great wars of Europe, the merest bloodhound courage made its possessors the envy of mankind, was not Pestalozzi repaid with poverty, and persecution, and obloquy, for all his knowledge, and his devotion, and his divine spirit of love?

Would it then, be any mistake; would it be a degradation of talent from noble to ignoble uses, to employ some of the mighty minds that adorn the profession of law, or some of the men who fill the chairs of our colleges, or are gathered among statesmen at the capitol of the nation, to invest the laws and devise the means by which mankind can be saved from poverty and wretchedness and crime, and made inheritors of the blessings which God bestows upon all who love and obey Him?

LET TEACHERS MAKE CAPITAL OUT OF DIFFICULT CASES.

Every man who has overcome a difficulty feels an honest satisfaction in his success; and the greater the difficulty overcome, the greater is the satisfaction felt. It requires but little strength to run down hill, and but little skill to sail down stream; but to scale the precipice, or to breast and overcome the impetuous current, requires vigor, skill and daring. Why should not teachers, like men engaged in other avocations, be inspired with a laudable ambition to triumph over obstacles. Abstract the occupation of teaching from its spiritual and moral relations; cut if off, for a moment, from its eternal consequences; discard, on the one hand, the ideas of health, competence, respectability and renown; and, on the other, those of poverty, superstition and remorse; of ruined, disgraced, agonized families; of innocent children, blasted in all their worldly fortunes and happiness by parental crimes and parental infamy,—set aside, we say, all these and kindred considerations, and let teachers look at the labors that are before them, as though they belonged to the natural sciences only, and were to be determined by sagacious and well conducted experiment, and the results to be obtained by philosophical induction; and then let teachers see if there be not the most powerful motives stimulating them to fidelity and perseverance.

We will try to illustrate our meaning. It is the expectation, as everybody knows, of young medical students, after having read diligently for a year or two, to be allowed to visit patients in company with their masters. It is considered a privilege to be permitted to attend the head physician of a general hospital, and hear clinical lectures. Here the young aspirants nourish a thirst for personal practice. They feel like the boy Ascanius, when he went out with his father to hunt:

"Optat aprum aut fulvum descendere monte leonem."

He longs for a wild boar, or a young lion, to rush down from the mountain and dare the terrors of his spear. So the young medical student longs for a case, whose difficulty shall proclaim his skill.

And who has ever been thrown amongst this class of young men, towards the close of their professional studies, or has mingled with young practitioners, while the M.D. at the end of their names was as fresh and bright as their newly-painted signs, has not witnessed the exultation and transport with which they describe their early cases, and the *secundem artem* treatment given to them. Oh, says one, what a beautiful case of fever I had last week. And I, says another, had the grandest hemorrhage. And I, says a third, had a god-send in the shape of a good case of croup. Fifteen minutes more and the child would have been dead. I'm established in that family, and there is a houseful of children. And so the lucky ones recount their exploits. Many years ago, we knew a young student, ambitious both of usefulness and fame, who went to Paris to complete his medical education. When he returned, among many other new and valuable things which he brought home was a stomach-pump. It so happened, that, within a few days after, a rich old man in the vicinity utterly lost the power of deglutition, and so was in danger of starvation while surrounded with abundance. The young doctor heard of the patient and hastened to his succor. He prepared a potation in the shape of some nice chicken-broth, and then applied the instrument; and as the old man felt the savory beverage flowing down his stiffened throat, and sweetly gliding around the epigastric region, and warming it into long-forgotten sensations, he rubbed his hands and pressed them against his hollow sides, and exclaimed, "Oh, this is life." The heart of the young doctor echoed back,—Oh, it is life to me as well as to you; for he felt it as warm and genial in his empty pocket as the patient did in his empty stomach.

With such zest and glow does the mere fledgling of a physician hail his good fortune in getting a difficult case, and his good judgment or his good luck in treating it. He does not abandon his patient because his case is one of extreme difficulty, and run to the health office, or to the academy of medicine, to enter a complaint against nature for contravening the laws of health, and thus subjecting him to labor of body and anxiety of mind. He does not fly into a rage and break his vials and gallipots, or put himself upon his dignity and stand aloof. He rejoices rather, in the desperateness of the malady, because it opens the way to more brilliant success. He rejoices at an opportunity to expend his skill on the meanest thing in human shape. If he can acquire money or fame by it, or test some ingenious speculation of his own, he will sit up all night by a loathsome bedside, in a foul room, until the disease of his patient has passed its crisis. And why is this? It is because he believes there are such things as an art and a science of healing, and that he, by deep study and meditation, can master them, and can show the world the difference between a doctor and a quack.

And why should not all teachers cherish a feeling akin to this, in regard to the toughest cases of stupidity and incorrigibleness that come under their care? We would not have them rejoice at the existence of weakness or wickedness; but where weakness and wickedness does exist, we would have them rejoice that it is their good fortune to have an opportunity to substitute strength for the weakness, and turn the vice into virtue. A physician exhibits not the slightest twinkle of pride, in regard to a whole town or city of healthy men and women, to whom he has never administered pill or potion; and whose good health, therefore, does not redound to his credit. But let him meet a man whom his art has saved from the grave; or, as it were, has exhumed after he was buried; and then he exults in the power and beneficence of his skill. He takes no pleasure in expelling a sick man from the hospital, but only in expelling sickness from the man. So teachers should aim not to expel a vicious boy from the school, but vice from the boy. Their ambition, the covetable points of honor and distinction with them should be, to bring forward the lagging and to reform the mischievous, to teach humility to the proud, and benevolence to the cruel, and the love of duty to the sinful.

So too, teachers should welcome improvements, from whatever quarter they may come. There is no surer proof of a narrow and contemptible mind, than to reject an improvement because of its origin. What would have been thought, in the case above stated, if the Medical College had come together and denounced the stomach-pump because it came from a monarchical government?

Who that has ever been acquainted with that class of public officers, whose duty it is to prosecute offenders under the criminal laws of the State, has not, scores of times, been a voluntary or an involuntary listener to their professional rehearsals and triumphs? In the early part of our professional life, as a lawyer, we were well acquainted with an eminent man, who had served the State for more than twenty years as a prosecuting officer. He was a grand recruiting sergeant for jails and state prison camps. At whatever court he stopped, thence proceeded the felon files to tenant prison cells. And with what elation of spirit would that old man spend a long winter evening, in recounting his triumphs over notable offenders, and his feats of intellectual gladiatorship with the eminent counsel who defended them. Here he would "fight his battles o'er again." He would dwell with fond minuteness upon every curious incident; tell how he disapproved an *alibi*, by proving an *alibi* of the witness himself; how he unquibbled the legal quibbles of the advocates, outwitted wit, and circumvented circumvention; until, by various, learned, astute and frustratory plans, he obtained a verdict of guilty from the jury, and a sentence from the court. Nay, if one would but attend a gathering composed of the lowest order of constables and police officers, he would hear them boasting of captured rogues and retaken plunder. It is well known that this class of officers, by study and practice, become keener than hounds in scenting, and sharper than eagles in seeing their prey. They learn the rogue's language; they study rogues' books,—Vidocq and others,—that they may know how to entrap them. They hold themselves ready, at a moment's warning, for the most hazardous expeditions. They make forced journeys, drive through drenching rains or drifting snows, send forward intelligence by lightning, and pursue it by steam, until at last they seize the culprit, recapture the spoils, and bring the rogue back to justice.

But the work of the teacher, though in some respects similar to this, is infinitely a nobler one. He is to pursue an evil disposition through all its moral labyrinths, just as a police officer ferrets out a culprit from his hiding-place. He is to unmask the falsehood of the heart in all its disguises of suppression, equivocation or deception. He is to cleanse the tongue from the filth of profanity and obscenity. He is to expose the inward beggarliness of ridiculing a poor child for his outward poverty. He is to show how base a thing is the pride of intellect, and the emulation that nourishes it. He is to make children perceive and feel, how much more noble is forgiveness than retaliation; and that, so far as the kingdom of heaven ever comes upon earth, the most honorable office in it will be that which best promotes the welfare of mankind. To accomplish these sacred purposes, cannot the teacher, like a prosecuting attorney, or a policeman, exhaust the knowledge of all professional books, learn new languages, watch his pupils in the streets as with the eyes of Argus, follow them to their pestiferous homes, court hardships by day and vigils

by night, so that, at length, he may bring back to the fold of the
Savior every lamb that has been intrusted to his care,—not having
lost one among the mountains, nor suffered one to be devoured by
wild beasts.

Let teachers, then, be inspired and not discouraged by the difficulties of their work. Whatever increases the difficulty to be overcome,
heightens the glory that overcomes it.

EDITOR'S FAREWELL.

The present Number closes the Tenth Volume of the Common School
Journal; and the Tenth Volume of the Journal closes the series.

The Editor had hoped that his leave-taking with his readers and
friends would be, on his part, a more extended interview than he is
now able to make it. He had hoped and intended to occupy the
present Number of the Journal with one heart-emanating, if not
heart-reaching appeal, addressed to all persons connected with the
cause of education, and designed not merely to stir up their minds
"by way of remembrance," but by way of anticipation also. But such
encroachments have recently been made upon his time, by calls that
seemed to forbid denial, that he has been obliged, first to postpone,
and then to renounce this cherished purpose. A few fragments of
hours, snatched from public engagements, or from repose, are all that
have been allowed him; and these he has occupied by throwing together
the fragmentary thoughts with which the present Number is filled.

A formal review of the history and purpose of the Journal seems
unnecessary. It came to the public, rather as their fate, than as
a consequence of their free-will. It was born, not because it was *wanted*,
but because it was *needed*. If it has been its happy fortune to carry
light where there was only darkness or twilight before; if it has, in
any case, sustained the spirit of the toiler sinking under his toil; if it
has tended, not only to kindle hopes, but to reveal some gleams of a
brighter future, for those who were desponding or despairing before;
if it has performed the office of a pioneer, plunging fearlessly into
wildernesses, driving out wild beasts and birds of evil omen, and
smoothing rough places into highways, so that civilization and happiness might eventually follow in its train;—if, in fine, the good which it
has done bears any assignable proportion to the desire of usefulness with which it has been conducted, then the Editor will not have
transferred his strength and his health into the pages in vain.

Though the Journal is but ten years old, yet compared with any other journal devoted to the cause of education in this country, its age is patriarchal. One,—the Albany "District School Journal," which was established about two years after this, having been nourished by the bounty of the State, still survives. But numerous others, subsequently commenced, have been sad remembrancers of the brevity of life. Some have died as soon as born, because they had no life, no vital organs within them; but others, and the far greater number, have perished from the bleak atmosphere,—the coldness, the congelation, into which they were born. May the survivors long live to earn the highest of all rewards,—the reward of well-doing;— and may their last days be their best days.

Our motto used to be, "The cause of education, the first of all causes." Recent events, however, of a national character, have forced upon the public attention the great truth, that before a man can be educated, he must be a free man. It is in obedience to this truth, that the Editor of the Journal now leaves the immediate field of education, to assist in securing, as far as one vote among two hundred and thirty votes, in one department of the national councils can do it, the FREEDOM OF MAN, in regions yet unoccupied by civilized races; so that the vast territories which are now roamed over by savage hordes may rise from barbarian life into civilization, instead of sinking, in this nineteenth century of the Christian era, from the depth of barbarism into the abyss of slavery.

It is no alienation, therefore, from the cause of education, but only to secure a sphere where education may "run and be glorified," that occasions this apparent departure from his long-loved field of labor. Than these causes, what can be nobler? For these causes who would not be willing to fall, though he should fall like Arnold of Winkelried, at the battle of Sempach,—his body "a sheaf of spears?"

With comprehensiveness of meaning that embraces both worlds, we wish our readers and friends, FAREWELL.

4.

The Higher Education

RESPONSIBILITY OF LEADERSHIP.

With the change in the organic structure of our government there should have been corresponding changes in all public measures, and institutions. About the expediency, and especially about the extent of that change, a wide difference of opinion prevailed. But the change being made, was it not the duty of its opponents to yield to the inevitable course of events, and to prepare for coming exigencies? And could not every really noble soul find an ample compensation for the loss of personal influence or family distinction, in the greater dignity and elevation of his fellow-beings? From whom should instruction come, if not from the most educated? Where should generosity towards the poor begin, if not with those whom Providence had blessed with abundance? Whence should magninimity proceed, if not from minds expanded by culture?

RESPONSIBILITIES.

An ignorant and degraded portion of society are to the intelligent what children are to parents; so, as parents are mainly responsible for the misconduct of their children, the intelligent are mainly responsible for the vices of the abandoned.

ANTIOCH COLLEGE: BACCALAUREATE ADDRESS
of 1857

Mann's Inaugural Address at Antioch College, delivered in 1853, was esteemed as a contemporary masterpiece, and, lengthy as it is, it repays study. It covered a multitude of subjects, offering a grand synthesis of Man as a physical, intellectual, and moral being. Though doubtless obsolete in details, the Address defines the problem of a college's function in timeless fashion. Mann's view of education as involving the whole *person denies the view that it ought to cater to and encourage specialist demands. The following address found Mann deep in the problems of practical college administration.*

THIS will be a memorable day in your recollections and in mine, and in those of all the friends of Antioch College. It is the first "Commencement Day" of our Institution. Four years ago, this College opened with no Undergraduate Class higher than the Freshman, and some of you were those Freshmen. To-day, therefore, finishes your academic career, and ushers you into that ampler sphere of honor and duty we call the "World." Hence to you, this must be a day full of tender recollections; full of inspiring anticipations. The great past and the greater future are struggling for mastery in your bosoms, and are heaving them with contending emotions. Even now, I imagine that you hear the trumpet of the battle of life sounding in your ears, and the voice of destiny summoning you to deeds of honor and usefulness, such as will make your *Alma Mater,*—your Nursing Mother,—rejoice to call you her FIRST-BORN.

In conferring upon a graduating class the honors of a College Degree, and in certifying that fact by the testimonial of a College Diploma, it is a well-established custom that the person standing in my place should make an Address to those standing in yours. In addition to this, I have been specially requested by you to comply with this time-honored usage. As you have so long and so faithfully complied with my requests, I do not feel at liberty to disregard yours.

On an occasion like the present,—which, in the history of any Institution, can never happen but once,—I feel called upon to discuss what seems to me the most important relation which can exist between a College and the Public. It is this:

What, in point of Moral Conduct and Character, has the public,—the community at large,—a right to expect from College Graduates?

Or, in different terms though identical in substance, What has the public, or community at large, a right to expect of College Faculties in regard to the Moral Conduct and Character of those upon whom they bestow the dignities and prerogatives of an Academic Degree?

In this question, it is plain to be seen that our conduct as a Faculty, and your supposed character as *Alumni* of this College, are involved.

What the *literary* and *scientific* character of graduates ought to be has been abundantly discussed. The present topic involves considerations of a far higher order.

A Diploma is a letter of credit addressed, not to an individual, but to the world. It purports to say, and it does, virtually if not expressly, say that its bearer has enjoyed superior advantages, and therefore that he is qualified to perform duties and to fill places of honor and trust, in some good degree proportionate to the advantages he has enjoyed. Hence it is plainly a certificate of educational pre-eminence. It seems to me equally clear, that it also imports good moral conduct and high moral character. Any interpretation that would allow a College Faculty to give this letter of credit to one profligate member of a class of *fifty,* would allow them to give it to *fifty* profligate members,—that is, to a whole class of profligates. If, by universal consent, the Diploma is *prima facie* evidence of the bearer's superior attainments,—liable of course to be rebutted by self-displays of ignorance,—then there is still stronger reason why it should be presumptive evidence of good habits, of sobriety and exemplariness of life. This should be so because the evils of vice are infinitely greater than the evils of ignorance. The plague of Egyptian darkness was bad enough, but the plague of the frogs and the lice and the murrain and the blood and the pestilence was a thousand times worse. Ignorance is a feeble accomplice or coadjutor with vice, in tormenting the world. They make a partnership, which, as the enemy of mankind, is comparatively powerless and contemptible. But an alliance between knowledge and vice dazzles, intoxicates, overwhelms with a Red Sea of ruin. When ignorance and vice league together, their most conspicuous products are —ridiculousness and nonsense. When talent and vice confederate, they lead a third part of the stars of heaven after them to perdition. If we must have the monkey's mischief, it is fortunate that he has only a monkey's brains with which to invent it. The martial spirit of a tiger is bad enough,—for, after man, I suppose the tiger to be the greatest military character in all zoölogy,—but if we must have the tiger's military proclivities, for God's sake, let us not have Napoleon's intellect to direct them. A College had a thousand times better indorse a score of dunces as learned than one villain as trustworthy. It is sufficiently calamitous to have a crawling, snail-paced reptile in the shape of man;—one who, though venomous, is incapable of scattering his venom wide and far; but to give the wings of Education to such a monster and turn him into a Flying Dragon, and accredit him to go over the earth and make ruin common,—this would seem to be the appropriate function of Pandemonium and the Underworld, but not of Colleges.

Is it not plain, then, that an official responsibility attaches to the Faculties of Colleges for the moral character of those on whom they confer the honors of a degree? It may, perhaps, show a very charitable and forgiving spirit towards a villain who has paid all his College bills, to give him a Diploma; but is it charitable towards the future victims of his villany, whose confidence may be won through the persuasiveness of that very recommendation? In pecuniary matters, the laws of the land provide that whoever volunteers to become sponsor of another's moneyed credit beforehand, shall be responsible for his payments afterwards. A recommendation of solvency is held to be a warranty for it. It obliges its author to make good whatever losses are fairly chargeable to the credit it obtained. It is an antecedent suretyship or guaranty, and the commerce of the world would be greatly restricted, the enterprise of upright and intelligent young men would be grievously crippled, were the indorsers of pecuniary ability to be absolved from pecuniary liability. But why should the precious and enduring interests of morality be estimated at a less value or protected by less stringent guaranties than the commodities of the market-place? If a seller who has been defrauded by an accredited purchaser may legally reimburse himself from the indorser's pockets, why should the character of a College Faculty escape rebuke, when a family or a community has its peace or its happiness invaded by one who bears a Diploma of honorable graduation fresh from its hands? If a pecuniary mulct punishes the one, why not a general outcry of condemnation the other?

It is a momentous fact that the Faculties of the Colleges in this country are stationed at the door of the three learned professions, and at the entrance, indeed, of all the great avenues to posts of honor

and emolument which life offers to men. They are therefore bound
to see that no one crosses the threshold of their sanctuary to enter
any of these walks of profit and renown who is addicted to low
and mean associations, or branded with the stigma of any flagrant
vice or misconduct; and those are the enemies of mankind,—not of
contemporaries only but of posterity,—who, because of parentage, or
wealth, or private friendship, or any other sinister motive whatever,
place the official seal of their approval upon dissolute, or profligate,
or intemperate characters. The Superintendent of the Mint dares not
send out a single piece of base coin stamped with the image and superscription of the government; for he well knows that his forgery of
a dime would cost him his official head. How, then, can a College
Faculty give currency to spurious characters without incurring common reprobation? How pollute their seal of honor by using it to
stamp impurity with the emblems of virtue? How pour the chrism
of education upon the head of full-blown depravity?

The thesis, then, which I submit is this: A vicious young man
is unworthy the prerogatives of a College education and the honors
of a College diploma. With my consent, he never shall have them.
Whenever or wherever brought into the relation of College teacher
to such a young man, I will provoke a divine and fatal quarrel with
him;—divine in its moral origin, fatal to his hopes of graduation.
Would any one dispute the soundness of this doctrine in regard to an
abandoned young woman? Why then, in regard to an abandoned
young man whose scope and power of harm-doing is so much greater?
As education, aye, even the reputation of an education, is a passport
to influential stations in society, not even that reputation should be
bestowed upon a vicious object. Let no association of ideas derived
from a man's literary or local antecedents give him facilities for gaining admission into circles he otherwise might never debase, or add
weight to an evil example, without whose influence he otherwise might
never beguile.

A College is a place where character is developed with fearful
rapidity. Seeds which might never, or not for years, have germinated at
home, spring into sudden vitality and shoot up with amazing luxuriance when brought within the actinic influence of numbers and of
institutional excitements. This explains why a College government
has a far more arduous task with each of its numerous pupils than
a parent with each of his small number of children. And hence, not

merely the expediency but the necessity for stronger antidotes and curatives than would suffice for domestic government.

In an humble condition, a young man may have principle or prudence enough to restrain him within the paths of rectitude. But if he desires to qualify himself for wider fields of honorable activity, and therefore seeks to master the literature that makes a scholar, and the science that makes a philosopher, and the laws and histories and economies that make a statesman, and if he thereby emerges from that humble sphere where the temptations are few and the ordinary supports of rectitude sufficient, and ascends into the region of great passions and great ambitions, where Fame waves her glittering prizes before his eyes, and Pride and Hope thrill him with their magnificent promises, and even a dim phantom of Failure stings him to madness; then, if he has not Moral Principle for his pole-star, if he is not inwardly sworn to an obedience to all the Divine Laws, he is a man predestined to perdition. Fate has already prepared her revenges for him. He falls like Lucifer son of the morning, and every beholder mourns that loftiness of his ascent whence sinful gravitations only plunge him into a deeper gulf of infamy. When, therefore, a youth first goes to College from the quiet circle and narrow horizon of home, and enters upon scenes beset with thick temptations,—where bodily appetites may find illicit indulgence and the soul's perversities may prompt to unhallowed speculations; where the rights of thought are in danger of being practically translated into the rights of passion, and the corollaries drawn from Free-agency shall be Free-license;— then, oh! how much he needs, and happy, thrice happy if he finds some ever-wakeful guardian and counsellor who can outbalance his present seducements to ruin by his yearnings after future honor and usefulness, and who, when the tempting Satans stand by his side, can teach him to wield the sword of Michael for their smiting.

Hence it is the duty of every teacher to explain to the pupils under his care,—just as far and as fast as they are able to understand him,—the universally acknowledged plan on which a human being is constructed. Man was made to be good;—if good to be happy, if not good to be miserable,—just as much as a swan's feet were made for swimming or a lark's wings for soaring. Every man has an animal nature, a lower tier of endowments, adapted to subordinate uses and gratifications. But all gratifications of this class are limited in their extent and short in their duration, and the universal law by which they are governed is that over-indulgence produces under-enjoyment. As we rise to the second order of faculties,—the intellectual,—the circuit or amplitude of gratifications is enlarged, their duration is prolonged, and the exquisiteness of enjoyment is enhanced. But it is only when a man becomes conscious of his divine capabilities; it is only when his moral and religious nature awakens or is awakened into activity that the area of his delights expands into boundlessness, that those delights become coextensive with eternity and brim to overflowing his ever-increasing capacities of rapture and ecstasy. Hence one of the first things to be taught to a young man is, that though he were possessed of all the wealth of the world, he cannot afford to be an inebriate and a glutton, because each present excess extinguishes a thousand future enjoyments. He is like one who has been invited to a banquet of the gods, but stops to gorge himself at a subterranean cook-shop on the way. Such a man might as well roll a hot iron over his tongue, cauterizing all its *papillæ*, and then complain that he has lost all the normal zests of the palate. It is a universal law that the plucking of a flower is the destruction of the fruit. The future is to be just as present as the present now is. Day for day, and hour for hour, the future will be worth more when it comes, than the present is now worth; because we shall then possess greater capacities of happiness and greater susceptibilities of pain than we now possess. So no man can afford to be a sensualist; for he exchanges nectar and ambrosia for garbage. Such is our constitution, that even for every bodily gratification, the last refinement of zest, the keenest edge of delight, is always derived from the soul's innocence and purity. Nay, a man cannot afford to be a philosopher, or an orator, or a poet, merely; for the highest achievements of talent and genius,—language, poetry, art, mathematics,—grand and enrapturing as they now seem to us, are only the tuning of the instruments with which the many-voiced orchestra of the soul shall hereafter peal its *Jubilate*. A great intellect without morals and religion, is but the *torso* of a Hercules.

I may be charged with entertaining a poetic idea of a College student. Even if so, I hope to be able to prove that it relates to didactic poetry rather than to romantic. The natural distinction is immense between the student and the worldling. The student sets things in the mind,—*within*. The worldling sets or establishes things outside of the mind,—*without*. The latter labors directly for material treasure; the former for immaterial. The one gathers of the perishable earth for the perishable body; the other, of the imperishable elements of the universe for the imperishable soul. Lands, goods, gold, are the pursuit of the one; ideas, truth, beauty, of the other. The one ministers to the senses and passions as if they were sovereign; in the other, all the senses and passions minister to the sovereign soul. Hence, from the very nature of the case, the student agrees to forego all gratifications incompatible with the soul's aspirings after excellence. The paths of the two diverge at a large angle, and they go different ways to pay their worship in different temples to different divinities. In the worldling's sphere of business or ambition, all is tumultuous, competitive, grasping and counter-grasping;—like drowning men, grappling and struggling, each to keep his own head above the waters, till, oftentimes, all sink together. In the student's sphere there is activity without strife; there is accumulation of wealth which makes no one poor; there is all the prowess and the triumph of conquest, with none of the miseries or humiliations of captivity. And these things are necessarily so, because in whatever pertains to earthly goods, there is a limit to quantity and an exclusiveness of ownership. Even justice often seems but little more than organized selfishness;—as that is yours, because this is mine. If I possess gold, or diamonds, or pearl, they are mine alone, and your crossing my threshold to obtain them is trespass, or theft, or robbery. If I gather luxuries in a foreign land, they must sail to my port, be brought to my city for my house, to enrich my table, wardrobe, or equipage. Not so in the polity or jurisprudence of the soul. A beautiful thought thrills the hearts of all mankind with one electric sweep, and every body is its rejoicing owner. A new discovery in Nature's laws gives winged velocity to every foot and puts a Titan's strength in every arm. When Fulton and his successors applied the power of steam to locomotion, did not we, who, in our power to traverse ocean and land, went to bed pygmies, wake up giants? Faust and Gutenberg bequeathed to all the art of embalming thought for immortality, and by a process stronger than any legal entailment made all men heirs of unspeakable wealth forever. Before Morse discovered the telegraph, I could think of my distant friend and bemoan our ignorance of each other's condition. Now, though he be at the distance of a thousand miles, I can converse with him *tête-à-tête*, across a continent as across a dinner-table. When Lord Rosse constructed his six-foot telescope, he enlarged the pupil of the human eye to the same diameter, revealing the wealth of immensity and enrapturing us with so much of the vision and glory of the regalia of God. In fine, the student does not deal with limited quantities and meagre possessions; for he is a citizen of that nobler Republic to which the richest Cubas and Central Americas are continually "annexed," without the meannesses, the piracies and the infamies of the freebooter. Dr. Kane achieving knowledge for all mankind, and not Capt. Kidd pirating for himself, is his exemplar. It is so even more emphatically in the subjective world of mind. A new spiritual or didactic philosophy, or a new poem, beautiful with pearl-colored words and weighty with ingots of thought, shines into all men's hearts like a new unveiling of the face of God. It feeds adoration as fuel feeds fire, and both author and reader are exalted towards the excellency they adore.

A young man of fair intelligence and an uncorrupted heart cannot have been in a College class for a single year without perceiving that he has crossed a boundary line and entered a new realm;—the realm of thoughts instead of the realm of the senses. His first lessons in philosophy teach him that he is in the midst of fixed and immutable principles. He sees that the laws of nature are but the thoughts of God. He knows that when he obeys the teachings of Omniscience, then Omnipotence indorses his success.

The reflecting student cannot have been in College for a single year, without discovering that there is a *periodicity* in his nature. Under the force of habit, the most difficult things become easy; and, at their stated times, they come, as it were, and ask to be done. Duties which at first cost a struggle pass quietly into routine. By persistence in rightdoing all the lower faculties of our nature become automatic, self-impelling, self-directing. By righteous self-control, our inordinate passions and appetites lose their vehemence, become tame and docile, and, at last, simply mechanical in their operations.

So of the intellectual faculties. Every cultivated mind which has arrived at mature age knows that what, at first, cost great efforts, is now performed without consciousness, or at least without the memory of consciousness. Ideas which once seemed heavy as the hills to lift, are now handled like toys. Heights to which the tired wing could scarcely soar, are now the common plane or level of thought, or are even looked down upon as valleys from an ascended hill. Combinations which could hardly be grasped with straining arms are now held in the hollow of the hand. Milton represents his devils as tearing up the hills by their shaggy tops and hurling them at their assailants. This, which would be a miracle to pygmies, would be pastime to Titans.

It is a proverbial saying that "habit is a second nature." Well was the question put, "What then is the first?" Despite Shakespeare, it is not difficult so to transform our functions that ginger will not be "hot i' the mouth." The intemperate man revolutionizes his whole physical nature more than God by his miracle did the stomach of Nebuchadnezzar, when he fitted it to digest grass. The glorious truth is, that habit has as much power to elevate as to debase us.

In view of these and kindred truths, the fact which impresses me with a sense of the Divine wisdom and goodness, more deeply than any other proof afforded by our whole organization, is this: Just in proportion as our nature is expanded and strengthened, all its earlier operations become automatic or mechanical. All customary duties are performed without conscious effort, as the heart beats or as the lungs swell and subside. All the physical and the lower portions of the intellectual and moral functions pass, one ofter another, out of the domain of the voluntary into that of involuntary nerves. There is no longer a necessity to charge memory with the performance of common duties. The time and the occasion bring the performance as cause brings effect. We have gauged our faculties to a prescribed kind of work, as an artisan gauges his machine, and then, without our special cognizance, and though the machine be left to itself, the work is done. Hence the higher capacities of the soul stand discharged from menial watching and anxiety. They are released for nobler employments or achievements, which, in their turn, as the soul is enfranchised for still loftier spheres of labor, will become normal and self-executing, and pass from the domain of consciousness and effort into that of spontaneity. It is in this way that the intellectual and moral character of man grows up, at the same time, into sturdiness and loftiness. He mingles his science with Omniscience or All-science, and his potency with Omnipotence, until one can hardly tell which is which. He incorporates himself into the body of the directing forces of the universe, moves with it in its eternal progression, and chants with it its everlasting hosannas. And yet,—such is the wonderful goodness of God!— with all this release from solicitude and care over those organs and faculties which have now been marshalled into the line of the divine forces and trained to keep step with them in their stupendous march, the true man is not bereft of a single flavor or perfume of any joy; not a single zest or appetency for all the delights of all his nature is deadened; not one thrill of rapture lost. Mark this, oh! man: it is disease, either of the body or the soul, that destroys all lusciousness and exquisiteness and ecstasy. But voluntary and conscious assent to God's laws consolidating by habitude into involuntary and spontaneous practice, marks the highest conceivable condition of our moral health. It is a health which is justified for being, in being, and therefore has the uncounted and ever-increasing joys of life gratuitously.

I have a thousand times been astonished at men's expression of astonishment, concerning noble deeds. When a righteous man spurns great temptations, when a subject defies the terrors of majesty, as Daniel defied Darius, or a stripling confronts a giant, as David confronted Goliath, the world cries out, What moral courage! what intrepidity! what self-sacrifice! In this, they change the truth end for end. To the habitually good man, to one who has taken the law of God for his guide, there is no more courage in doing right than there is in the flow of rivers or the ascent of flame. To do the contrary would demand the sacrifice,—sacrifice greater than suicide to a lover of life.

But this mighty power for good, like mighty oaks, has its feeble beginnings, its tiny germ. More than anywhere else, it begins in self-control;—in a subjugation of the bodily appetites and desires. It cuts off the hydra heads of passion and cauterizes the living wound that they may not sprout out anew. Each fresh acquisition of strength gives ability for greater effort, and greater effort elaborates new strength; until, at length, all the mutinous and insurgent forces of the soul are brought into consentaneous action with the Higher Law. The habitual sovereign over his own desires becomes like king Mithridates who could drive sixteen yoke of horses in his chariot at once, and, with rein and bit, could snap the under jaw-bone of any one of them that attempted to prance or caricole out of the harness.

Thus, my young Friends, by this gracious law of the good of God, the passive and the active side of man's nature support and glorify each other;—like the banyan, whose every branch sends down a rooted column into the earth, for strength, and whose every column sends up a towering crown into the sky, for beauty. If, as the poets say, old age is the autumn of life, surely the old age of such a life is like a tropical autumn,—its orchards and groves brilliant with flowers while bending with fruits.

Hence the very air and bearing of the true student, on being withdrawn from scenes of grossness and sensuality and being introduced into those of grand ideas and lofty emotions, will *import* that he now begins to disdain the trivialities and follies of which, in his unregenerate state of worldly-mindedness, he was enamoured. Amid the jostlings which before would have unbalanced him, he now stands in firm equipoise; for his thoughts are of the august processions of nature's works. With each new philosophic truth which he learns and with each new thrill of love for his fellow-men which he feels, he perceives that so much of God's nature has passed into him; and hence, so far, he feels, like his Creator, strong and happy. What the world flatters as "moral intrepidity" is becoming his habitual, normal state of mind; for he sees the vast chain of cause and effect that binds the past and the future eternities in its adamantine grasp, and he therefore knows that every righteous act thrown into the great current of Providential events, though swept beneath the surface for a thousand years, will be watched by the All-seeing Eye, and will, at last, emerge, a ministering seraph for his everlasting honor and glory.

The vivifying light of great thoughts and pure emotions cannot long exist in the human mind without permeating and illuminating the tenement that contains it. The pure heat of mental and moral fervor dissipates grossness, or it vitrifies what it cannot evaporate, turning opacity into transparence. How often have I witnessed this beautiful process in members of this Institution,—a transmutation of pottery into porcelain,—as the student's glowing love for knowledge smelted off the impurities of the worldling. Not Moses alone, coming down from holding communion with God on Mount Sinai, wears a shining face, but every man who holds communion with lofty thoughts and feeds his soul with the manna of righteousness, radiates from his countenance something of the resplendence of heavenly light.

The true student working under wise instructors, at proportioned labors, always succeeds; and, at every success, a shout of victory and a song of gratification is uttered and sung to his inward ear. Hence who can be happier than the student, especially the religious-minded student, not with clamorous revelries, but with the alternation of growing strength and acknowledged victory, steady in their succession as the systole and diastole of the heart!

While, however, I would vehemently condemn all brawling jollities, or sports unworthy the nobler faculties of man, let me advance an earnest plea, in behalf of elegant and refined mirthfulness. I love cheerfulness and hilarity, and wit founded upon the subtile and almost magical relations of things. Wit is an intellectual faculty, and God placed its organ at the outer angle of the forehead so that it may look all ways for subjects of merriment. Kingsley, than whom a more religious man has not written in our day, and whose love of nature is only less than his love of humanity, suggests that there are certain animals whom God created in the spirit of fun. I like the Homeric idea that the gods of Olympus loved a joke. I refuse my approval only because their jokes were unworthy of gods. The element of wit, like that of benevolence or veneration, is within us, and the sources of its legitimate gratification are all around us and inexhaustible. The subtile genius who can discern startling or incongruous relations and thus create delightful surprises, is, next to him who can discern a new truth, a benefactor to mankind. A jocose physician will restore more patients by his jokes than by his physic, and a witticism that hits the mark will disperse a mob quicker than bullets that hit the men.* How exhilarating to think of some master-stroke of wit, started thousands of years ago, descending along the path of time, crackling and coruscating, creating new explosions of laughter before the old ones have died away, expanding both mouth and heart of all men, until, in our day and time, it flaps and vibrates all living diaphragms, and is then destined, like a *feu de joie*, to run down the line of all future generations. Ignorance and the brutishness of ignorance, crime and the retributions of crime, can alone extinguish this love of mirthfulness in the heart of man. It is bad enough to see a *man* who always looks as Adam may be supposed to have looked the morning after the fall, but a *child* that never laughs is one of the saddest sights in the world.

But mirthfulness should always be associated with the higher faculties. When allied with the lower or animal propensities of men, it is as debasing as it is elevating when associated with the higher nature. It should always be employed to adorn benevolence and wisdom, and to increase our scorn for falsehood and our righteous detestation of hypocrisy. To be attracted by one of the most attractive

---

*After the French revolution of 1848 which dethroned Louis Philippe, Lamartine, who had been placed at the head of the Provisional Government, and who had enjoyed unbounded popularity, suddenly incurred the vengeance of the Parisian mob, who marched forthwith to the Hotel de Ville, where Lamartine and his colleagues were in council, and demanded the presence of their foredoomed victim. No sooner had he appeared on the balcony than a wild roar, like the noise of many waters, filled the air: "*His head*," "*His head*," shouted the angry mob. "*My head*," said Lamartine, "*would to God you all had it on your shoulders!*" The infinite contrast of ideas between trampling his head under their feet for vengeance, or wearing it on their shoulders for wisdom and guidance, transformed them, suddenly as another Pentecost, and he escaped.

of all things, warm-blooded laughter,—and when you expect to see a Hyperion, to behold, instead, only the foul eyes of a Satyr leering out upon you, is one of the sorest and most grievous of moral affronts. There can be no greater misalliance than that of genius and vice, or, what is almost as fatal, that of education and vice.

What is remarkable and most pertinent to our purpose here, is, that almost all those living and enduring treasures which now constitute the world's *"capital stock of wit,"* have come from the scholar. In this single department, the true student finds a thousand-fold compensation for all the coarse buffooneries and vulgar jollifications of the world. But let him remember that his wit, in order to be enduring, must be genuine, heart-exhilarating, truth-flashing, virtue-protecting, vice-exposing;—not the empty laughter of Bacchus nor the loathsome grinnings of Silenus.

Nothing unveils a man's character so suddenly and so surely as what he laughs at. Laughter is so unpremeditated and spontaneous, that it turns the soul inside out before one has time to think. The moral nature of that man needs to be constructed, who laughs at what is obscene, profane, or wicked. The sardonic grin is painful as the bite of a viper. The hyena laughs, the saint laughs; what an infinitude of moral distance lies between them!

The earnest College student, under proper intellectual and moral illuminations, and however unfortunate may have been his early education and associations, will soon give evidence that he is undergoing a refining process of character. His first change will be to repudiate and spurn all those monkeyisms of "trick" and "prank" and "practical joke," as they are called, which descend in College life from one low order of students to another,—the legacy of folly to fools. We all know that there are Colleges in this country whose vicinity to poultry-yards and hen-roosts is more formidable than if every building on the College premises were a burrow for Samson's foxes. The doctrine of the "Golden Rule," as applied to the whole *risible* nature of man, is simply this: *"That is not fun, which is not fun for both sides."*

For the coarse allurements of sense, the student has the serene and refining joys of sentiment. For the precarious and spasmodic delights which seem to come fortuitously to one who lives in what appears to him to be a world of chance, the student knows that he lives in the midst of everlasting laws, as beneficent as they are immutable, and that he has the power so to adjust events to moral forces as to produce happiness with far more certainty than a manufacturer can make cloth from wool or a miller flour from wheat. To his anointed vision, therefore, all vice is an insanity, because it is the palpable exchange of good for evil, and all virtue is a demonstration, because it is the palpable exchange of evil for good.

The student sees arguments for the immortality of the soul, such as the uneducated mind can never comprehend, and hence he derives motives for purity of heart and rectitude of life whose sovereign grasp and hold of the moral nature no one else can know. This is of unspeakable worth; for without the doctrine of a retributive immortality, I look upon all the divinest aspirations after excellence, and the most enduring moral heroism, as only a fleeting pageantry;—almost as unsatisfying to the spontaneous yearnings of the human heart, almost as disproportioned to the grandeur of the human soul, as the feats of Punch and Judy in a puppet-show. Without the doctrine of a retributive immortality, I look upon this midnight concave of starry worlds around us, with the magnificent sweep of their orbits and the unerring periodicity of their returns, as no better than a game at marbles.

I hope I may be permitted to say that one of the dearest ambitions of my past life has been to secure a full, generous, Common School education to every child born within the boundary of our free republican institutions. Nor did I ever feel the necessity and the preciousness of such an enterprise more deeply than now. The mission of the Common School is one of the grandest, the most beneficent of missions. Its first office is that of such a formation of character as will supersede the necessity of reformation. But in the present state of society, it has quite as much to do in pruning as in training. The vicious sentiments and noxious habits into whose midst so many children are born, and which, therefore, they imbibe as inevitably as they do their mother's milk;—these, it is the sacred function of the Common School to extirpate and abolish. For this purpose, every child should pass into life through their avenue; and I believe this country will soon see the necessity of requiring that every child, not voluntarily educated by its parents, should be compulsorily educated by the State.

So far our path of duty seems plain. But at this point, or soon after reaching this point, I come to a halting-place, where we should rest and take counsel as to the future. When our youth have passed through the Common School, and also through the Academy or Preparatory School, and have at length enrolled their names in College books, then it is almost universally true that their characters have taken their bent,—that they have got what Dr. Paley calls "a holding turn," so that from their existing elements we can predict their future orbits with a kind of astronomical certainty. At this period, in my opinion, their time of educational probation draws to a close.

Even here, however, let us lean to the side of hope and mercy. Even here, stern as is the duty we owe to the world, and Brutus-like, self-blinded in our judgments to all the appeals of parental affection, as we ought to be; yet here, where the student does first enter upon his collegiate career, I desire to put in one plea of charity in his behalf. If his character be in apparent equipoise between right and wrong;— nay, though the wrong threatens to overbear the right; yet if the scale trembles as though some electric thrill of duty still pulsated and struggled within it; if the elective moral affinities still leave it doubtful whether they will crystallize around the nucleus of evil or of good; then, for humanity's sake, for God's sake, ply all of your skill which the wisest and most loving can command, exhaust the whole armory of earthly and of heavenly motives, to recall and to save. Spare until you despair. But if all these appliances fail; if expostulations and tearful yearnings are flouted back; if rebukes administered in love only beget mutiny or defiance; then let the unrelenting blow fall;—let it fall; and though it fall on child or brother, on patron or friend, let it fall. I proclaim it to be an offence against public morality for any College to graduate a vicious young man. When, therefore, a College student persists in criminal habits, when he will walk straight forward towards a criminal life, I hold that the fulness of time has come to execute upon him that passage of Scripture which says, "Every tree which bringeth not forth good fruit is hewn down and cast into the fire."

But it may be said we should not withhold education from the profligate or the base-minded; *for he may change his character.* I reply, let him change his character first. If the Prodigal Son returns tearful and penitent, run to meet him and kill the fatted calf and make general jubilee. But if he comes home only to have his infamous diseases cured, and to get another outfit for another infamous expedition, he is a false father who furnishes the supplies.

And here rises before us, at full length, that great theme which I wish I had time more adequately to discuss: the Power of Colleges over the welfare of mankind, through the influence of those whom they educate, or refuse to educate.

On its Colleges, far more than on its Legislatures, does the well-being of the country depend,—on its education more than on its Legislation. Education has become an essential element of success in all enterprises. No cause, not even the highest and purest, can prosper, in our day, without making education its ally. Nine tenths of all the leading men, in Church and State, in this community and in all communities, have become leaders among men, and speak "with authority" to men, because of the education which Colleges conferred upon them. Almost the only considerable exception to this rule among us, is found in the low region of partisan politics.

Now if it were universally understood, as it so easily might be, that no College would ever honor by a degree, or long retain upon its rolls, any student who would drink, gamble, or blaspheme, or lie;—any one who prefers "toys and lust and wine" to the exalted satisfactions of truth and duty, of order and sobriety;— then every young man who should resolve to enter College would prepare himself for that purpose in his habits just as much as he would in his classics. As a necessary prerequisite, all candidates would bring themselves within the action of antidotal or reformatory influences. In short, in order to obtain the position, they would comply with the required conditions.

Are there any parents among us who, through wealth, or pride, or general turpitude of character, would not subject their children to our moral tests or rear them up to our moral standards, let them found a College on their own account, and have an academical Botany Bay all to themselves, with Judas and Tom Paine and Brigham Young for a Faculty, and some queen of the Cyprians,—some Fanny Ellsler or Lola Montes,— as head of the Female Department.

In the first place, a College which graduates a bad young man imposes upon one of the noblest instincts of human nature. There is scarcely any natural sentiment more firmly seated in the heart of man than that of reverence for knowledge. In all ages, ignorant men have defied learning and granted an apotheosis to those whom they esteemed morally great and good. How unnatural, then, how sacrilegious, to profane these divine promptings of the unsophisticated heart of mankind, by sending out Pharaohs and Potiphars instead of men like Moses and women like Deborah, as guides and leaders of the people!

Dr. Paley says that "to send out an uneducated child into the world is little better than to turn out a mad dog or a wild beast into the streets." I never could understand how a man of such strong sense as Dr. Paley should intimate that a bad child is but "little *better*" than "a mad dog or a wild beast." Why, my friends, there is virus enough in one bad man, with his Gorgon head, to strike the whole canine race with hydrophobia, could he be brought into mesmeric relation with them; and all the wild beasts in mountain and jungle are infinitely less perilous than one debaucher of public morals. The most formidable and fatal of all monsters to be found on land or sea, is a learned, eloquent, clear-headed, vile-hearted man.

A College Faculty, then, I say, ought to confer the honors and the prerogatives of a degree upon no one whose conduct and character while an undergraduate, has not promised that he will throw his influence on the side of right in the affairs of the world. In regard to the common virtues and vices that bless or that torment society, a graduate of a College should be more than a neutral; he should not be a mere zero which other men may place at the left hand of their digits.

A College should be a nursery for the principles of sobriety and for all noble aspirations, whence vigorous scions can be taken wherewith to ingraft the wild stock of popular appetite and passion, which otherwise might grow into public inebriation and licentiousness. Even for this life, there can be no foundation on which to build enduring eminence and fame but Christian morality. The most brilliant career, indeed, which is not sustained by the everlasting principles of righteousness and a benevolent life, is but dizzy and rudderless aeronauting. For a few months or perhaps years, a godless impostor may balloon himself over the heads of the people; but nature's laws are persistent as well as irresistible; the steady-working omnipotence of gravitation cannot be overcome by gas or parachute, and the height of his ascent will only measure the demolition of his fall.

What an enormity it is that our Colleges, which annually send forth hundreds of young men to the rostrum, the forum and the pulpit, should ever be guilty of overt acts of treason against the highest welfare of the community by fitting depraved men for positions of emolument and power. Under ordinary circumstances, a College may feel obliged to *receive* those who present the usual credentials. But no College is obligated to *retain* them. If applicants are welcomed, residents may be sifted. Undergraduates must be filtered;—the grovelling, the vile, the depraved must be rooted out from the useful, the honorable, the exemplary, and the latter only commended to the confidence and honors of society. They must be winnowed with so rough a wind that all ergot and smut will be blown away. We can bear, perhaps, a little of the chaff of weakness, but none of the poison of corruption. In the ancient polity of the Jews, if a father had a son who was a glutton or a drunkard, he was directed to take him before the priest, and if the offence was proved against him, all the people were commanded to stone him to death, in order, says the sacred narrative, that "all Israel shall hear and fear."

Where do immoral students go when they graduate, and what do they become? If not entirely consumed by their vices, and so cast upon the dunghill as having lost head as well as heart, they usually seek the professions, aiming at wealth in them, or for political distinction through them. And what will a corrupt-minded physician do? Through the hope of health and the terrors of disease, he is admitted, as it were by compulsion, to domestic intimacies and familiarities from which even the dearest and most trusted of friends are excluded. What barriers then, but those of the most sacred honor and fidelity shall prevent him from being another serpent blasting another Eden?

So if religious sentinels stationed upon the watchtowers of Zion, sleep when they should watch, and cry "Peace, Peace," when the Philistines of every vice beleaguer God's citadel, then sudden ruin must overwhelm the heritage they were appointed to protect.

In College, the future lawyer learns the lore of many tongues, and he is trained and practised in wielding the massive armor of eloquence. What social devastation, then, can he commit; or rather, what can he not commit, if he turns the whole phalanx of his qualifications against the cause of truth; and, finding the eyes of the goddess of justice to be blind, smites off her arms also? Whenever the bar array legal rule against moral right, they organize iniquity. The professional defenders of guilt are worse than the original perpetrators they defend. Every lawyer who knowingly rescues a criminal from condign punishment becomes, both by legal and moral definition, an accessory after the fact. One who habitually sells his services to all guilty applicants, is an accessory before the fact, and the sign fastened upon his door is a public advertisement of himself as a suborner of crime. How few offences would be committed, even in the present corrupt state of society, but for these two tempters!—first, the hope of escaping detection, and second, a reliance upon the professional chicanery of some Old Bailey lawyer,—of which, the latter is by far the more persuasive seducer to crime. The bar could do more than all legislators, courts, and executive officers together, to prevent the perpetration of crime,—by simply refusing to defend it. If ever the scales of custom and habit fall from the eyes of the community, they will see that the unscrupulous and every-ready defender of male-factors, is himself the greatest malefactor in society. His evil spirit is omnipresent, promising to screen the offender; and when the old forms of indictment charged the culprit with "being moved and insti-gated by the wiles of the devil," the literal meaning of that phraseology was, that he was thinking of some lawyer who would save his neck. The evil spirit of such a lawyer is present whenever confederates league together, shaping their plans to commit the offence yet escape the conviction. He muffles the step of the burglar on his midnight errand of plunder; he whets the knife of the assassin; he puts a lighted torch into the hands of the incendiary.

Some of the most awful and heaven-defying vices that destroy the peace of society and turn all the sweets of life into bitterness, are only College vices full-grown;—the public manhood of the academic childhood of guilt. The expert gamblers at State or National capitals are recruited from the ranks of those who played cards at college and studied Hoyle more than they did their lessons. The student of licen-tious reading and conversation grows into the fashionable roué or chronic debauchee, as naturally as adders grow out of eggs; and if, to physical sensualism he adds a sort of metaphysical turpitude, he becomes a political profligate, or a whole or half-way advocate of the doctrines of Free-love, that superfetation of diabolism on polygamy. There is no such deadly enemy of mankind as a wicked, profligate genius equipped with learning; for he fascinates many of the noblest faculties of youth, and thus leads them to rebel against the moral element in their nature, the noblest faculty of all. He embellishes with all the adornments of wit and imagination and elegance the paths that lead to the chambers of death. The Jack Sheppards in romances make the Jack Sheppards on the highway, and the Don Juans in poetry the Don Juans in society, as certainly as hyenas beget hyenas or vul-tures vultures. I well remember a set of College students who emulated Lord Byron's fiery and misanthropic genius, and imitated their idol so far as to—wear his shirt-collars and practise his amours. Now why should such incarnate vice be robed in the fascinations and armed with the glittering weapons of knowledge? Do we want our youth to grow up into such characters as William Congreve or Richard Steele?

A few years ago, there were three ambassadors of these United States, resident at European courts, *at the same time*, who were all notorious public drunkards,—two of whom had hardly a lucid interval while they professed to *represent their country* abroad. Think you they did not drink alcoholic beverages in College? Think you when they studied electricity and magnetism, they did not mistake demijohns for Leyden jars, and use brandy bottles for a voltaic pile? They were the men to sit around a table and take shocks. And thus the offences of the student's private room became at length the opprobrium of the nation.

That wisest and most valiant band of reformers this country has ever known,—the glorious advocates of Temperance,—how have their divine labors for the redemption of mankind from the direst of all mortal curses, been baffled and brought to nothing by anti-temperance and non-temperate legislators and courts! It is a notorious fact, respecting those judges who have been foremost in declaring all prohibitory liquor laws to be unconstitutional, that their public functions smell of their private habits. They uphold and stimulate the manufacture and sale of intoxicating drinks by the double encouragement of protection as judges and potation as men. They pronounce laws to be repugnant to the constitution of the State, while, in fact, it is only their own self-abused constitution that is repugnant to the law. In nine cases out of ten, in ninety-nine cases out of a hundred, the College life of these men foreshadowed the unutterable calamities which their judicial decisions have inflicted upon the world. The standard of College morals ought to be such, and it easily may be such, that no undergraduate would dare to drink alcoholic beverages, or to have them in his room, any more than he would venture to erect a lightning-rod on the top of his head and take a walk in a thunder-storm.

I know very well what is said, and said on high authority too, about judges being the expounders of law and not the makers of it; that their function, in all cases, is to declare what the law is, and not what it should be.* But we all know that a judge's brain is something more than so many pounds of avoirdupois of concrete law. We all know that in a very large class of cases, the character of the man is always

---

* "The judicial department has no will in any case. Judicial power, as contradistinguished from the power of the laws, has no existence. Courts are the mere instruments of law and can will nothing. . . . Judicial power is never exercised for the purpose of giving effect to the will of the judge, but always for the purpose of giving effect to the will of the Legislature; or, in other words, to the will of the law."—Chief Justice Marshall: *Osborne* vs. *Bank of the United States,* 9 Wheaton's Rep., 366.

visible in the decision of the judge. On any point of natural equity and justice, the law is not the same thing when coming from Lord Hale and from Lord Jeffreys. On the subject of human liberty, the law is not the same when coming from the Supreme Court of the United States and when from Wisconsin or Vermont.

Everybody knows that new classes of cases are constantly arising, where there are no precedents to be followed, but one is to be made; and where, therefore, the court will deduce their principles from sobriety or from inebriety, and will seek their analogies in liberty or in despotism, in Christianity or in Paganism, according to their own natural and acquired affinities. In all such cases, the judge exercises almost the entire functions of legislator and judge combined. The decider will be sure to impress his own moral lineaments upon his decision. If he be a wise and a good man, virtue through all her realms will rejoice at his living oracles; but if he be an ungodly man, the sun will not take your daguerreotype more exactly than his expositions of law will picture the vileness of his moral image. No matter what the law of the land may be, if you have judicial monsters upon the bench, you will have judicial monstrosities in their adjudications.

Now what I affirm is, that College Faculties ought never to graduate students who by overt acts during their collegiate career, forebode disaster and disgrace to the world. By so doing, they sink snags in the stream of human progress, against which many a precious bark freighted with immortal riches will strike and go down. The bestowment of higher forms of knowledge upon worthy objects is binding as a sacrament, but the priest who knowingly celebrates the nuptials between learning and wickedness is guilty of sacrilege.

When a College sends some great Dagon of intellect into the community, who by force of erudition and talent reaches the high places of judicature or statesmanship, and there perfidiously prostitutes his logic and eloquence to dethrone national justice and enthrone national iniquity, who debauches the public morals by suborning religion to become the defender of national crimes, and who sets the most contagious and fatal of all examples before the young,—that of a union between talent and intemperance or licentiousness,—that College inflicts a wound upon the very vitals of the State, for which the graduation of a thousand men of common-place virtues can never atone.

I know I am about to present an opinion which conflicts with the historic and the contemporaneous practice of this country. But believing it to be founded in eternal truth, I have no option to withhold it. All our earlier Colleges (and most of their successors have followed their example) aimed to indoctrinate their students into special denominational tenets, instead of establishing the great principles of practical morality and securing obedience to them. They ignored the everlasting truth that a man's creed grows out of his life a thousand times more than his life out of his creed. It was one of the profoundest of philosophical remarks, "If any man will do His [God's] will *he shall know of the doctrine.*" A man's creed may be long or short, but is not the autograph of a virtuous life a signature which will pass current in all worlds?

It is said that there are in this country, at this time, fifty organized, different, Christian sects. If each one of these had the power, it would, to-day, extinguish all conflicting dogmas of all rival sects, stamp its own faith upon all mankind, and secure its universal dominion to the end of time by perpetual entailment. Each one is now doing its utmost by influence, talent, money, missions, to supplant all others by itself. There are great differences among them in regard to toleration, great differences in regard to the means supposed to be legitimate for effecting the purposes of proselytism and self-perpetuation; but I doubt whether a single sect exists which would not, to-day, could the question be determined by a major vote, assume the awful, the tremendous responsibility of petrifying into its own likeness the religious faith of the world, for the residue of time, shorter or longer. But if truth be ONE and not MANY, then all but *one* of these faiths,—possibly all of them,—are wholly or partially wrong. Forty-nine out of the fifty must be more or less wrong,—possibly the fiftieth also. All but one, then, and perhaps all, are desperately struggling to impose upon the world, as truth, what is not true. This is mathematically demonstrable.

Meanwhile truth exists as certainly as God exists. There it lies, outside or partially outside of all, or of all save one. While each denomination is shouting, "Ho! all ye, we alone have truth," there outside or partly outside of them all, lies the glorious and divine, yet trampled and bleeding body of truth, foresaken and contemned by those who have gone after false gods. Now if this truth, which certainly exists, is ever to be recognized and welcomed, and its priceless blessings enjoyed by the world, the common course of God's providence leads us to suppose that it will be discovered and enthroned through human instrumentality; for the Christian world is not now looking for any new, miraculous revelation. Yet all the organized instrumentalities that exist are now struggling, agonizing to perpetuate, each one its old error, none to install with divine honors that new truth which alone can make men free.

Now, how are mortals to discover truth? I answer, that to seek for it in the right spirit is the only guaranty of a successful search. And the most important elements in this spirit are, a supreme love of truth and the power of impartial thought. To be capable of impartiality of thought opens all the avenues to truth. Incapability of it closes them all. Yet all the Christian sects, and almost all Colleges and private schools, at this day, are training the children and youth under their care to be incapable of impartial thought. They are divesting them of their intellectual impartiality, not only as between different denominations compared with each other, but also as between different denominations on one side and truth on the other. This they do by stamping the peculiarities of their own faith as early and as deeply as possible upon the uninformed mind, as though that faith were infallibly true, and by stigmatizing all conflicting ones as certainly false.

And could all the Christian sects so far succeed as to repel all proselyting incursions into their own territory, and to transmit their own creed down through their own sectarian lineage, for a thousand or for ten thousand years to come, then, even after all that lapse and waste of time, would not Christendom still present the same Ishmaelitish and shameful spectacle of warring sects, it does today? Each one would still be waiting for that millennium when its own dogmas would over-ride the world, while, practically, all would be uniting to barricade the only avenue by which the true millennium can ever enter. In the mean time, outside this most unchristian realm of strife, the glorious majesty of truth would linger and mourn, like a fond father waiting for the return of his Prodigal Son, and longing to bestow upon him a boundless heritage of blessings.

This commitment of the ingenious nature of a child to a blind partisanship; this forcible seizure of the young mind, taking it out of the class of honest inquirers, and training it to a dogmatic presumptuousness of assertion respecting deep mysteries, which, from its feeble powers and narrow vision, it is impossible for it to understand; this veiling of its eyes against the light of truth, and then teaching it to affirm what it cannot see;—this, indeed, is a profanation of all the holiest instincts of the soul; this is sacrilege!

In our present state of knowledge, whether secular or divine, there are numerous questions respecting the nature and attributes and providence of God which cannot be answered with a preemptory affirmative or negative, and it is treason to the sacred majesty of truth itself to teach a child to affirm or deny, as though he understood, what as yet it is impossible for him to understand. When children who have been educated in this way become adults, they always defend with passion what they cannot defend with argument; their logical resources are not reason and conscience, but the fagot and the torture; or as near to these as the laws of our country will allow.

The undeveloped nature of childhood is always trusting. Like the callow brood, it opens its mind, whether the mother brings poison or nourishment. All unintelligible doctrines are equally acceptable to it. It welcomes with the same readiness the dogma of the Immaculate Conception or the Ptolemaic system of astronomy; Transubstantiation or Hindoo cosmogony. If a tough kernel of religious error be dropped into the receptive nature of a child, all the tendrils and filaments of thought and sentiment and affection twine round it, clasp it, infold it, imbed it; and there, in the centre of being, it hardens until it becomes insoluble by truth; pharmacy has no lotion that can dissolve and wash it away, and if the psychological dissector attempts to remove it, he must cut so deep into the vitals as to destroy the life of religion itself in the soul.

That elevation and comprehension of mind, that power of impartial thought which would train the rising generation to the love and quest of truth, instead of blindly defending what, without consideration, it has prejudiced to be true, cannot be expected from Mohammedans or Pagans; it ought, however, to be expected from Christians; but, unhappily, in this respect, the sectarian and the heathen are on the same level.

And history informs us that it is only those who abjured more or less of their father's faith,—such as Luther and Melanchthon, Robinson and Wesley,—who have ever added any new stores to the world's treasure-house of truth. Yet these are the very men on whose heads fell all the thunders of the Church. Would not their additions to truth have been discovered more easily and more early, would not vastly more new truths have been discovered, had not sectarians and bigots universally plucked the eyes of impartiality out of their children's heads as soon as they were born?

In this connection, how instructive is the history of Physical Science! How slow were its advances, and what blank centuries intervened between one discovery and another, until dogmatic teaching was supplanted by the Spirit of Inquiry! Then, how thick and fast came the luminous revelations whose several splendors make the concentrated effulgence of the present day. But for that revolution, we should be teaching Aristotle's Physics to-day;—that the planets move round the earth in circles, because the circle is the only perfect form of motion, and Nature's abhorrence of a vacuum,—the very doctrine that made the human mind the vacuum it denied.

But shall nothing be taught as truth, lest we should teach error? This would be the opposite extreme. This would be the counterpart of the world's present false method, which is to teach those points most positively and most laboriously in regard to which there is the least agreement. Here, too, the improved methods of scientific investigation and inculcation are to be followed. What the great body of accredited scientific expounders agree in, we teach as truth. If there are two schools, we announce the prevalent doctrine, but never fail to qualify it by a full and fair statement of the dissenting authorities. So while we announce, as settled, all the great points in which the whole Christian world substantially agrees, (and which I believe all acknowledge to be the most numerous and the most important,) yet when we encounter controverted points, we ought frankly to state the great names and fairly to present the arguments adducible for each, conducting the case magnanimously towards absent antagonists, and as we would have them conduct the same exposition towards us; so that the new, unsophisticated, unpreoccupied mind of the learner may see all sides and may hence be able to hold the balances more steadily, than our minds, debased by early prejudice, were ever able to do. In this way, the mind is trained and fitted for using the instruments of logic and reason and conscience for the discovery of truth. By dogmas and creeds and catechisms, it is trained and fitted, not for the discovery of truth, but only to find arguments in defence of doctrines prejudicated to be true.

But it may be replied, the youthful heart is so prone to evil that if it be not filled with great and saving truths as early as possible, it will fill itself with great and ruinous errors. But first, are they *truths* which are submitted to it, or are they only one set of doctrines out of fifty, forty-nine of which must be more or less false; and possibly all may be? And again, why will not the supposed innate depravity deny and profane what is submitted to it as absolute truth, as certainly and even more fatally than it would, if the same views were submitted to it, among others, as having claims to be true? If there be an inborn,

connate impulse to profane and blaspheme all divine beauty and
excellence, shall that spirit be kept as long as possible away from the
object and the opportunity of its terrible indulgence; or shall it be
turned at once into the Holy of Holies? If a child has vehement destructive propensities, until those propensities can be curbed or tamed,
shall his toys be costly or cheap, of iron or of glass?

But the teacher cannot be impartial. He will have his views of
truth, and unconsciously if not designedly, through the force of nature
if not of will, he will give predominance to his own opinions. But if a
man conscientiously believes he ought to act the part of a judge and
not of a lawyer, why can he not obey this dictate of conscience as
well as any other? The difficulty suggested would arise only when one
should hypocritically assume to perform the noble functions of the
judge in holding the balances while his hand still trembled with the
interested passions of the advocate.

One more suggestion will close the argument on this topic. What
is the course of the wisest governments and of men in a case closely
analogous? When an exciting cause is to be tried in a civil court,
does not every judge examine the jurors upon oath, to learn whether
they have expressed or formed an opinion on the merits of the case, and
does he not set aside as unworthy to be upon the panel, those who
have formed such opinion? Every man sees and feels the reasonableness of this course. Yet this is just the reverse of what is done in regard
to controverted religious doctrines, in most of our private schools,
Sabbath schools, Colleges, and Theological Seminaries. Hence Truth,
claiming by divine warrant to be heard, is silenced; error, worthy
of annihilation, is perpetuated, and hostile sects, the scandal of the
Christian religion, are increased in numbers and virulence.

Claiming, then, no innate superiority of the present over the
past, but only believing that, from our more advantageous stand-point,
we can see some things which our predecessors could not, we cannot
refrain from expressing the opinion that our Colleges commit one
of the greatest possible educational errors, when they attempt to
transfer belief or disbelief ready made, to the minds of youth, on
points, respecting which great bodies of wise and good men entertain
different opinions. Ought not those institutions rather to expend their
utmost resources in inspiring the youthful mind with a supreme love
of truth as the divinest of all possessions earthly or heavenly, and in
training them to the power of impartial thought, that greatest of all
mortal achievements? Are not these the most certain instrumentalities

by which, in the providence of God, new truths will be revealed and old errors purged away? Let Colleges, then, bend their energies to secure, not uniformity of a supposed good creed, but universality of known good morals. Conscience has a higher function than intellect; the love of truth is better than the love of logic. When the true morality of Christianity prevails, the true doctrines of Christianity will not be far away. What Jeremy Taylor calls "a heap of miracles," performed every day, would not prevent the thoughts of men from conflicting, but the Spirit of Love is everywhere the same, and this may be inculcated upon all.

"BE ASHAMED TO DIE UNTIL YOU HAVE WON SOME VICTORY FOR HUMANITY"

Baccalaureate Address of 1859

In his last address to a graduating class, Mann spoke literally from the edge of the grave. His words had always reflected his high ideals and aspirations. But in his fighting years, in his struggles with adversity, misunderstanding, and lack of sympathy, he had employed rugged phrases, indignation, barbed example. Now, before death, his purest motives and anticipations rose to the top. He no longer controverted. He appealed. He exhorted. His final words to his students and countrymen became his most famous and the watchword of his College. To his wife, his last words were "Sing to me, if you have the heart."

AFTER journeying together for so many years on our passage through life, we are about to part. Another day, ay, another hour, and we separate. Would to God I could continue this journey with you through all its future course! There is no suffering of a physical nature which I could survive, that I would not gladly bear, if thereby I could be set back to your starting-point,—to the stage of life where you are now standing. When I think, after the experience of one life, what I could and would do in an amended edition of it; what I could and would do, more and better than I have done, for the cause of humanity, of temperance, and of peace, for breaking the rod of the oppressor; for the higher education of the world, and especially for the higher education of the best part of it;—woman: when I think of these things, I feel the Phoenix-spirit glowing within me; I pant, I yearn, for another warfare in behalf of right, in hostility to wrong, where, without furlough, and without going into winter-quarters, I would enlist for another fifty-years' campaign, and fight it out for the glory of God and the welfare of man. I would volunteer to join a "forlorn hope" to assault the very citadel of Satan, and carry it by storm, and bind the old heresiarch (he is the worst heresiarch who does wrong) for a thousand years; and if in that time he would not repent, of which I confess myself not without hope, then to give him his final quietus.

But alas! that cannot be; for, while the Phoenix-spirit burns within, the body becomes ashes. Not only would the sword fall from my hand; my hand would fall from the sword.

I cannot go with you. You must pursue your conquering march alone.

What, then, can I do? Can I enshrine my spirit in your hearts, so that when I fall in the ranks (as I hope to fall in the very front ranks of this contest), and when my arm shall no longer strike, and my voice no longer cheer, you may pursue the conflict, and win the victory?—the victory of righteousness under the banner of Jesus Christ. This transferrence of my enthusiasm, of the results of all my experience and study, into your young and athletic frames, is what I desire to do; what, as far as my enfeebled strength allows, I shall attempt to do.

But, first, the new circumstances under which we assemble to-day; the new men whom I see on this stage occupying the seats of official dignity and honor; or, where the individual men are not new, the new functions they have come here to execute; in fine, the new auspices under which this commencement is held,—demand a word.

This is Antioch College still, the same as we have known and loved it heretofore; but, according to the doctrine of metempsychosis, it is by the transmigration of the old soul into a new body. The old body, with its works (that is, its scholarships and its debts, and its promises to pay without paying), is dead; and in its stead we have the ressurrection of a new and glorified body,—a body without scholarships, without debts or pecuniary trespasses of any kind.

But this beneficent change has not been accomplished without a great struggle. In contests where the antagonist powers of good and evil come into collision, especially where the conflict is waged on a conspicuous arena, the respective combatants will summon their auxiliaries from above and below. We feel as if, during the last two years, our enemies had enlisted their most potent allies against us, but such as bore no tokens of coming from above. We feel as if the cause of right and truth had at last triumphed; and therefore, though ready to forget and forgive, we feel as if we have a right to congratulate ourselves, and as if it were a duty to thank Heaven for our success.

But I return to my purpose of striving to transfuse into your bosoms, for the life-work that is before you, some of the thoughts and emotions that have animated me.

Answer these questions! O youth just starting on your earthly and your immortal career:—

What are the sources of my welfare? What, also, are the sources of my misery?

There are two sources of human happiness. There are two also of human misery.

There is the happiness that alights upon us without any agency or forethought of our own. It comes to us, or wells up within us, ready-made and complete; and our first consciousness of it is in the joy it bestows. Such is the spontaneous, unbought happiness of infancy and childhood; the happiness which a mother's beaming face sends thrilling through the frame of a babe; the happiness which is felt when a father's strong arm rescues a child from danger and from fear; the happiness which we have in the natural gratification of all our senses and faculties.

The other kind of happiness is that which comes through our own procurement or co-operation, where, while God does his part, he leaves us to do our part; and so our gratification is the joint product of both divine and human agencies.

Hence, of human happiness, there are two sources, the Heaven-derived and the self-derived,—Heaven supplying us with the means; or, what is far more common, our happiness is the result of the inter-flow and commingling of both,—Heaven's bounty and our effort or instrumentality; the first performing the incomparably larger share of the work, though the latter an indispensable share.

So there are two sources of human misery. One kind befalls us. It comes upon us as an aerolite might fall out of the skies upon a man's head; as the tortoise which the eagle carried aloft in its talons, and dropped upon the bald cranium of Æschylus, and cracked it; as hereditary diseases come upon children; or as all the curses of a bad government or a false religion descend upon innocent generations, or as Adam's fall, whether we understand it literally or allegorically, plunged the human race into unmeasured depths of woe. A child is born blind, or deaf and dumb, or shallow-pated, or with faculties more askew than limbs and features can be: unspeakable misery results; but it comes in the course of Providence, and the victim must submit and endure, trusting to the remunerations of eternity.

"For God hath marked each anguished day,
And numbered every secret tear;

And heaven's long age of bliss shall pay
For all his children suffer here."

The second source of misery is, like the second source of happiness, self-derived. It is the result of voluntary ignorance or crime;
though in regard to misery, as in regard to happiness, vastly the
larger portion results from an admixture of the two causes,—the
providential and the personal. Now, both for such results of happiness and misery as spring from our own character and conduct, we
must take care of our own character and conduct. By so doing, we
can obtain a maximum of the one, and avoid all but a minimum of
the other. For such results as are exclusively of divine origin, we must
learn to obey God's laws; for a perfect knowledge and a perfect
obedience of God's laws would introduce all possible happiness into
the world, and eliminate all possible misery from it.

And, for this purpose, it is among our highest privileges to know
that God operates by uniform rules. No matter if theologians and
metaphysicians do divide God's providential dealings with men into
the natural and the supernatural: each must fall under the domain of
law. This is so, because it is impossible to conceive of a being, possessed
of such glorious attributes as we ascribe to the Almighty, who should
act otherwise than uniformly; because he must always act out of his
unchangeableness. Hence fixedness and certainty must pervade the
supernatural not less than the natural domain. This fixedness and
uniformity of operation are all that is meant by *law*. Hence a knowledge of his laws is attainable by man; and if a knowledge of, then
also a conformity to them. To an intelligent apprehension, the Diety
seems moving onward from everlasting to everlasting, not with devious,
ziz-zag motions, but in one right line; not with mutability and fluctua-
tion of purpose, but one vast plan, so perfect in the beginning, that it
needs no revision, addition, or expurgation.

To those who regard either the natural or the supernatural as
not regulated by law, the Diety must seem adroit only, and not wise;
as rescuing his own system from ruin by expedients and makeshifts,
such as a bungling craftsman resorts to to operate a bungling machine.

But why any evil or misery in the world at all? Why not universal impassibility to pain? Why not man necessitated to be happy?—
every nerve of his sensitive nature pervaded by delight, as every
corpuscle of his body is by gravitation. Why not his soul a compound
of spiritual joys as his body is of chemical ingredients? Nay, why not

happiness, passive and spontaneous, congenital, anti-natal, eternal, without effort or wish for good, or resistance of evil, on our part, and man made virtuous and saintly in this life, and carried into immortality and transcendent bliss in another, as a dead-head, and all the saints only so many spiritual lazzaroni?

Had not God begun at zero in creating the race, where should he have begun? Should he not have bestowed language on children at birth, so that they might have told their mothers the seat of their pains, and thus have taken only one medicine, instead of all in the pharmacopoeia? Should not children have had enough knowledge of metals to abstain from eating arsenic for its sweetness? Should they not have possessed enough knowledge to keep out of fire and water, and to count to a hundred, and thus have fallen outside of Blackstone's definition of a fool?

But suppose all men to be born at a certain advanced point of development, at a certain height in the scale above zero, would they not then be encompassed with a new circle of inconveniences and privations, quite as serious and annoying, and quite as earnestly demanding the *manus emendatrix*, the "amending hand," as Sir Isaac Newton called it? And so, at whatever degree along the ascending scale man might be launched into being, he would, at that point, feel an apparent necessity of having been started at a higher point, until nothing could satisfy his demands but to have been created with the infinite perfections of a God. Surely this is as strong as the mathematicians' *reductio ad absurdum*. The only uncomplaining point to begin at is to begin so low, that there is no ability to complain. Hence man is created at the point of blank ignorance, that he may have the felicity and the glory of ascending *the whole way*. Had he been set up any number of steps in the stairway of ascension, so much as he rose to higher elevations would have been lost from the perceptions of contrast and the emotions of sublimity. A mountain can never appear so grand to one born on its top as to one who was cradled in the vale, but has climbed to its summit.

Here, then, we see how evil comes upon our race. We are created with numerous appetences; all like so many eyes to desire, and like so many hands to seize, their related objects in the external world. The external world superabounds with objects fitted to gratify and inflame these internal appetences. And now these beings, fervid and aflame with these desires, are turned loose among these objects, without any knowledge of what kind, in what quantity, at what time, they are to be taken and enjoyed, but with free agency to take what, when, and as much as they please. Bring these four elements into juxtaposition,—the thousand objects around, the inward desire for them, the free will to take them, and complete ignorance of consequences,—and how is it possible to avoid mistakes, injuries, errors, crimes? With only one radius in which to go right, with the whole circumference of three hundred and sixty degrees in which to go wrong, and without innate knowledge of what is right and what wrong,—for a being so circumstanced never to err is just as impossible as for an infinite number of dice to be thrown an indefinite number of times, and always to come up sixes. Take any one man out of the thousand millions of men now on the earth, and his appetite for food and drink is not adapted merely to one aliquot thousand-millionth part of all the viands and fruits and beverages upon the earth: it is adapted to all edibles and drinkables alike; and without knowledge, and something more than knowledge, he will seize them where he can find them.

Consider all the property of the world—gold, gems, palaces, realities, personalities—as aggregated into one mass. Our natural love of this property is not confined to one quotient, using all mankind as a divisor; but it is adapted to the whole dividend, and without knowledge, will demand it. "Male and female created He them." One man to one woman, one woman to one man, is the law. But each of one sex to all of the other is the adaptation; and without knowledge, and something more than knowledge, chemistry has no affinities, mathematics have no demonstrations, more certain than that polygamy, Mormonism, Freeloveism, with all their kindred abominations, will be the result. Among all the young sparrows ever hatched, shall "never one of them fall to the ground without your Father." And, because one does fall, shall we say God's system is imperfect? Does not the Preacher say, "Shall those who remove stones not be hurt therewith, and they who cleave wood not be endangered thereby?" Who could foreknow that nettles would sting, until some person made a very sudden and perhaps improperly worded report of the fact? Shall all mankind use edge-tools, and no man's fingers ever be cut? How is an ignorant colony to avoid a malarious district until the fever shall have scorched and the ague shall have shaken enough witnesses to swear that region in open court to be the putative father of quotidian, tertian, or quartan? Why shall the convenience of lead service-pipes be abandoned, until the poisoned water shall have been caught, *flagrante delecto*, scattering colics and paralyses? After seeing the hardening effect of fire on clay, how can a man tell, without experience, that it will not produce the same effect on wax? That is, in physical matters, how shall an agent, free to do what he *will*, and ignorant of what he *ought*, escape error, and consequent damage? With an impelling force behind and no guiding light before, and with one only goal to be reached, how shall the engineer avoid fatal deviations right or left, or a no less fatal crash against obstacles in his path? How should the first builder of houses, as a defence against cold and storm, foresee disease through loss of ventilation?

In matters of pure intellect, how could the first generations understand all astronomy by looking into the heavens, or all geography and geology by seeing the surface of the earth? Why should they not accredit the evidence of their own senses in regard to the diameter of the sun and moon, and therefore believe that a man could carry one of them under one arm, and the other under the other arm to balance it? Why not explain eclipses of sun and moon by saying that a great dragon had swallowed them? Why not believe in all the chimeras and absurdities of astrology? Why not believe that the whole framework of the heavens rotates daily about the earth, as it seems to do? If a man cannot see around the curvature or rotundity of the globe, nor penetrate downward through its numerous strata, why not believe it to be flat and thin, and to have four corners, and to have been made, with all its appendages, in six secular days? And, if the muscles of man grow weary by labor, why not suppose that the Deity grew weary also, and ordained a sabbath for bodily rest? And when the passions flash their intense light of love or hate, of admiration or of disgust, upon the objects around us, can reason be always achromatic, and blend the whole emotional prism of rays into that white light through which alone the divine complexion and features of truth can be truly seen?

Still less in divine affairs could it be expected that a new-born being, occupying but a point in space, should fathom the depths of immensity; or, occupying but a point in time, should comprehend the eternities before and after. And when this frail child of an hour hears the thunder's roar, and sees the heavens ablaze, and feels the earth shake, and the forests bend, and oceans toss, and he is unable to form a conception of a spiritual God, why should he not fall down and worship the first thing which his own ignorance makes mysterious?

Oh beautiful idolatry, when it springs from a devout and reverent soul as yet unilluminated by knowledge! for, when the true God shall be revealed to such souls, they will cover the earth with the beauty of holiness, and fill the heavens with the fragrance of worship. Polytheism grew up because men had not minds large enough to conceive of one God capable of all these terrestrial and celestial marvels, and therefore they had to divide his attributes among thousands, even millions, of deities.

And, with all the numerous appetites and propensities innate in every man, how shall he maintain an equilibrium of exercise and of indulgence between them, and how a subordination of the lower to the higher, until the errors and miseries of the wrong paths, rising up before him like fire, shall have turned him back again and again to seek the right one? How should a man know, until some one shall have tried the experiment, that fire will burn, or water drown, or that alcohol will intoxicate, and opium narcotize, or that the only difference between a filthy tobacco-user and a vile green tobacco-worm is, that, while the worm never comes up towards the man, the man constantly goes down towards the worm? How, before trial or experiment, could it be known that dyspepsia is a non-conductor of knowledge, and that next to the calamity of being *non compos* in the brain is that of being *non pos* in the stomach? How, before observation, could it be known that avarice, among the worldly passions, is the most destructive to every sentiment of honor and nobleness in the heart of man, and that bigotry, beyond all other spiritual crimes, destroys most thoroughly all mercy and godliness in the soul; that a man may be a thief, and yet, according to the proverb, have some vestige of honor; that he may be a robber, and not despoiled of all generosity; that he may be a libertine, and yet have some filial or social affections; that an epicure can be generous after dinner, and a conqueror have a circle of favorites? And again: we know that the heathen pagans and savages open their heaven to the good man, come whencesoever he will; but a miser would keep the Omnipotent at work through all eternity creating wealth for himself, and the bigot would harry him with prayers to invent new tortures for heretics, and both remain surly with disappointment.

This combination then, I say, of inward appetites reaching outward, of innumerable outward objects adapted to the inward appetites, with free will and with ignorance of consequences before trial, necessitates mistakes which are physical evil, necessitates errors which are intellectual evil, and necessitates these violations of God's law which are moral evil. This theory vindicates the providence of God in the creation and government of man for the existence of what we call evil, by showing that, with beings at once finite and free, it was inevitable.

But, if evil is inevitable, how is man accountable for it? If moral evil *must be*, is it not absurd to call men wicked? Nay, is it not monstrous forcibly to set a man down in a certain place, or to put him in a given state of mind, and then pronounce him sinful for being there?

This is our solution of that Sphinx riddle: *Though evil be inevitable, it is remediable also; it is removable, expugnable.* Nor does it follow, because evil necessarily now is, that it must necessarily always be; nor because it must continue for a given period, longer or shorter, that it must continue forever. Most of the evils of mortals are terminable because they are exterminable. A farmer can rotate his crops: he can root out brier and thorn, and cultivate wheat. Legislatures make laws to prevent the recurrence of evils, to bar them out, to abolish them. Satirists lash the evil-doer with their terrific thong, and force him to desist from shame when he will not from principle. Oppressed nations invoke God, and dethrone the oppressor. Pioneers hunt out wild beasts.

Nor is it with great evils only, such as threaten life and limb, wealth or good name, that men combat. They take cognizance of the smallest annoyances, and remove or remedy them. They assuage hunger and thirst: in heat they seek the shade; in cold, the fire. Every man seeks to take a mote out of his eye, or to banish a fly from his nose; and, if his soul were large enough, he could just as well remove or abolish the evils of war, intemperance, bigotry, oppression, as to drive a snake from his path.

This, then, is the conclusion of the matter: Men are not responsible for the evils they have not caused, and cannot cure; *but they are responsible for the evils they consciously cause, or have power to cure.* I am no more responsible for what Cotton Mather and his coadjutors did at the time of the Salem witchcraft, or for what Pharaoh did at the time of the Israelitish exodus, or for what my very much respected but unfortunate great grandparents, Adam and Eve, did in the Garden of Eden at the time of the interview with a distinguished stranger in disguise,—I am no more responsible for any of these things than I am for the law of mathematics, by which, if unequals be added to equals, the results will be unequal, or by which, if the dividend is not a multiple of the divisor, you must have a fraction in the quotient.

But our power to diminish evils, to extirpate evils, one after another, creates the *obligation* to diminish and to extirpate. This duty is oftentimes coincident with selfishness or self-love; that is, it is both our duty and our desire to gratify some natural appetite or propensity. But sometimes our duty conflicts with the appetites or propensities of the lower nature. In either case, the duty is no less sovereign. In either case, obedience is indispensable to our permanent well-being. In all cases, God commands the performance of duty at all hazards and all sacrifices. As, if matter is to exist, there must be extension and solidity; so, if rational happiness is to exist, there must be a knowledge of God's laws, and an obedience to them. Whenever one perceives a law in Nature or in Providence, it is as though the heavens opened, and a voice from the Most High came audibly down, calling us by name, and saying, *"Do!"* or *"Forbear!"* Not the children of Israel only, but every man, stands at the foot of Sinai, and must hear the commandments of the Lord; not ten only, but ten thousand; not Decalogue only, but Myrialogue; and must obey them, or die. For God's law is omnipotent as well as eternal, and we are co-eternal subjects of it. Nor is it to be supposed that he has one law of cause and effect for this world, and another law of cause and effect for the next world, but that there is no law of cause and effect between the two worlds. Better and far nearer the truth would it be to say that this world is cause, and the next world effect. Shall the acts of a man—great virtues or great crimes—live forever upon earth in their good or evil consequences, but shall the actor, the man himself, perish? Shall a grain of wheat buried in the integuments of an Egyptian mummy two thousand years ago, if now exhumed and planted, germinate, and connect the reign of Sesostris with the nineteenth century, but shall the soul of him whose body was buried with that kernel of wheat pass into nonentity? Shall a diamond adorning the shroud of some ancient king of Persia be restored to the light in our day, and again flash and blaze in the sunbeams, but shall the soul of the king himself live no more forever? God's laws abide forever, and we abide forever under them; and hence it is our highest conceivable interest as well as duty to conform, to inosculate our lives, our characters, ourselves, to them. In many things, the average of human knowledge shows this to be true already: additional enlightenment will demonstrate its truth in all things. A man inherits houses or lands. If his estate needs rounding out at any point, he adds to it, and symmetrizes its boundaries; and, if disproportioned in its kinds of production, he turns forest into tillage, or tillage into forest: if his house offends taste, or frustrates convenience, he modernizes it into beauty and fitness. So if a man, on waking up to conscious comparisons, finds himself abnormal, or distorted from the common type,—afflicted, for instance, with *strabismus*, or noncoincidence of the optic axes,—he applies to the surgeon, has the contracted muscle cut, and he no longer squints: so, if club-footed, or suffering under any other pedal malformation, he goes to an orthopedist, who, by the wonders of his art, reshapes the foot into simulation to the common pattern. If we have an unsightly or distorted feature, does not the smallest modicum of common sense teach us to cure or at least to palliate it? If wounded or diseased in body, do we not seek to be healed or cured, and submit to privation and pain to be made whole? See one of America's noblest and brightest sons, for an injury to the brain, which mad brutality in the council-halls of the nation had sacrilegiously inflicted on him,—see him seeking restoration in foreign lands, and going to the terrific *moxa*, the fire-cure, as to his daily meals; and why? Because he hoped, from these fire-thrills through all his nerves, for a rehabilitation of the brain, and then for that other and hallowed fire in the cause of freedom and humanity such as touched Isaiah's lips. And if all this is done and borne for intellectual recuperation, nay, for the body that perishes, what ought not the scholar,—he who is indoctrinated into the knowledge of cause and effect, into the wondrous and saving knowledge of God's laws,—that knowledge which fuses the two worlds into one, and makes death only an event in life,— what ought not he to do or dare for the exaltation and grandeur of the soul?

And this brings me to the second stage of my inquiry: How shall we obtain happiness, how avoid misery?

I answer, in the briefest and most comprehensive formula, By knowing and obeying the law of God; for, in regard to all the higher forms of happiness, his plan seems to be to make men earn their own; he furnishing them with an outfit of capital and implements, or, as a business-man would express it, stock and tools.

The babe recognizes God's laws. Before it has any conception of divine attributes or a Divine Being, before it can articulate the Holy Name, it recognizes one of the most central of all laws,—that by which, under like circumstances, like causes will produce like effects. One well-executed burning of its fingers in a taper's blaze is sufficient: it needs no second lesson in that liturgy forever. Let a morsel of delicious food stimulate the papillæ of its tongue, and old age cannot obliterate its memory. So, but contrariwise, of the caustic or bitter. How soon the infant learns to call for water when it is thirsty, or to turn to the fire when it is cold! The boy learns the law of his sports. Sir Isaac Newton did not understand the law of resistance better than the slinger. A *ninny* farmer knows that, though he should sow the sea with acorns, and harrow them in with the north wind, he could not raise a forest of oaks upon its surface. A man may own all the coal-fields of Pennsylvania, or all the wood of the Hartz Mountains; but, without oxygen, he will freeze in the midst of them all. If a man will turn his bars of railroad iron into natural magnets, his road must run north and south. It may lie east and west to all eternity without their polarization. To create a visual image, the light must come to a focus on the retina of the eye, and not on the tympanum of the ear. Shadows are not projected towards the illuminating body, nor does an echo precede the sound that awakes it.

Not less true is it, that if a man will enjoy health, strength, and longevity, he must know and observe the hygienic conditions of diet, air, exercise, and cleanliness. A sound brain *cannot* be elaborated from a hypochondriac or valetudinarian body, nor systems of sound philosophy be constructed in an unsound brain. Good digestion is part and parcel of a good man; though it does not follow from this that pigs are Christians. Rum-blasted or tobacco-blasted nerves become non-conductors of volition; and a porous and spongy brain can no more generate mental fire than a feather can beget lightning. Weak parents can no more be blessed with strong children than wrens can hatch eagles; and it is impossible for a child to detach himself from the qualities of his ancestry, as impossible wholly to break the entail of hereditary qualities, as it would be in a court of law to prove, at the time of his birth, the *alibi* of himself or his mother. Ezekiel notwithstanding, personal qualities are descendible; and, if the fathers will eat sour grapes, the children's teeth will be set on edge. It has been objected to Swedenborg, that he once introduced the Divine Being on an unworthy occasion. He says, that, when once dining in his chamber, the Adorable Majesty appeared before him, and said. "Swedenborg, do not eat so much." Was this an unworthy occasion?— *a dignus non vindice nodus?* I deny the justness of the criticism. It is one of the wisest revelations which that coffee-inspired prophet ever had. If a company of one hundred families would set themselves to-day profoundly and devotedly to the work of exemplifying God's physiological laws, they would, in five generations of continued fidelity to them, govern the world.

These conditions of prosperity, of achieving good and avoiding evil, pervade the intellectual and moral world. A man must know his faculties; he must know the subordination of the lower to the higher, and his practice must accord with his knowledge.

There are two grand laws respecting mind-growth, more important than the laws of Kepler. The first is the law of symmetry. The faculties should be developed in proportion. Their circumference should be round, not polygonal; they should be balanced, not tilted. Every faculty is firmer set when it receives support from *all* others. Every faculty acts with infinitely more vigor when the other faculties sympathize and co-operate. A man who has one arm spliced to the other, giving him the length of both in one, while the armless fingers are attached to the scapula; a man who is Daniel Lambert on one side, weighing seven hundred pounds, and Calvin Edson, weighing only forty pounds, on the other,—is not more deformed than a man who is all intellect and no sentiment, or all sentiment and no intellect. Heretofore the kingdom of knowledge may have been enlarged by a distortion of the faculties,—by concentrating a sufficient energy upon one power and in one direction to achieve a discovery which could not have been achieved had that energy been equally distributed among all. But hereafter an entire realm of new discoveries will be opened and the errors of former discoverers rectified by that brighter illumination, when the rays of all the faculties shall converge to a focus upon the object of inquiry,—as in that remarkable case which occurred in Boston as but yesterday, where the laws of music and of electricity were invoked to solve an acoustic problem in the heart's beatings which had baffled all the science of Europe.

It is this relative disproportion of the faculties which has given rise to so many of the errors and even the crimes of the race, individual and national. If a body of seventy-two city brokers were now appointed to publish a septuagint edition of the New Testament, they would leave out the four Gospels, and insert in their stead the last best edition of the most approved interest tables. It is this accumulation of all excellence around one egotistic idea which makes an Englishman believe that Divine Providence always operates in subserviency to the British Constitution. It is this same exaggeration of a national sentiment which leads the French nation to look forward to a judgment-day, when men will be separated to the right hand and to the left, not because they have or have not given food or drink or clothes to the needy, not because they have visited or failed to visit the sick or imprisoned, but according as they have been or have not been soldiers in the Grand Army. The descendant of the Puritan is disposed to believe in the doctrine of vicarious atonement, because this getting every thing and giving nothing is such a sharp bargain,—very much the same plan on which the Puritan ancestor treated the Indians. So the national foible or infirmity of our people—its over-grown vanity and pride—stands on a parallel with the haughtiness of the Spaniard, the vainglory of the Frenchman, and the egotism of the Englishman.

The first grand law of the faculties, as a whole, then, is the law of symmetry. An obedience to this law will yield immense happiness, and avoid immense misery.

The next law is as important as the first. It is that all our faculties grow in power and in skill by use, and that they dwarf in both by non-use. By growth, I mean that they pass out of one state into another, as a grain of corn grows or passes from the embryo germ to the plumule, from the plumule to the stalk, to the flowering tassel, to the bountiful ear.

What was Benjamin Franklin at birth? Would he have sold for any thing in any Christian market? Could he have been forced upon a debtor as legal tender, even for the smallest charge in the debt? Would any artist have purchased him for his studio, or any philosopher for his cabinet of natural history? No chemist could have turned him to any account in his retorts. He was destined for far other retorts than theirs. But he grew. From being a lump of flesh weighing so many pounds avoirdupois, he took on other qualities and attributes, each transcendent, culminating over the preceding. By and by he became Benjamin Franklin *plus* the English alphabet, then Benjamin Franklin *plus* the multiplication-table. By industrious days and laborious nights, by observation and reflection, by noble abstinence from foul excesses, by divine energy of will in temperence, in diligence, in perseverance (better than the theologic perseverance of the saints, because it was his own), he gathered knowledge, accumulated stores of experience, grew wise on observation and lucubration, until soon he became that Benjamin Franklin whose name the lightning blazons from one part of the heavens unto the other, and to whom every summer cloud in all the zones and to the end of time shall thunder applause. See the offshoots of this growing man at this point of his development! Morse, House, Field, are his own brain-begotten children. The lightning is nimbly at work to-day in the shops of ten thousand artificers. It strikes alarm-bells, and warns sleeping cities that conflagration and a fiery death are at their doors. It measures longitudes as no geometer or astronomer could ever measure them; and before another twelve-month shall have passed, by a new application of that elemental force which ran along Franklin's kite-string, a cable shall unite the Eastern and Western Hemispheres, along whose electric threads shall fly to and fro such "winged words" as Homer never dreamed of. Then he grew into that Benjamin Franklin who signed the Declaration of American Independence; then into that Benjamin Franklin who signed the treaty of peace that acknowledged the independence and sovereignty of these United States; an act extorted from a sovereign, which made *him* more than sovereign,— the *pater patriæ* of a country peopled with sovereigns. Then he became Benjamin Franklin *plus* the Constitution of the United States.

What growth was here! what excelsior strivings and triumphs from day to day! what ascension from glory to glory! not to cease even with death; for in all Christendom there is not now, nor ever hereafter will be, a child born of woman, who has not and will not have more of well-being and less of ill-being on earth because Benjamin Franklin lived; that is, because of his industry, fidelity, and temperance when he was a boy; because of his integrity, wisdom, and philanthropy when a man.

Now, each class and profession of men has a different stand-point from which it surveys the world, and to which, in its peculiar position, the world presents its immense variety of aspects. To a hack-driver, the living freight which a steamboat or railroad-train pours into a city are worth twenty-five or fifty cents apiece. The barber feels ties of brotherhood, and the gates of his soul open with welcome, towards that part of the human race that shaves. The manufacturer of playing-cards thinks it terrible Puritanism to condemn what Burns calls the "Devil's pictured buiks;" and the printer of Bibles is a most zealous member of the Bible Society. When a shoemaker is requested to fit a tiny pair of shoes to an infant's feet, he sees a row of prospective and gradually enlarging shoes stretching out into futurity. So the tailor sees a lengthening vista of coats, and the hatter of hats, for all their customers. All these are seen as clearly as Æneas saw Marcellus far away in the coming generations.

So it is easy to take an ancestor who lived a thousand years ago, and see his lineal descendants diverging and radiating from him, children and grandchildren,—each line or lineage reaching in solid rank and file down to the present time; one branch honorable, another proud, another base. These are realities.

But in view of this law of growth, and of the rapidity of its increments, no less real to me is the spectacle presented by every young man, especially by every young man who receives the nutriment and invigoration of college-life. Radiating from every such young man as from a central point, I seem to see long-extended lines of the forms of men,—such forms as he may enter and occupy, and so become the men they represent. It is as though these lines shot out from him as from a centre to a circumference; only there is no circumference, for the lines lengthen outward into endless perspective. Stand up, young man, and let us behold the forms of men, noble or ignoble, lofty or mean, saintly or satanic, which beleaguer you, and into which your soul enters as you pass on in your life, from glory to glory, or from shame to shame! Here, shooting out in one direction, I see an ascending series, an upward graduation of noble forms, figures of lofty stature and mien. Health and strength are in all their limbs; fire, ardor, aspiration, gleam from every eye; the light of virtue shines from every face; each life is pure. What a throne for majesty is every brow! Beneficence is in every hand. See how each individual in that long-extended rank excels the last, as it rises and towers, and is lost at last to our view, but lost only where earth meets heaven!

But what do I see on the other side? Another line, compact like the former, shooting outward from the same centre, but stamped and branded with all those types of infamy that can be developed from the appetites,—gluttony, intemperance, sensuality, debauchery, agony and ignominy unspeakable! O God! I rejoice that I can see no farther into the perdition beyond. These, *these*, young man, are the forms which you may grow into and become. Choose to-day whether you will pass through this succession to honor and bliss, or this to shame and despair.

This young man proposes to be a lawyer. Shooting outwards from him on either hand are compact files of those who disgrace or those who honor the noble profession of law. This line begins with a pettifogger, a chicaner, a picaroon,—one whose study and life it is to throw the cloak of truth over the body of a lie, like that lawyer of whom a malefactor said, "I have counted the chances, and concluded to commit the crime, for I know *he* can get me off;" and it ends in an Old-Bailey or Five-Points solicitor, sold to the service of Satan, content to take half his pay in money, and the rest in pleasure of wickedness,— like the man who was a great lover of swine's flesh, who said he wished he were a Jew, that he might have the pleasure of eating pork and committing a sin at the same time. Another radiating file begins with examples of honor, equity, truth-loving, and ends in a chief justice such as Holt or Marshall or Shaw.

Another means to be a public man. His first transformation may be into a demagogue, half-sycophant, half-libeller, a pimp and pander of power, a peculator, an embezzler, a robber of mails or mints, a polyglot liar; or he may pass into those types whose systems of political economy have humanity for their end, and wealth for their means only; who know no castes or classes or nobility, excepting those who bear God's patent of intelligence and virtue.

This young man looks to the sacred desk. Next to him, on one side, stands the chameleon preacher, the color of whatever he touches. His soul is a religious *camera-obscura*, reflecting back only the souls of those who pay his salary. He cannot preach against the crimes of to-day,—the crimes that flout heaven, the crimes that crush life out of the human heart. He can only preach against the "exceeding sin-fulness of sin,"—now and then hurling a terrific bolt at Jeroboam or Judas. *They* are personages not very likely to disturb the sacred quiet of *his* parish. But what a glorious column of forms of men stands on the other side!—true disciples of Jesus Christ, constituted of piety, philanthropy, and wisdom,—men who, for truth's sake, can bear revilings and a crown of thorns, can look without shrinking upon the cross, nay, can die upon the cross if need be. But, oh! when the sanctifying hour of death has passed, then the revilings become world-wide homages; the crown of thorns, a crown of amaranth, blossoming forever in the air of heaven: even the accursed cross is made sacred in the eyes of men.

Thus it ever is when men make sacrifices in the cause of duty. First comes the temptation; which if resisted, the transfiguration follows. The stern fulfillment of duty enrages the wicked, and they execute crucifixion: and then comes the ever-glorious ascension: and even the memory of the Joseph of Arimathea who cared for the dead body of the martyr is gratefully and forever embalmed in the hearts of men.

Crowding thick around you, my young friends who go forth from here to-day, I see these various classes and characters of men whom I have attempted to portray. Select which you please. Trans-migrate through the forms of one class into ever-increasing nobleness and dignity, ascending to all temporal honor and renown, to end in the glories of immortality; or plunge through the other, from degradation, to perdition that is bottomless.

I need not carry out the parallel with regard to the young ladies who are before me, and who are candidates for graduation to-day. For them, if they will have the courage to lift themselves out of the frivolities of a fashionable and a selfish life, each one, in her own sphere and in her own way, may become another Isabella, securing an outfit for another Columbus for the discovery of another hemisphere wherewith to bless mankind,—more honorable to the queenly helper than the bold navagator. . . .

The last words I have to say to you, my young friends, are these:—

You are in the kingdom of a Divine Majesty who governs His realms according to law. By His laws, it is no more certain that fire will consume, or that water will drown, than that sin will damn. Nor is it more sure that flame will mount, or the magnetic needle point to the pole, than it is that a righteous man will ascend along a path of honor to glory and beatitude. These laws of God pervade all things, and they operate with omnipotent force. Our free agency consists merely in the choice we make to put ourselves under the action of one or another of these laws. Then the law seizes us, and sweeps us upward or downward with resistless power. If you stand on the great table-land of North America, you can launch your boat on the head waters of the Columbia, or the Mackenzie, or the St. Lawrence, or the Mississippi; but the boat, once launched, will be borne *towards* the selected one of the four points of the compass, and *from* all the others. If you place your bark in the Gulf Stream, it will bear you northward, and not southward; or though that stream is as large as three thousand Mississippis, yet you can steer your bark across it, and pass into the region of the variable or the trade winds beyond, to be borne by them.

If you seek suicide from a precipice, you have only to lose your balance over its edge, and gravitation takes care of the rest. So you have only to set your head right by knowledge, and your heart right by obedience, and forces stronger than streams or winds or gravitation will bear you up to celestial blessedness, Elijah-like, by means as visible and palpable as though they were horses of fire and chariots of fire.

Take heed to this, therefore, that the law of God is the supreme law. The judge may condemn an innocent man; but posterity will condemn the judge. The United States are mighty; but they are not almighty. How sad and how true what Kossuth said, that there had never yet been a Christian government on earth! Before there can be a Christian government, there must be Christian men and women. Be you these men and women! An unjust government is only a great bully; and though it should wield the navy in one fist and the army in the other, though it should array every gun in the armories of Springfield and Harper's Ferry into one battery, and make you their target, the righteous soul is as secure from them as is the sun at its zenith height.

While, to a certain extent, you are to live for yourselves in this life, to a greater extent you are to live for others. Great boons, such as can only be won by great labors, are to be secured; great evils are to be vanquished. Nothing to-day prevents this earth from being a paradise but error and sin. These errors, these sins, you must assail. The disabilities of poverty; the pains of disease; the enervations and folly of fashionable life; the brutishness of appetite, and the demonisms of passion; the crowded vices of cities, thicker than their inhabitants; the retinue of calamities that come through ignorance; the physical and moral havoc of war; the woes of intemperance; the wickedness of oppression, whether of the body or of the soul; the Godlessness and Christlessness of bigotry,—these are the hosts against which a war of extermination is to be waged, and you are to be the warriors. Never shrink, never retreat, because of danger: go into the strife with your epaulettes on.

At the terrible battle of Trafalgar, when Lord Nelson, on board the "Victory," the old flag-ship of Keppel and of Jervis, bore down upon the combined fleets of France and of Spain, he appeared upon the quarter-deck with his breast all blazing with gems and gold, the insignia of the "stars" and "orders" he had received. His officers, each a hero, besought him not thus to present himself a shining mark for the sharpshooters of the enemy, but to conceal or doff the tokens of his rank. "No," replied Nelson: "in honor I won them, and in honor I'll wear them!" He dashed at the French line, and grappled with the "Redoubtable" in the embrace of death. But, when the battle had raged for an hour, a musket-ball, shot from the mizzen-top of the enemy, struck his left epaulette, and, crashing down through muscle and bone and artery, lodged in his spine. He knew the blow to be fatal; but as he lay writhing in mortal agony, as the smoke of battle at intervals cleared away, and the news was brought to him that one after another of the enemy's ships—the "Redoubtable," the "Bucentaur," the "Santa Anna," the "Neptune," the "Fougueux"— had struck their colors, his death-pangs were quelled, joy illumined his face, and for four hours the energy of his will sustained his vitality; and he did not yield to death until the fleets had yielded to him.

So, in the infinitely nobler battle in which you are engaged against error and wrong, if ever repulsed or stricken down, may you always be solaced and cheered by the exulting cry of triumph over some abuse in Church or State, some vice or folly in society, some false opinion or cruelty or guilt which you have overcome! And I beseech you to treasure up in your hearts these my parting words: *Be ashamed to die until you have won some victory for humanity.*